Rebecca
◆◆◆ Sitton's

Spelling
Sourcebook™ 2

Your Guide for
Teaching
and Extending
High-Use
Writing
Words
1–400

ISBN 1-886050-01-5
©1995–Rebecca Sitton
Egger Publishing, Inc.
P. O. Box 4466, Spokane, WA 99202
Phone: 509-534-1000 FAX: 509-534-6971

Dear Educator,

I have created the *Spelling Sourcebook* Series for you as an alternative to traditional workbook spelling. It is your source for teacher-customized spelling instruction designed to complement the writing-rich classroom. You can develop your own research-based, spelling-for-writing program using the *Spelling Sourcebook* options and resources.

Begin with *Spelling Sourcebook 1.* This specific guidebook tells you how to develop and implement your own spelling program using high-frequency writing words. The seventeen Articles of Part 1 include options for dividing the high-use words across the grades, organizing a flexible schedule for teaching the words, and establishing practical expectations for spelling accountability in writing; guidelines for effectively using research-based procedures, informing parents and involving them in the new program, and handling lower and higher achievers; and suggestions for authentic and performance-based spelling evaluations. Part 2 of *Spelling Sourcebook 1* is the reference section. It features 1200 high-frequency writing words listed in their order of frequency of use, practical spelling rules, game and writing ideas, and a review of valid spelling research with a complete bibliography. The final section, Part 3, has your blackline master forms for instruction and record keeping.

Spelling Sourcebooks 2, 3, and *4* are your activity books. They provide abundant suggestions for teaching and extending the high-use words within a literature-based, language-centered classroom. This book, *Spelling Sourcebook 2,* includes ideas for words within the frequencies 1–400. *Spelling Sourcebooks 3* and *4* follow with ideas for words 401–800 and 801–1200. There are no student books. You don't need them with the *Spelling Sourcebook* Series.

I invite you to participate in the *Spelling Sourcebook* methodology. This nontraditional, commonsense approach to spelling will help your students learn to spell where it counts . . . in their everyday writing!

If you have questions, contact me. If you'd like to share your experiences using the *Spelling Sourcebook* Series, contact me. Or if you'd like information on the spelling seminar I present to educators that highlights the concepts of the *Spelling Sourcebook* methodology, contact me. I'd like to hear from you.

Sincerely,

Rebecca Sitton
South 2336 Pittsburg
Spokane, WA 99203
(509) 535-5500

Your Guide to the Contents

About the Spelling Sourcebook Author

Rebecca Sitton is an internationally recognized authority on spelling instruction. She applies research-based spelling strategies to instruction within an integrated, language-centered curriculum that offers students many opportunities for writing.

Rebecca has experience teaching in both regular and special education, was a Chapter I teacher, and served as a school district Language Arts Coordinator. Currently, she is a free-lance educational consultant and staff development trainer to numerous school districts and regional education agencies. She serves as an instructor for the Bureau of Education and Research, providing seminars to educators throughout the United States and Canada. She teaches at the university level and is an author of numerous published educational materials.

Published Materials by Rebecca Sitton

Spelling Sourcebook Series, Northwest Textbook, 503 639-3194

Spelling Sourcebook Video Series, Northwest Textbook, 503 639-3194

Increasing Student Spelling Achievement — seminar guidebook, Northwest Textbook, 503 639-3194

Increasing Student Spelling Achievement Audio Tape Program, Bureau of Education and Research, 1 800 735-3503

Spelling Workshops Series correlated to HEATH READING, D.C. Heath, 1 800 235-3565

Instant Spelling Words for Writing Series, Curriculum Associates, Inc., 1 800 225-0248

Stop and Think— Life-Skills Literacy Series, Curriculum Associates, Inc., 1 800 225-0248

QUICK-WORD™ materials, Curriculum Associates, Inc., 1 800 225-0248
  QUICK-WORD™ WORDSHOP Activity Series
  QUICK-WORD™ Handbook for Everyday Writers
  QUICK-WORD™ Handbook for Everyday Writers (Canadian Edition)
  QUICK-WORD™ Handbook for Everyday Writers (Spanish Edition)
  QUICK-WORD™ Handbook for Beginning Writers
  QUICK-WORD™ Handbook for Practical Writing

Story Pictures Plus Series, Curriculum Associates, Inc., 1 800 225-0248

Storybooks Plus Series, Curriculum Associates, Inc., 1 800 225-0248

About Spelling Sourcebook 2

What is the purpose of Spelling Sourcebook 2?

Spelling Sourcebook 2 lists Core Words 1–400 in their order of frequency of use in everyday writing (see *Spelling Sourcebook 1* pages 77–82 for the complete *Sourcebook* word bank of 1200 Core Words and discussion of how they were compiled). Following each of the 400 Core Words, multiple activities are suggested for teaching the words and "springboarding" to related language learning. Here is a sampling of the activity idea options.

What kinds of activities are included?

literature—books and follow-up activities that reinforce and extend the Core Words

writing—motivational writing ideas that require students to apply their spelling skills in writing activities

vocabulary building—activities that "springboard" from the Core Words to introduce other forms of the words, synonyms, antonyms, homophones, homographs, prefixes and suffixes, roots, multiple meanings, clipped words (plane/airplane), and words often confused (then/than)

research activities—ideas to stimulate research, writing, and oral reporting

visual activities—visual discrimination and perception activities

word origins—activities that encourage an understanding of word histories, eponyms, and foreign words and phrases

dictionary skills—activities that promote competent use of dictionaries and other writing references, including lessons on alphabetical order, multiple meanings, pronunciations, and syllabication

phonetic analysis—activities that reinforce sound-symbol correspondence of consonant, vowel, and digraph sounds; and awareness of silent letters

structural analysis—activities for exploring compounds, contractions, double letters, and palindromes; affixes and word parts; and patterning activities

thinking skills—activities that help students explore word relationships through sequencing, analogies, and sorting; exercises that encourage students to discover multiple meanings of words; and creative and expository writing

spelling rules—activities that teach reliable rules, or generalizations, with opportunities to apply the rules to new words

Why is it most effective to present words in the order of their frequency of use in writing?

For the tightest bond between spelling and writing, the Core Words should be taught in their order of frequency of use in writing, just as they are listed. This ensures that the words with the greatest long-term spelling power are learned before words with less utility in writing (see *Spelling Sourcebook 1,* Article 2, page 9).

What are the grade levels of the Core Words in Spelling Sourcebook 2?

The grade levels to which these Core Words can be assigned varies. Dividing the words into grade levels is a decision for the program developers to make as they customize *Spelling Sourcebook 1's* Core Word bank to meet the needs of a specific group of program users (for guidelines for grade level options see *Spelling Sourcebook 1,* Article 2, page 9 and Article 16, page 67).

How will the activities challenge better spellers? ◆ Many of the activities in *Spelling Sourcebook 2* are designed for better students who are minimally challenged by learning to spell the Core Words on their spelling pretests and posttests or previews and reviews (for an explanation of the Self-Corrected Test and guidelines for administering it, see *Spelling Sourcebook 1*, Article 4, page 21). The activities in *Spelling Sourcebook 2* extend learning beyond the Core Words to word banks, skills, and application opportunities that develop understandings about our language and its effective written use (for additional ways to challenge better students, see *Spelling Sourcebook 1*, Article 11, page 49, and Article 12, page 51).

How will the activities meet the needs of less able spellers? ◆ Some of the activities in *Spelling Sourcebook 2* are included for typical learners, but there are also activities for students who need extra reinforcement with spelling and language concepts (for additional ways to meet the learning needs of students with spelling problems, see *Spelling Sourcebook 1*, Article 13, page 53). These students will particularly benefit from the activities that develop visual skills. Though many skills are interwoven for spelling facility, the visual modality is the dominant skill for spelling success (for additional visual development ideas see *Spelling Sourcebook 1*, Article 7, page 29). These students also benefit by being included in the discussion of the language-learning activities and projects generated by the typical and more-capable learners. Language facility is acquired through example and practice.

Is it necessary to teach all of the activities? ◆ No one should teach all the suggested activities in *Spelling Sourcebook 2*; there are too many. Rather, the activity ideas are a menu of options from which to choose as an integrated spelling and language program is taught. The most effective instruction for most students would employ a variety of activities so that the students receive a balanced curriculum of skills and their application.

How should activities be selected for instruction? ◆ The teacher makes the activity decisions, just as the teacher decides how many Core Words to include in a unit and the time frame for teaching a unit (see *Spelling Sourcebook 1*, Article 2, page 9). The instructional philosophy of the teacher and the needs of the students should provide the guidelines for activity selections— which activities to include in the program, which students should be assigned which activities, and the format of the activities.

Are the activities designed for independent seatwork or teacher-directed instruction? ◆ *Spelling Sourcebook 2* does not stipulate the instructional format for the activities. Teachers may choose to assign activities as independent work for individual students or students in small cooperative-work groups; or use the activities as teacher-directed instruction to individuals, small groups, or the whole class. An activity that would be appropriate for independent work for some students might also only be effective with teacher direction for other students. The teacher, not the program, makes this decision.

How is review achieved? ◆ The activity ideas incorporate systematic review of concepts and words, especially those that routinely present a persistent spelling challenge. However, teachers can increase the review as necessary by teaching activities for previous words that were not selected for initial instruction and systematically including selected review words on current spelling preview or review tests. This review complements the built-in *Sourcebook* system for review and mastery of specific words students misspell or misuse in their writing (see *Spelling Sourcebook 1*, Article 8, page 33, Article 9, page 39, and Article 11, page 49).

What are student expectations for accurate spelling and use of words in the writing activities of Spelling Sourcebook 2?

As writing activities are assigned from the suggestions in **Spelling Sourcebook 2**, students should be reminded to proofread their work. Which words are unacceptable for students to misspell or misuse in their writing? The answer depends upon the kind of writing lesson it is.

The **Spelling Sourcebook** suggestions for writing consist of everyday writing experiences and topics for writing-as-a-process assignments. In both situations, students are afforded spelling references for the words for which they are accountable—words unacceptable to misspell or misuse. However, selected activities could be used for a "no-reference" writing piece in which a spelling reference is not provided to students (see **Spelling Sourcebook 1**, Article 10, page 45).

Spelling accountability for everyday writing is for the current list of Core Words, any technical reference words (see **Spelling Sourcebook 1**, Article 3, page 17), as well as students' Priority Words (see **Spelling Sourcebook 1**, Article 8, page 33, and Article 9, page 39). One hundred percent accuracy in spelling is not expected on everyday writing pieces for developing writers. However, writing-as-a-process assignments progress through various stages of refinement to the final copy—a perfectly proofread piece void of all errors. In most instances, the teacher can decide which format to employ as writing is assigned. In general, when a class-made or student book is a suggested activity, a "published" work is developed through writing-as-a-process toward an error-free final copy.

Which activities in Spelling Sourcebook 2 provide the best information for spelling assessment?

Grading the activities that are selected for instruction from **Spelling Sourcebook 2** is a small factor in total spelling assessment. In fact, most of the activities aren't designed to be completed for a grade. Among the activity options, the most important evaluative information would be derived from students' spelling on the assigned writing activities. Spelling mastery, as defined by the **Sourcebook** methodology, is achieved only in writing. The writing activity ideas offer opportunities for authentic evaluation, as well as for performance assessment (for spelling evaluation guidelines see **Spelling Sourcebook 1**, Article 10, page 45).

How does Spelling Sourcebook 2 complement Spelling Sourcebook 1 to ensure spelling mastery?

Spelling Sourcebook 2 provides abundant language-integrated ideas for making spelling instruction a meaningful complement to the writing-rich curriculum. But the activities do *NOT constitute a total spelling program*. The activity options simply support the **Spelling Sourcebook** methodology outlined in **Spelling Sourcebook 1**. Implemented together, **Spelling Sourcebook 1**, the program design; and **Spelling Sourcebook 2**, the support activities for words 1–400, offer commonsense strategies for ensuring language learning and spelling growth where it really counts—in writing.

Activities to Teach and Extend High-Frequency Core Words 1–400

1 the

Visual Skill-Building, Art

◆ Have students cut *the* words from magazines and newspapers. Then paste them on construction paper to make a collage. Point out *he* inside each *the*.

Writing Words, Predicting Spellings, Capitalization

◆ Ask each student to name an object in the room. Write the names of the objects on the chalkboard using this model: _____ desk. Have students predict the spellings of words as they are written. Ask students to write the word *the* on the chalkboard preceding their word. Then make sentences such as *The desk is blue*. Note with students that *The* has a capital letter when it begins a sentence.

2 of

Usage, Predicting Spellings

◆ Have students think of times they use the word *of* (glass *of* milk, made *of* wood, *of* course). Write the *of* phrases on a chart, asking students to predict spellings as the words are written. Have students read the phrases. Then ask them to look and listen for more examples to add to the collection. *Of* has multiple uses in English, many of which are idiomatic.

Visual Skill-Building, Writing Words

◆ Write *of* on the chalkboard, and draw an outline around the word to accentuate its shape. Provide students with graph paper (or use the blackline master on page 108 of *Spelling Sourcebook 1*). Have students write *of* and *the* in the boxes and outline the shape of the words (see Letter Grid Games on page 88 of *Spelling Sourcebook 1*).

3 and

Sound-Symbol Awareness, Vocabulary Skills, Writing Rhymes, Choral Reading

◆ Write _ *and* on the chalkboard. Have students add beginning letters to make new words (*band, brand, grand, hand, land, sand, stand, strand*). Discuss unfamiliar words. Write rhymes with students, using the patterned rhyming words. Then read them chorally.

Book Tie-In, Creating a Book, Reading

NA Follett

◆ Use *Some Things Go Together* (Charlotte Zolotow, Harper, 1978) as a model for a class-made book, *Go Togethers*: cup *and* saucer, salt *and* pepper. Have students read the class book.

4 a

Sound-Symbol Awareness, Writing Words, Art, Reading, Creating a Book

◆ Discuss the letter *a* as a word and as a letter. Show students several popular alphabet books, and note the words illustrating the letter *a*. Then have students make their own "Aa page" by writing a word that begins with the letter *a* and illustrating it. Compile the results into a class-made *A Book* (see page 138, Creating Classroom Books). Expand the activity to other letters.

Art, Writing a Sentence

◆ Draw random lines on a blackline master titled "What is it?" Have students create a picture incorporating the lines into their drawing. On the paper, have students answer the question by writing: *It is a _____*. Provide spelling assistance as needed. Display the results on a bulletin board.

5 to

Art, Creating a Book, Reading

◆ Make the cover for a class-made book titled *I like to . . .* Then have each student create a page by drawing a picture of what he or she likes to do. Have students label each picture with this sentence: *I like to _____*. Provide spelling assistance as needed. Have students read the book.

Homophone Usage,
Writing Sentences

❖ Introduce one homophone of *to*, the number *two*. Then on the chalkboard write the following sentences and have students choose the right word for each blank:

He went _____ (to) bed.
She likes _____ (to) play.
I ate _____ (two) apples.
I have _____ (two) books
Give it _____ (to) me.
She is _____ (two) years old.

Have students write sentences using *to* and *two*. The word *too* can be introduced later. Until then, help students differentiate *to* and *two* as they write.

6 *in*

Book Tie-In, Creating a Book
NA Follett

❖ Use *What's Inside* (Duanne Daughtry, Knopf, 1984) as a model for a class-made book. Peas are *in* pea pods, teeth are *in* mouths, letters are *in* words.

Making Predictions,
Predicting Spellings, Book Tie-In

❖ Ask students what creatures they might find down inside some tall, tall grass. List the creatures on the chalkboard, asking students to predict the spellings as the words are written. Then read the boldly illustrated book *In The Tall, Tall Grass* (Denise Fleming, Holt, 1991), which describes the movements and sounds of various creatures living in the grasses.

Book Tie-In, Antonyms
NA Follett

❖ Use *By The Sea* (Michelle Koch, Greenwillow, 1991) to introduce the concept of opposites, or antonyms. Focus on *in* and *out*.

Sound-Symbol Awareness,
Vocabulary Skills, Reading

❖ Write _ *in* on the chalkboard. Have students add beginning letters to make new words (*fin, pin, shin, chin, skin, thin, spin, grin, tin, sin, win*). Discuss unfamiliar words. Then have students read the words and use them in oral sentences.

7 *is*

Book Tie-In, Creating a Book,
Reading

❖ Use the book *A Hole Is to Dig* (Ruth Kraus, Harper, 1952) to reinforce *a* (4), *to* (5), and *is*. The book introduces concepts such as "grass *is* to cut" and "a face *is* to make faces." Ask students to write definitions using the same frame: *A _____ is to _____.* Compile the results into a class-made book for students to read.

Book Tie-In,
Visual Skill-Building
NA Follett

❖ Use *Is It Something? Is It Nothing?* (Jeni Basset, Watts, 1989) to reinforce the concept of zero. Have students identify their spelling word in each of the questions.

Writing Words

❖ Use *is* and review words 1–6 for the Mystery Words game (see *Spelling Sourcebook 1,* page 89).

8 *you*

Visual Skill-Building,
Writing Words

❖ Write *you* on the chalkboard, and draw an outline around the word to accentuate its shape. Provide students with graph paper (or use the blackline master on page 108 of *Spelling Sourcebook 1*). Have students write *you* in the boxes and outline its shape (see Letter Grid Games on page 88 of *Spelling Sourcebook 1*). Have students review words 1–7 using the word shape activity. Ask students to find the two words that have the same shape (*in, is*).

Visual Skill-Building ⟡ Point out that *you* includes the letter *u*. Have students write *you* and circle the letter *u* in the word.

Book Tie-In, Vocabulary Skills, ⟡ Use *All About You* (Catherine and Laurence Anholt, Viking, 1992) to develop
Writing a List, vocabulary skills related to everyday activities. Then have students list in
Public Speaking writing and report orally to the class about things they often do after school.

9 *that*

Sound-Symbol Awareness, ⟡ Write _at on the chalkboard. Have students add beginning letters to make new
Writing Rhymes, words (*bat, cat, fat, hat, mat, pat, rat, sat, brat, chat, vat, flat*). Write rhymes
Choral Reading with students, using the patterned rhyming words. Then read them chorally.

Sound-Symbol Awareness ⟡ Ask students to find a review word that begins with the same sound and letters
as *that* (*the*, 1). Then have students brainstorm for more words that begin with
the same *th* sound. Choices may include *this, these, those, them, they,*
there/their, then.

Apostrophe, Book Tie-In ⟡ Write *that's* on the chalkboard, and explain that it is spelled using two familiar
N⁴ Follett words, *that* and *is* (7). Discuss the use of the apostrophe (contractions will be
introduced with 76). Then use *That's Good! That's Bad!* (Margery Cuyler, Holt,
1991). The story repeats the title phrases through a series of lucky escapes.

10 *it*

Book Tie-In, Visual Skill- ⟡ Use *There's an Ant in Anthony* (Bernard Most, Morrow, 1980) to reinforce the
Building, Writing Words concept of words inside words. Then help students collect words with *it* inside
(*little, city, kitten, sit, it's, with*). Review the words *the* (1), *and* (3), and *that* (9),
using the words-in-words activity. Have students write the words and the words
found inside each.

Sound-Symbol Awareness, ⟡ Ask students to write *it*. Then have them follow these directions to write new
Writing Sentences and review words:
Change one letter of *it* to make *in* (6).
Change one letter of *it* to make *is* (7).
Add one letter to *it* to make *fit, sit, hit, bit.*
Change one letter of *it* to make *at.*
Change one letter of *it* to make *if.*
Have students write sentences using some of the words they made.

11 *he*

Antonyms ⟡ Review the antonyms *in* (6) and *out*. Then introduce the antonyms *he* and *she*.
Book Tie-In, ⟡ Use *Alphabeasts: A Hide and Seek Alphabet Book* (Durga Burnhard, Holiday,
Visual Skill-Building 1993), a gamelike book in which alphabetical animals are hidden in pictures.
After students have practiced their visual skills on the animal puzzles, introduce
the Word Look-Alike game to reinforce the words *he, of* (2), *to* (5), *in* (6), *is* (7),
and *it* (10). Make a blackline master of the rows shown on page 10. Do the first
two rows with students, asking them to circle the words in each row that match
the underlined word. After they have completed a row, have them turn the paper
over, picture the underlined word, and write it. Have them complete the
remaining four rows as seatwork.

he	be	he	hi	ha	be	me	we	he	ho	the
of	if	of	to	off	of	for	do	oh	ok	off
to	ho	do	of	to	go	so	to	too	do	two
in	on	an	in	is	if	hi	in	tin	it	in
is	as	so	is	sit	us	is	its	as	is	is
it	if	of	in	at	to	it	hi	is	its	it

12 *for*

Writing Sentences, Reading
- Write on the chalkboard: *Books are for reading.* Use it as a model for creating sentences with students: _____ *are for* _____ (Horses are for riding, Apples are for eating, Balls are for throwing). Have students read the sentences.

Homophone Usage, Writing Sentences
- Review *to* (5) and its homophone *two.* Write *for* on the chalkboard and the number word *four.* Then write the following sentences and have students choose the right word for each blank:

    These _____ (four) books are _____ (for) you.
    It is time _____ (for) the _____ (four) of us to go.
    I like _____ (to) play with my _____ (four) friends.
    Take _____ (two) apples _____ (for) your lunch.
    The _____ (four) boys went home at _____ (four) o'clock.
    This is _____ (for) you _____ (to) eat.

    Have students write sentences using the homophones *four, for, two,* and *to.*

13 *was*

Visual Skill-Building, Writing Sentences
- Play the Hidden-Word Game. Write a long sequence of nonsense letters on the chalkboard in which there are many *was* words:

    tswasguhwasopiwasbkfjwasvtwasitsawwaswinbdwasswimkdwas

    Let students take turns circling *was* in the sequence of letters. Then make a Hidden-Word Game blackline master for students to complete using *was* and selected review words 1–12. For each sequence of letters, tell students which word to circle and how many of the words there are to find in the sequence. Then have students write the circled words in a sentence.

14 *on*

Book Tie-In, Sound-Symbol Awareness, Art, Writing Words
- Use the alphabet book *On Market Street* (Arnold Lobel, Greenwillow, 1981), which introduces objects one can buy on Market Street . . . from apples to zippers. Ask students to create pictures of more shops labeled with the shop names for an "On Market Street" bulletin board.

Book Tie-In, Antonyms
- Use *Inside, Outside, Upside Down* (Jan and Stan Berenstain, Macmillan, 1983) to reinforce antonyms. Review the antonyms *in* (6) and *out,* and *he* (11) and *she.* Extend the concept of opposites to *on* and *off.* Then introduce antonyms for review words: *to* (5) and *from, you* (8) and *me* or *I, that* (9) and *this, for* (12) and *against.*

15 *are*

Visual Skill-Building, Predicting Spellings

Write the letter *r* on the chalkboard. Explain that there is a letter *r* and a word with the same name, *are*. Have students write *are* and circle the *r* in the middle. Let students take turns contributing sentences that use the word *are*. Write the sentences on the chalkboard, underlining *are* in each sentence. Ask students to predict the spellings of selected words in the sentences as they are written.

Book Tie-In, Creating a Book, Reading

Use *Are We Almost There?* (James Stevenson, Greenwillow, 1985), a humorous tale of two animal children enduring a long car ride to the beach. Follow up with students writing a "Long Trip" story to compile into a class-made book for them to read.

16 *as*

Writing Similes, Art

Write color similes with students: *As* green *as* grass, *as* white *as* snow, *as* orange *as* pumpkins. Have students choose one simile to write and illustrate. Display the results on a bulletin board.

Book Tie-In, Writing Reasons

Extend the concept of similes with *As Right As Right Can Be* (Anne Rose, Dial, 1976), a silly story about how the purchase of a pair of shoelaces leads to buying a new house and furniture to match. Ask students to decide whether this story is a true or make-believe tale and to write a reason for their choice.

Sound-Symbol Awareness

Write _*as* on the chalkboard. Ask students what they need to add to make the word say *was* (13). When the *w* is added, ask, "But do we say *WAS*?" (pronounce with short *a*). "No! We say *WAS*" (pronounce with short *u*). Then make the word *has*. Note with students the similarities among the letters of the three words *as*, *has*, and *was*, but the inconsistency of the sound of *a*. Conclude that spelling English words does not always make sense.

17 *with*

Reading, Writing Phrases

Have students read and review the go-together book created with *and* (3). Create pairs that go together using *with* as the connector: bread *with* butter, fish *with* water, clouds *with* raindrops.

Sound-Symbol Awareness, Predicting Spellings

Write *with* on the chalkboard. Underline the letters *th*. Provide clues for students to name these *th*-ending words: *earth, strength, mouth, north, south, teeth, tooth, Fourth of July, breath, path, math, bath, cloth*. Write the words on the chalkboard as they are guessed, asking students to predict the spellings.

Book Tie-In, Making Inferences

Use *With the Wind* (Liz Damrell, Orchard/Jackson, 1991), a story of a physically handicapped boy's feelings of freedom riding a horse with the wind. Point out the *with* in the book's title. Following the reading, ask students to tell what connection the book title has to the story content.

18 *his*

Visual Skill Building

Write *his* on the chalkboard. Ask students to find a review word inside (*is* 7).

Antonyms

Introduce the antonym of *his*, the word *her(s)*.

Sound-Symbol Awareness, Writing Sentences

Ask students to write *his*. Then have them follow these directions to write new words:

Change one letter of *his* to make *has*.

Change one letter of *his* to make *him*.

Add one letter to *his* to make *this*.

Have students write a sentence for each word they made.

19 *they*

Visual Skill-Building ◈ Write *they* on the chalkboard. Ask students to find two review words inside: *the* (1), *he* (11).

Antonyms ◈ Introduce the antonym of *they*, the word *we*.

Visual Skill-Building, Writing Words ◈ Write *they* on the chalkboard, and draw an outline around the word to accentuate its shape. Provide students with graph paper (or use the blackline master on page 108 of **Spelling Sourcebook 1**). Have students write *they* in the boxes and outline its shape (see Letter Grid Games on page 88 of **Spelling Sourcebook 1**). Then have students make a word shape for one of their review words, exchange papers with a partner, and see if the partner can fill in the boxes with the appropriate word.

20 *at*

Reading ◈ Have students read the rhymes they made as they studied *that* (9).

Writing Words, Book Tie-In ◈ Write *_at* on the chalkboard. Ask students to write words with this pattern. Make a cumulative list on the chalkboard. Then read *The Cat in the Hat* (Dr. Seuss, Random House, 1957) to discover how many of their *_at* words are used in the rhyming story.

Book Tie-In, Making Inferences, Predicting Spellings ◈ Introduce *At the Frog Pond* (Tilde Michels, Harper, 1989) by showing students the cover of the book and reading the title. Write students' ideas of what might happen "at the frog pond." Have students predict spellings as words are written. After reading the book, compare the content of the story with the written predictions.

21 *be*

Art, Writing A Sentence, Public Speaking ◈ Brainstorm for characters in the students' favorite stories (Little Red Riding Hood, Chicken Little, Alexander). Then ask students to choose a story character they would like to *be*. Have students draw a picture of their choice and write this sentence: *I want to be _____.* Then have students tell why they made the choice they did.

Homophone Usage, Writing Sentences ◈ Introduce the homophone of *be*, the insect *bee*. Have students use the homophones in oral and written sentences to differentiate them. Review *to* (5) and *two*, and *for* (12) and *four*.

22 *this*

Visual Skill-Building ◈ Find words inside *this* (*his, is, hi*). Use the words-in-words activity with review words *the* (1), *that* (9), *for* (12), *was* (13), *his* (18), and *they* (19).

Choral Reading, Writing Words, Book Tie-In ◈ Write the words for the Mother Goose rhyme "This Little Pig Went to Market" on the chalkboard, drawing a fill-in blank each time the word *this* is used. Have the class chorally read the poem while different students write the word *this* in the blanks. Use the same technique for the refrain in "London Bridge": ". . . go *this* way and that way . . . " Use the book *London Bridge Is Falling Down* (Peter Spier, Doubleday, 1957).

Antonyms ◈ Review the antonym of *this*, the word *that* (9).

23 *from*

Book Tie-In, Writing Stories,
Creating a Book, Reading
Use *From Me to You* (Paul Rogers, Watts, 1988), a story a grandmother tells to her granddaughter that highlights events in her life of eighty years. Have each student ask an older person to briefly relate an event from the past. Ask students to write a story of the event. Compile the anecdotes into a class-made book, *From Me to You*, modeled after Rogers' book. Then have students read their contributions to the class.

Antonyms
Review the antonym of *from*, the word *to* (5).

24 *I*

Book Tie-In, Writing Stories
Use *I Am Eyes Ni Macho* (Leila Ward, Scholastic, 1987), a tale of a Kenyan child. Use the story as a catalyst for students' writing about themselves. Title each writing piece with the name of its author: "I Am _____."

Capitalization
Discuss capital and lowercase letters. Point out that the word *I* is always written with a capital *I*.

Homophone Usage,
Writing Sentences, Book Tie-In
Introduce the homophone of *I*, the word *eye*. Have students use the homophones in oral and written sentences to differentiate them. Use *Eye Spy: A Mysterious Alphabet* (Linda Bourke, Chronicle, 1991), in which clues are hidden in the pictures. The guessing-game book intermingles word play, including homophones, into the artwork and alphabet story.

25 *have*

Book Tie-In, Creating A Book,
Reading
Use *Pickles Have Pimples* (Judi Barrett, Atheneum, 1986) as a model for a class-made book of associations: "chicks *have* peeps, beds *have* sleeps." Have students read the new book.

Sound-Symbol Awareness,
Writing Words
Write *have* on the chalkboard. Ask students to identify the letter *e*. Point out that the *e* cannot be heard when *have* is said. Count the letters they see (4) and the letters they hear (3). Ask students to find and write words from books they are reading that have a silent *e* at the end.

Multiple Meanings,
Book Tie-In
Have can be used in more than one way. Illustrate this with *A Turkey for Thanksgiving* (Eve Bunting, Clarion, 1991), in which Mrs. Moose says she'd like to have a turkey for Thanksgiving and Mr. Moose invites a real one to join the moose family for their holiday feast.

26 *or*

Art, Book Tie-In
Have students make and label pictures of a favorite food (strawberry yogurt, popcorn, raisins). Play a game with the pictures. In a pocket chart place the word *or*. Then select two food pictures to place on either side. Say, "Do you want _____ *or* _____ ?" Students take turns choosing a food picture. Each time a food picture is chosen, replace it with another until all the pictures have been chosen and every student has had a turn. Extend the activity with *Would You Rather* (John Burningham, HarperCollins, 1993), an interactive book of choices that features *or.*

Visual Skill-Building, Writing Words

◆ Play the Word Look-Alike game introduced with *he* (11). Ask students to circle the words in each row like the underlined word. Then they turn the paper over, picture the underlined word, and write it.

<u>or</u>	on	of	or	to	at	of	and	or	on	or
<u>at</u>	of	on	to	at	and	it	at	it	at	of
<u>be</u>	we	to	at	to	be	he	be	of	be	me
<u>was</u>	with	as	was	saw	was	as	we	with	was	saw
<u>of</u>	to	of	off	on	oh	off	or	no	of	for

27 *by*

Sound-Symbol Awareness, Writing Words, Vocabulary Skills, Writing Rhymes, Choral Reading

◆ Write _y on the chalkboard. Have students add beginning letters to make new words that rhyme with *by* (*dry, fry, cry, sky, pry, sly, spy, shy, my, try, fly*). If rhyming words are suggested that do not follow the same spelling pattern, write them in a separate list (*pie*). Discuss unfamiliar words. Write rhymes with students, using the rhyming words. Then read them chorally.

Sound-Symbol Awareness, Predicting Spellings

◆ Ask students to name words that begin with the letter *b* as in *by*. Write the words on the chalkboard, asking students to predict the spellings as the words are written.

Homophone Usage, Writing Words

◆ Introduce the homophone of *buy*, the word *by*. Write the following sentences on the chalkboard, asking students to choose the right homophone for each blank:

Sit _____ me. (by)
The book was read to us _____ the old man. (by)
Mom is going to _____ a new dress. (buy)
The parade went _____ our house. (by)
_____ six apples at the store. (Buy)

28 *one*

Book Tie-Ins, Writing Words, Creating a Book

◆ Use *Moja Means One: Swahili Counting Book* (Muriel Feelings, Dial, 1971), to introduce number words through the sights and sounds of East Africa. Then write the number words *one* through *ten* and corresponding numerals on a chart. Say a number, and ask students to write the correct number word using the chart as a reference. Follow up with a book of original poems about numbers one through ten, *An Old-Fashioned 1 2 3 Book* (Elizabeth Allen Ashton, Viking, 1991), or *One Prickly Porcupine* (Odette and Bruce Johnson, Oxford, 1992) to use as a model for students' illustrated number books.

Homophone Usage, Writing Words, Writing Sentences

◆ Introduce the homophone of *one*, the word *won*. Write the following sentences on the chalkboard, asking students to choose the right homophone for each blank:

I have _____ apple. (one) Who _____ the race? (won)
They _____ the game. (won) She is _____ year old. (one)

Review previously introduced homophones: *to* (5) and *two*, *for* (12) and *four*, *be* (21) and *bee*, *I* (24) and *eye*, *by* (27) and *buy*. Have students use the homophones in oral and written sentences to differentiate them.

29 *had*

Sound-Symbol Awareness, Writing Words, Vocabulary Skills, Writing Rhymes

✦ Write _ad on the chalkboard. Have students add beginning letters to make new words (*bad, dad, lad, fad, mad, pad, glad, sad*). Discuss unfamiliar words. Have students write rhymes using the patterned rhyming words and read them to the class.

Sound-Symbol Awareness, Writing Words, Vocabulary Skills

✦ Write *ha_* on the chalkboard. Have students add ending letters to make new words (*has, ham, hat, hatch, hash, hand, have* [25]). Discuss unfamiliar words.

Visual Skill-Building

✦ Play the Hidden-Word game introduced with *was* (13), using *had* and selected review words.

30 *not*

Book Tie-In, Writing Reasons

✦ Use *Do Not Open* (Brinton Turkle, Dutton, 1981), about a bottle found on the shore and labeled "Do Not Open." Follow up by creating a "Do Not _____" rule list with students. It may include Do Not Disturb, Do Not Run, Do Not Bend, Do Not Touch, Do Not Feed the Animals, Do Not Cross, Do Not Enter. Then have students choose one rule, write where it might be found, and write reasons why it is a good rule.

Homophone Usage, Book Tie-In, Making Inferences

✦ Introduce the homophone of *not*, the word *knot*. Note the silent *k*. Have students find *not* inside of *knot*. Use *Knots on a Counting Rope* (Bill Martin, Jr. and John Archambault, Henry Holt, 1987), a Native American tale. Following the reading ask students to tell what connection the story title has to the book content.

Writing Words

✦ Introduce Bingo to students, using *not* and selected review words (see **Spelling Sourcebook 1**, page 87).

31 *but*

Book Tie-In, Writing Reasons

✦ Use *But Martin!* (June Counsel, Faber, 1984), a science-fiction tale. Follow up by asking students to decide whether this story was true or make-believe and to write reasons for their choice.

Visual Skill-Building, Writing Words

✦ Write *but* on the chalkboard, and draw an outline around the word to accentuate its shape. Provide students with graph paper (or use the blackline master on page 108 of **Spelling Sourcebook 1**). Have students write *but* in the boxes and outline its shape (see Letter Grid Games on page 88 of **Spelling Sourcebook 1**). Ask students to find the review word that has the same shape as *but* (*had* [29]). Then have students make a word shape for one of their review words, exchange papers with a partner, and see if the partner can fill in the boxes with the appropriate word.

32 *what*

Visual Skill-Building, Writing Words

✦ Write *what* on the chalkboard. Cover the *w*. Ask students to write the new word *hat*. Then cover the *h* and have students write *at*. Have students find and write words inside selected review words.

Writing Riddles, Creating a Book, Reading
✦ Ask students to create "What Hat?" riddles by writing clues to identify a person who traditionally wears a special hat (cowboy, police officer, nurse, motorcyclist, baseball player, firefighter, witch, Santa, king or queen, snowman, bride, chauffeur, Uncle Sam, pilgrim, swimmer, baby, surgeon, or graduate). Compile the riddles into a class-made book with the clues on one side of the paper and a student-drawn picture of the answer on the opposite side. Have students read their book aloud.

Book Tie-In
✦ Use *What Shape?* (Debbie MacKinnon, Dial, 1992), a companion to *What Color?* and *What's Inside?* to develop concepts and reinforce the word *what.*

Book Tie-In, Choral Reading, Writing Words
✦ Good for choral chanting, *Polar Bear, Polar Bear, What Do You Hear?* (Bill, Martin, Jr., Holt, 1991) is reminiscent of Martin's *Brown Bear, Brown Bear, What Do You See?* Reinforce the spelling of *what* by creating a cloze activity in which students fill in *what* in the rhyming text.

33 *all*

Word Analysis, Writing Words, Reading
✦ Write _all on the chalkboard, and note with *the* students that *all* is the first spelling word to have double letters. Ask students to find and write words from their reading books that have double letters. Write some of these words on the chalkboard, underline the double letters, and have students read the words. Point out as the words are read that students *hear* one letter but *see* double letters.

Sound-Symbol Awareness, Vocabulary Skills, Writing Rhymes
✦ Write _all on the chalkboard. Have students add beginning letters to make new words (*ball, call, fall, hall, mall, tall, stall, small, wall*). Discuss unfamiliar words. Have students write rhymes using the patterned rhyming words and read them to the class.

Antonyms
✦ Introduce the antonym of *all,* the word *none.* Review selected antonyms.

Book Tie-In, Writing Stories, Creating a Book, Reading
✦ Use *All Wet! All Wet!* (James Skofield, Harper, 1984), about a boy who goes for a walk in the rain. Ask students to write about a time when they got "all wet." Compile the stories into a class-made book of the same name. Have students read their contributions to the class.

34 *were*

Writing Questions and Answers, Question Mark, Predicting Spellings
✦ Ask students to help compose question-and-answer sentences using *were* (Where <u>were</u> the books? They <u>were</u> at home.) Write the sentences on the chalkboard, asking students to predict the spellings of selected words. Point out the use of the question mark. Then have students write a question and answer using a review word in each.

Visual Skill-Building, Writing Words
✦ Play the Hidden-Word game introduced with *was* (13), using *were* and selected review words.

Writing Words
✦ Introduce Race Track Spelling (see **Spelling Sourcebook 1,** page 90) with *were* and selected review words.

35 *when*

Visual Skill-Building
✦ Have students find and write words inside *when* (*hen, he*).

Book Tie-In, Creating a Book, Reading, Public Speaking
◆ Use *When We Grow Up* (Anne Rockwell, Dutton, 1981), a book about what a group of classmates plan to do when they are older. Then have students write what they'd like to do when they grow up. Compile the results into a class-made book of the same name. Then have students read their page to the class and tell why they made the choice they did.

Book Tie-In, Writing a Story Ending
◆ *When the Rain Stops* (Sheila Cole, Lothrop, 1991) can be followed up with students writing what they'd like to do when the rain stops. The girl and her father in the story decide to go outside to pick blackberries. Save the story ending until after students write.

Sorting Words
◆ Have students play Word Sorts (see *Spelling Sourcebook 1*, page 92) using these words: *when, what* (32), *that* (9), *they* (19).

Begin Grade 2

36 *we*

Book Tie-In, Visual Skill-Building, Writing Words
NA Follett
◆ Use *Find the Canary* (Neil and Ting Morris, Little, 1983), in which a canary is cleverly hidden in a series of pictures. After students have practiced their visual skills on the canary puzzles, play the Word Look-Alike game. Ask students to circle the words in each row that are like the underlined word. Then they turn the paper over, picture the underlined word, and write it.

<u>we</u>	me	be	he	we	we	me	be	ow	he	we
<u>on</u>	no	an	in	on	no	am	oh	do	on	of
<u>what</u>	that	white	when	hat	what	who	what	hot	why	what

Antonyms, Writing Words
◆ Review the antonym of *we*, the word *they* (19). Review selected antonyms by asking students to write the antonym for a given word.

37 *there*

Writing Jokes, Book Tie-Ins, Creating a Book, Reading
NA Follett
◆ Have students write "knock-knock" jokes to reinforce *there*. Use *Knock! Knock!* (Colin and Jacqui Hawkins, Aladdin, 1991) and *Knockout Knock Knocks* (Caroline Levine, Dutton, 1978) as models for the jokes. Compile the jokes into a class-made book titled *Who's There?* Have students read the jokes they contributed, and have the class try to guess the answer.

Antonyms
◆ Introduce the antonym of *there*, the word *here*. Note that *here* is inside *there*.

Visual Skill-Building, Writing Words
◆ Write *there* on the chalkboard, and draw an outline around the word to accentuate its shape. Provide students with graph paper (or use the blackline master on page 108 of *Spelling Sourcebook 1*). Have students write *there* in the boxes and outline its shape (see Letter Grid Games on page 88 of *Spelling Sourcebook 1*). Then have students make a word shape for one of their review words, exchange papers with a partner, and see if the partner can fill in the boxes with the appropriate word.

38 *can*

Book-Tie-In, Word Analysis, Predicting Spellings
NA Follett
◆ Use *Since Lulu Learned the Cancan* (Orel Protopopescu, Green Tiger, 1991) for a for-fun introduction to *can*. Point out the words *cancan* and *Lulu*, and ask students to name other words that contain repetitive letter sequences (*yo-yo, mama, papa, Mimi, choo-choo*). Write the words on the chalkboard, and have students predict their spellings as they are written.

Book Tie-In
NA Follett
◆ Use *Pretend You're a Cat* (Jean Marzollo, Dial, 1990), in which rhyming lines describe thirteen different animals: "Can you bark?/ Can you beg?/ Can you scratch/ With your leg?" Have students guess the animals as the story is read.

Sound-Symbol Awareness,
Vocabulary Skills, Writing
Rhymes, Reading
◆ Write _an on the chalkboard. Have students add beginning letters to make new words (*Dan, fan, man, Nan, pan, ran, tan, than, plan, van*). Discuss unfamiliar words. Have students write rhymes using the patterned rhyming words and read them to the class.

Multiple Meanings,
Book Tie-In, Writing Sentences
◆ Review the concept that the same word can mean more than one thing. Write these sentences on the chalkboard, and discuss the different meanings of *can*:

Put the <u>can</u> in the trash.
I <u>can</u> read.

✓Follow up with the book *Can Do, Jenny Archer* (Ellen Conford, Little, 1991), in which Jenny participates in a can-collecting contest. Then have students write sentences using *can* in different ways.

39 *an*

Visual Skill-Building
◆ Use the _*an* list generated with *can* (38) to have students find the word *an* inside each of the words.

Word Usage, Writing Sentences
◆ Give examples of *an* used instead of the word *a* (words beginning with vowels: *apple, orange, inch, elephant*). Ask students to look for examples of *a* and *an* in classroom books and share the examples they found. Then have students write sentences that use *a* and *an*.

40 *your*

Visual Skill-Building
◆ Have students write *your*. Then have them find *you* and *our* inside *your*.

Visual Skill-Building, Filling
Out a Form
◆ Create a personal data form for students to complete. Include the following: your name, your address, your phone number, your birthday, your favorite color, your favorite food, your favorite book, your best friend. Before they complete the form, ask students to circle each *your* on the data sheet.

Writing Words
◆ Play Mystery Word (see **Spelling Sourcebook 1**, page 89). Use *your* and selected review words.

41 *which*

Word Analysis, Writing
Sentences
◆ Write *which* and *witch* on the chalkboard. Contrast the words. Have students write a sentence using each word.

Book Tie-In
NA Follett
◆ Use *Which Pig Would You Choose?* (Edith Kunhardt, Greenwillow, 1990), a pattern book in which students participate in the reading by making choices for clothing, meals, and chores.

Writing Words
◆ Introduce the spelling game Red and Green (see **Spelling Sourcebook 1**, page 90). Use *which* and selected review words.

42 *their*

Homophone Usage,
Writing Sentences, Creating a
Reference Chart
◆ Reinforce the concept of homophones with *Eight Ate: A Feast of Homonym Riddles* (Marvin Terban, Ticknor, 1982). Review the homophone of *their*, the word *there* (37). Have students use the homophones in oral and written sentences to differentiate them. Create a large classroom reference chart with context sentences for the proper use of *there* and *their*. Review selected homophones, and add context sentences to the chart for those that present a problem.

Writing Words	◆ Introduce the All-Play Spelling Bee (see ***Spelling Sourcebook 1***, page 86). Include *their* and selected review words.

43 *said*

Book Tie-In, Writing Rhymes, Choral Reading *NA Follett*	◆ Use *"There Are Rocks in My Socks," Said the Ox to the Fox* (Patricia Thomas, Lothrop, 1979), a for-fun rhyming story with multiple opportunities for students to predict what might happen next. Use the title as a model for student-made sentences: *"There's a pie in the sky," said Mr. Fry to a guy.* Have students chorally read the rhyming sentences.
Idiomatic Usage, Writing Explanations	◆ Ask students to explain in writing what they think it means to say (then discuss): Easier said than done. No sooner said than done.
Visual Skill-Building, Writing Words	◆ Write *said* on the chalkboard, and draw an outline around the word to accentuate its shape. Provide students with graph paper (or use the blackline master on page 108 of ***Spelling Sourcebook 1***). Have students write *said* in the boxes and outline its shape (see Letter Grid Games on page 88 of ***Spelling Sourcebook 1***). Expand the activity to include selected review words.

44 *if*

Book Tie-In, Creating a Book	◆ Use *If I Ran the Zoo* (Dr. Seuss, Random, 1950), a classic tale featuring animals you wouldn't expect to see in your city zoo. Follow up with students creating class-made books that feature stories and pictures of animals you wouldn't expect to find in a zoo . . . in a forest . . . in your home as a pet.
Book Tie-Ins, Hypothesizing, Writing Speculations *NA Follett*	◆ To explore fantasy and reinforce the word *if*, pose questions to students, such as "If you had a magic carpet, where would you go?" This question and others are asked in the book *Imagine That! Exploring Make-Believe* (Joyce Strauss, Human Sciences, 1984). Have students write their answers. Follow up the lesson with *If Dinosaurs Came to Town* (Dom Mansell, Little, 1991), a whimsical tale in a modern-day setting.
Sound-Symbol Awareness, Writing Sentences	◆ Ask students to write *if*. Then have them follow these directions to write review words: Change one letter of *if* to make *of* (2). Change one letter of *if* to make *in* (6). Change one letter of *if* to make *is* (7). Change one letter of *if* to make *it* (10). Then have students write a sentence for each word they made.

45 *do*

Writing Lists	◆ Make a daily class "To Do" list for several consecutive days. Then have students make a personal "To Do" list, including things outside of school they wish to remember to do.
Homophone Usage, Writing Sentences	◆ Introduce the homophones of *do*, the words *due* and *dew*. Have students use the homophones in oral and written sentences to differentiate them.
Other Word Forms, Book Tie-In, Suffix Practice *NA Follett*	◆ Introduce common other word forms of *do*: *did, doing, done, does, didn't, doesn't, don't, doer*. To reinforce *doing* and the *ing* suffix, use *Seeing, Saying, Doing, Playing: A Big Book of Action Words* (Taro Gomi, Chronicle, 1991). Have students write words with the *ing* suffix.

46 *will*

Book Tie-In, Multiple Meanings, Writing Sentences

◆ Write the book title *Will's Mammoth*. Talk about *Will* as a nickname for *William*. Explore other meanings for *will*. Then read *Will's Mammoth* (Rafe Martin, Putnam, 1989), an imaginative story of Will and his many mammoths. Then have students write sentences that use *will* in different ways.

Sound-Symbol Awareness, Vocabulary Skills, Writing Sentences

◆ Write *_ill* on the chalkboard. Have students add beginning letters to make new words (*bill, chill, dill, drill, fill, gill, grill, hill, Jill, kill, mill, pill, quill, thrill, sill, spill, still*). Then write *w_ll* on the chalkboard and have students add new vowels to make new words (*wall, well*). Then write *wi_* on the chalkboard and have students make more new words by changing the last letter (*wig, win, wit, witch, with, wind, wish, wick*). Provide word clues for assistance. Discuss any unfamiliar words. Then have students use some of the words they made in sentences.

Word Analysis

◆ Write *all* (33) on the chalkboard. Review the double *l* in *all* and *will*.

47 *each*

Sound-Symbol Awareness, Predicting Spellings, Vocabulary Skills, Writing Sentences

◆ Write *each* and underline the *ch*. Brainstorm for other words that end in *ch* (*which* [41], *church, much, watch, inch, rich, such*). Write the words and have students predict the spellings as they are written. Underline the *ch* in each word. Then brainstorm for words that begin with *ch* (*church, children, child, chair, chief, chapter.*) Write the words and have students predict the spellings as they are written. Underline the *ch* in each word. Discuss any unfamiliar words. Then have students make sentences with some of the words they made.

Book Tie-In

◆ Use *Each Peach, Pear, Plum* (Allan and Janet Ahlberg, Viking, 1992), a picture book guessing game, to reinforce the word *each*.

Writing Words

◆ Play Race Track Spelling (see **Spelling Sourcebook 1**, page 90) with *each* and selected review words.

48 *about*

Book Tie-In, Visual Skill-Building

NA Follett

◆ Use *The Turn About, Think About, Look About Book* (Beau Gardner, Lothrop, 1984) which engages students in making visual discoveries as pictures are turned about and thought about. Point out *about* in the book's title and *out* inside *about*.

Idiomatic Usage, Writing Explanations

◆ Ask students to explain in writing what they think it means to say each of these expressions (then discuss):

> It's nothing to write home about.
> Go about your business.
> Keep your wits about you.
> It's about time!

Writing Sentences

◆ Introduce the game Questions and Answers (see **Spelling Sourcebook 1**, page 90), using *about* and selected review words.

49 *how*

Book Tie-Ins, Writing Directions, Creating a Book

◆ Introduce students to how-to books with *Ed Emberley's Great Thumbprint Drawing Book* (Ed Emberley, Little, 1977), which shows how to make thumbprint art, or *Fun With Paper* (Robyn Supraner, Troll, 1981), about how to make paper crafts, or *The Little Pigs First Cookbook* (Cameron Watson, Little,

NA Follett

1987), which has easy recipes. Follow the directions in one of the books to do an activity together. Then review the directions, and write them on a chart. Then ask students to write directions for something they know how to do and would like to share with others. Compile the written directions into a class-made "How-To" book.

Sound-Symbol Awareness, Writing Sentences
Note with students that *about* (48) and *how* have the same vowel sound, but one uses *ou* and the other *ow* to spell the sound. Ask students to collect other words that have this sound spelled in these two ways. Answers may include *mountain, hour, south, out, found, house*; and *down, now, brown, power, crowd*. Have students write selected *ou* and *ow* words in sentences (Our brown house is on South Street).

50 *up*

Book Tie-In, Writing Stories
NA Follett
Use *Up and Up* (Shirley Hughes, Lothrop, 1986), a wordless picture book about a girl wishing to fly. Have students write stories to fit the pictures.

Antonyms
Introduce the antonym of *up*, the word *down*.

Idiomatic Usage, Writing Explanations
Ask students to explain in writing what they think it means to say each of these expressions (then discuss):

What's up?
Time is up.
to be up a creek without a paddle
to give up
to be a cut-up (See literature entry below.)
to crack up (See literature entry below.)

Book Tie-In, Writing a Sequel
✓Use *The Cut-Ups Crack Up* (James Marshall, Viking, 1992), a book about the pranksters Spud and Joe. Follow up with a class-written sequel about the Cut-ups.

51 *out*

Book Tie-Ins, Antonyms
Use *Exactly the Opposite* (Tana Hoban, Greenwillow, 1990) to reinforce opposites. Pair *out* with *in* (6). The songbook *Go In and Out the Window* (Dan Fox, Henry Holt, 1987) can introduce students to the song of the same name.

Book Tie-In
Write *out* on the chalkboard. Then write *outer space*. Introduce *Spacey Riddles* (Katy Hall and Lisa Eisenberg, Dial, 1992), which focuses on riddles about outer space.

Visual Skill-Building, Predicting Spellings, Vocabulary Skills, Writing Sentences
Write the word *about* (48) on the chalkboard, and underline *out*. Then ask students to predict the spellings of *shout, without, stout, pout*. Discuss unfamiliar words. Then have students write the words in sentences.

52 *them*

Sound-Symbol Awareness
Review previously introduced words that begin with *th*: *the* (1), *that* (9), *they* (19), *this* (22), *there* (37), and *their* (42). Ask students to add more words to the *th* list. Include *then* (53) and *these* (58).

Visual Skill-Building
Find words inside *them* (*the, he, hem*). Extend the activity to *your* (40), *there* (37), *what* (32), and *this* (22).

Writing Words	✦ Play Bingo (see ***Spelling Sourcebook 1***, page 87) using *them* and selected review words.

53 *then*

Sound-Symbol Awareness	✦ Review the *th* words generated with the study of *them* (52). Have students read the words and contrast the sounds made by the *th* (*think, thought* [unvoiced]; *this, then* [voiced]).
Visual Skill-Building, Writing Sentences	✦ Play the Word Look-Alike game. Ask students to circle the words in each row that are like the underlined word. Then they turn the paper over, picture the underlined word, and write it.

<u>then</u>   than   them   this   hen   than   then   them
<u>them</u>   them   the   they   ten   them   than   then
<u>there</u>   their   then   here   there   those   their   there
<u>their</u>   the   there   this   their   them   there   their

Next, have students write each of the underlined words in a sentence.

Idiomatic Usage, Writing Explanations	✦ Ask students to explain in writing what they think it means to say each of these expressions (then discuss):

every now and then
and then some
then and there

Antonyms	✦ Introduce the antonym of *then*, the word *now*.

54 *she*

Sound-Symbol Awareness, Predicting Spellings, Writing Sentences	✦ Brainstorm for other words that begin with *sh* (*shoe, ship, should, show, shut*). Write the words on the chalkboard, asking students to predict the spellings as the words are written. Present to students this tongue twister: *She sells sea shells down by the seashore.* Then ask students to write tongue twister sentences using *she* and the *sh* words.
Antonyms	✦ Review the antonym of *she*, the word *he* (11).

55 *many*

Visual Skill-Building	✦ Ask students to write words they can find inside *many* (*man, an, any*). Expand the activity by asking students to find words inside selected review words.
Antonyms	✦ Introduce the antonym of *many*, the word *few*.
Writing Questions	✦ Ask students "How Many?" questions that can be verified, such as:

How many days before spring vacation? How many red stripes on the flag? How many children in second grade are named David?

Then have students write "How Many?" questions. Answer the questions as a class.

Idiomatic Usage, Writing Explanations	✦ Ask students to explain in writing what they think it means to say each of these expressions (then discuss):

Too many cooks spoil the broth.
to have too many irons in the fire

56 *some*

Compound Words, Visual Skill-Building, Book Tie-Ins, Writing Descriptions, Writing Speculations

NA Follett

◆ Write *some* on the chalkboard. Tell students that *some* is "sometimes" connected to another word. Introduce the term *compound word* and provide familiar examples. Then ask students to brainstorm for compound words that begin with *some* (*someone, something, somewhere, someplace, somebody, sometime,* and *sometimes*). Write the compounds on the chalkboard, and underline *some* inside each word. Then use *The Something* (Natalie Babbitt, Dell, 1970), a fantasy tale about something in the dark. Follow up with students writing a description of something they think is lurking in the dark nearby. Also use *Somebody and the Three Blairs* (Marilyn Tolhurst, Orchard, 1991), a humorous story parallel to the familiar "Goldilocks." Introduce the book by asking students to speculate in writing who they think the "Somebody" in the book title is.

Homophone Usage

◆ Introduce the homophone of *some*, the word *sum* (only if it is a word used with students in math).

Idiomatic Usage, Writing Explanations

◆ Ask students to explain in writing what they think it means to say each of these expressions (then discuss):

> Use some elbow grease.
> to catch some Zs
> to raise some eyebrows

57 *so*   *NA Follett*

Book Tie-In, Writing Tall Tales

◆ Use *If You Say So, Claude* (Joan Nixon, Warne, 1980), a humorous tall tale. Use it as a model for writing other "If You Say So, _____" tall tales.

Homophone Usage, Writing Sentences

◆ Introduce one homophone of *so*, the word *sew*. Have students use the homophones in oral and written sentences to differentiate them.

Idiomatic Usage, Writing Explanations

◆ Ask students to explain in writing what they think it means to say each of these expressions (then discuss):

so be it	so far, so good
so much the better	so-so
so long	so-and-so

58 *these*

Sound-Symbol Awareness, Writing Sentences

◆ Review *th* words (see *them* [52]). Ask students to use the *th* words in the Sentence Puzzles game (see ***Spelling Sourcebook 1***, page 91).

Antonyms

◆ Introduce the antonym of *these*, the word *those*.

Alphabetical Order, Book Tie-In, Writing Words

◆ Discuss alphabetical order with students. Use *From Acorn to Zoo: And Everything in Between in Alphabetical Order* (Satoshi Kitamura, Farrar, 1992), which poses questions with clues for students to answer. Follow up with students writing each set of words in alphabetical order:

these	many	when	these	what
out	into	these	of	these
about	these	are	have	your

59 *would*

Visual Skill-Building, Writing Questions

◆ Write *would* on the chalkboard, and underline the *ould*. Ask students if they can identify other words that have the *ould* spelling pattern (*could, should*). Ask students to write the *ould* words in sentences that ask a question.

Homophone Usage, Writing Sentences
✦ Introduce the homophone of *would*, the word *wood*. Have students use the homophones in oral and written sentences to differentiate them.

Writing Sentences, Book Tie-In
✦ Write the classic tongue twister, *How much wood would a woodchuck chuck if a woodchuck could chuck wood?"* Then ask students to write it and then try to say it fast. Have students research other tongue twisters, or write original ones and then ask a classmate to say the twisters fast. One source may be *Six Sick Sheep: 101 Tongue Twisters* (Joanna Cole and Stephanie Calmenson, Morrow, 1993).

Remember . . .

Develop spelling accountability as students write—see **Spelling Sourcebook 1**, Article 8, page 33. Spelling mastery is achieved ONLY when students can spell and use words consistently correctly in writing.

60 *other*

Predicting Spellings
✦ Write *other* on the chalkboard. Then ask students to predict how these words would be spelled: *mother, brother, another*.

Idiomatic Usage, Writing Explanations
✦ Ask students to explain in writing what they think it means to say each of these expressions (then discuss):

in one ear and out the other
on the other hand
There are plenty of other fish in the sea.

Writing Words
✦ Use the All-Play Spelling Bee (see **Spelling Sourcebook 1**, page 86) with *other* and selected review words.

61 *into*

Compound Words, Writing Words
✦ Note with students that *into* is their first compound spelling word (*compound word* introduced with [56]). Have students write *into* and underline the two word parts. Then have them brainstorm for and write other compound words.

Idiomatic Usage, Writing Explanations
✦ Ask students to explain in writing what they think it means to say each of these expressions (then discuss):

to toss your hat into the ring
to get into full swing
out of the fry pan and into the fire
to vanish into thin air
to burst into tears

62 *has*

Writing Sentences
✦ Write these sentences on the chalkboard:

An elephant has a trunk.
A book has pages.
A car has wheels.

Ask students to make more sentences following this model: _____ has _____.

Sound-Symbol Awareness, Writing Sentences
✦ Write *has* on the chalkboard. Ask students to follow these directions to write new and review words:

Change one letter of *has* to make *was* (13).
Change one letter of *has* to make *his* (18).
Change one letter of *has* to make *hat*.

Then have students write a sentence for each word they made.

Visual Skill-Building,
Writing Sentences

♦ Play the Hidden-Word game introduced with *was* (13), using *has* and selected review words.

63 *more*

Word Analysis,
Writing Words

♦ Point out the final silent *e* of *more*. Then review previously introduced words with final silent *e*: *are* (15), *have* (25), *one* (28), *were* (34), *there* (37), *some* (56), and *these* (58). Ask students to add more words to the final silent *e* list, and save it for review with *like* (66), *time* (69), and *make* (72).

Idiomatic Usage,
Writing Explanations

♦ Ask students to explain in writing what they think it means to say each of these expressions (then discuss):

Don't bite off more than you can chew.
to wear more than one hat
There's more than meets the eye.

Antonyms, Creating a Word
Puzzle, Writing Words

♦ Introduce the antonym of *more*, the word *less*. Then review selected antonyms and their partners. Have students make a word search puzzle using antonym pairs: They hide one antonym partner in the puzzle and write the other partner as a word search clue (see Letter Grid Games, *Spelling Sourcebook 1*, page 88).

Idiomatic Usage, Writing
Explanations, Book Tie-In

♦ Ask students to write what they think it means to say "more or less." Then use *A Million Fish. . . More or Less* (Patricia McKissack, Knopf, 1992), a tall tale that illustrates the saying.

64 *her*

Antonyms

♦ Review the antonyms of *her(s)*, the words *him* and/or *his* (18).

Writing Questions and Answers

♦ Have students play the game Questions and Answers (see *Spelling Sourcebook 1*, page 90) using *her* and selected review words.

Sound-Symbol Awareness,
Writing Sentences

♦ Write *her* on the chalkboard. Ask students to follow these directions to write new and review words:

Add one letter to *her* to make *here*—He is over *here*.
Add one letter to *her* to make *hers*.
Change one letter of *her* to make *hen*.
Add two letters to *her* to make *there* (37) — She is over *there*.
Add two letters to *her* to make *their* (42) — This is *their* dog.

Then have students write a sentence for each word they made.

65 *two*

Homophone Usage,
Writing Sentences

♦ Review the homophones *two* and *to* (5). Reinforce *two* and *to* by asking students to write sentences using the homophones.

Book Tie-In, Creating a Book,
Reading

NA Follett

♦ Use *Two Is for Dancing: A 1 2 3 of Actions* (Woodleigh Hubbard, Chronicle, 1991). The number story progresses to the number twelve: "One is for dreaming, two is for dancing." Follow up by having students write their own books using the same sentence pattern. Have students read and show their books to the class.

Book Tie-In, Writing Reasons

♦ Use *Two of Everything* (Lily Toy Hong, Whitman, 1993), a Chinese folktale. Then have students write why they would like to have two of something.

66 *like*

Multiple Meanings,
Writing Sentences

♦ Discuss the different meanings of *like*. Check a dictionary with students for verification. Have students write the different meanings in sentences.

NA Follett

Book Tie-In,
Writing Explanations

◆ Use *The 329th Friend* (Marjorie Sharmat, Four Winds, 1992), and then ask students to write the lesson of the story. Help students conclude that the story shows us that you must like yourself in order to genuinely like others.

Predicting Spellings, Word
Analysis

◆ Write *like* on the chalkboard. Then have students predict the spellings of *bike, lake, life, and line*. Note the final silent *e*. Review the final silent *e* words already generated (see *more* [63]).

Other Word Forms, Spelling
Rules, Writing Sentences

◆ Introduce common other word forms of *like*: *likes, liked, liking, likely, likable*. Point out that the final *e* is dropped in *liking* and *likable*. Introduce this spelling rule to students (see *Spelling Sourcebook 1*, page 85). Have students use the other word forms in oral and written sentences.

Writing Words

◆ Introduce the game Connect the Dots (see *Spelling Sourcebook 1*, page 87). Use *like*, its other word forms, and selected review words.

67 *him*

Sound-Symbol Awareness,
Writing Sentences

◆ Write *him* on the chalkboard. Ask students to follow these directions to write new and review words:

Change one letter of *him* to make *ham*.
Change one letter of *him* to make *his* (18).
Change the first part of *him* to make *swim*.
Change one letter of *him* to make *hid*.

Then have students write a sentence for each word they made.

Antonyms

◆ Review the antonym of *him*, the word *her* (64).

68 *see*

Book Tie-In, Writing Sentences,
Creating a Book, Reading

◆ Use *Brown Bear, Brown Bear, What Do You See?* (Bill Martin, Jr., Holt, 1992) to introduce a writing activity in which students use their own name:

Brown Bear, Brown Bear, What do you _____ (see)?
I _____ (see) a red bird looking at me.
_____ , _____ , What do you _____ (see)?
I _____ (see) a _____ looking at me.

Have students illustrate their writing. Compile the results into class-made or student-made books (see page 138, Creating Classroom Books). Have students read the books.

Homophone Usage, Writing
Sentences, Book Tie-In

◆ Introduce the homophone of *see*, the word *sea*. Have students use the homophones in oral and written sentences to differentiate them. Use the alphabet book *Under the Sea From A to Z* (Anne Doubilet, Crown, 1991) to introduce sea life.

Other Word Forms,
Writing Sentences

◆ Introduce common other word forms of *see*: *sees, saw, seeing, seen*. Have students use the other word forms in oral and written sentences.

69 *time*

NA Follett

Book Tie-Ins, Writing Words

◆ Use *My First Book of Time* (Claire Llewellyn, Houghton, 1992) and *What Time Is It, Dracula?* (Victor Ambrus, Crown, 1992) to explore time in an original way. Follow up with students collecting pictures of time pieces for a bulletin board. Have students label each time piece with the time it shows using words, not numerals.

Idiomatic Usage,
Writing Explanations
Ask students to explain in writing what they think it means to say each of these expressions (then discuss):

to give someone a rough time
to kill time
in the nick of time
to get time off

Predicting Spellings,
Word Analysis
Write *time* on the chalkboard. Ask students to predict the spellings of *tame, lime, tile, tide, tire,* and *dime.* Note the final silent *e.*

70 *could*

Visual Skill-Building, Writing
Words, Writing Sentences
Compare the spelling of *could* with *would* (59) and *should.* Write the words on the chalkboard, and draw an outline around each word to accentuate its shape. Provide students with graph paper (or use the blackline master on page 108 of **Spelling Sourcebook 1**). Have students write the words in the boxes and outline their shape (see Letter Grid Games on page 88 of **Spelling Sourcebook 1**). Then have students make word shapes for review words, exchange papers with a partner, and see if the partner can fill in the boxes with the appropriate words. Next, have students write sentences using these words.

Writing Words
Play the game Red and Green (see **Spelling Sourcebook 1**, page 90). Use *could* and selected review words.

Alphabetical Order,
Writing Words
Ask students to write each set of words in alphabetical order:

you	would	could	each	from	more	what
could	many	these	two	said	could	other
about	could	other	could	could	like	could

71 *no*

Book Tie-In
To introduce *no,* use *N-O Spells No!* (Barbara Baker, Dutton, 1991), an easy-reader tale about sibling rivalry.

Book Tie-In, Writing Reasons
Use *No Jumping on the Bed!* (Tedd Arnold, Dial, 1987), a story about Walter, who jumped so hard on his bed he landed in the apartment below. Have students think of a *no* rule at home or school. Then they write reasons why they think the rule is a good one or a bad one.

Homophone Usage,
Writing Sentences
Introduce the homophone of *no,* the word *know.* Have students use the homophones in oral and written sentences to differentiate them.

Antonyms, Writing Words
Introduce the antonym of *no,* the word *yes.* Review selected antonyms by asking students to write the antonym for given words.

Sorting Words
Have students play Word Sorts (see **Spelling Sourcebook 1**, page 92) using these words: *no, we* (36), *not* (30), *now, were* (34), *went.*

72 *make*

Book Tie-In, Writing a Sequel
Use *Dial-a-Croc* (Mike Dumbleton, Orchard, 1991), a story about a funny scheme to make money. Ask students to write a silly sequel about another interesting way to use an animal friend to make extra coins.

Predicting Spellings, Vocabulary
Skills, Word Analysis
Write *make* on the chalkboard. Then ask students to predict the spellings of *take, bake, cake, fake, lake, rake, flake, stake, quake, shake, male,* and *made.* Discuss the meanings of any unfamiliar words. Note the final silent *e* in each of the words.

Other Word Forms, Word Analysis, Spelling Rules, Writing Sentences

✦ Introduce common other word forms of *make*: *makes, made, making, maker*. Point out that the final *e* is dropped in *making, timing* (69), and *liking* (66). Review this spelling rule with students (see **Spelling Sourcebook 1**, page 85). Have students use the other word forms in oral and written sentences.

Book Tie-In, Making Signs

✦ Write *maker* on the chalkboard. Explore these words with students: *dressmaker, troublemaker, homemaker, signmaker*. Then read *The Signmaker's Assistant* (Tedd Arnold, Dial, 1992), about Norman, who becomes a signmaker and creates mass confusion with his mischievous signs. Follow up with students noting the signs they see in their neighborhood and then making those signs to display on the bulletin board.

73 *than*

Idiomatic Usage, Writing Explanations, Book Tie-In

✦ Ask students to explain in writing what they think it means to say each of these expressions (then discuss):

Your eyes are bigger than your stomach.
Don't bite off more than you can chew.
Actions speak louder than words.

NA Follett

Use *Bushbaby* (Adrienne Kennaway, Little, 1991) to illustrate the saying "Your eyes are bigger than you stomach."

Sound-Symbol Awareness, Writing Sentences

✦ Write *than* on the chalkboard. Ask students to follow these directions to write new and review words:

Change one letter of *than* to make *thin*.
Change one letter of *than* to make *that* (9).
Change one letter of *than* to make *then* (53).
Remove one letter of *than* to make *tan*.
Remove two letters of *than* to make *an* (39).

Have students write a sentence for each word they made.

74 *first*   *NA Follett*

Book Tie-In, Writing Sentences

✦ Use *Happy Thanksgiving Rebus* (David Adler, Viking, 1991), a story within a story that uses a rebus format to tell about the first Thanksgiving. Have students follow up by writing sentences using the rebus format.

Writing Sentences, Usage

✦ Have students write cause-and-effect phrases: *First seeds, then flowers. First kittens, then cats. First clouds, then rain. First _____, then _____.* Point out the use of *then* (53), often confused with *than* (73).

Predicting Spellings, Writing Words

✦ Write on the chalkboard *first, second, third, fourth, fifth, sixth, seventh, eighth, ninth, tenth*. Have students predict the spellings as the words are written. Next to each word, have students write the word's corresponding number word and numeral.

Antonyms

✦ Introduce the antonym of *first*, the word *last*. Have students write what they do first each morning and last each night.

75 *been*

Visual Skill-Building, Writing Words

✦ Write *b_ _n* on the chalkboard. Ask students to fill in the vowels to make *been*. Then cover the word, and have them write it from memory. Extend this letter fill-in activity to review words, including *was* (13), *from* (23), *what* (32), *your* (40), *said* (43), *about* (48), *many* (55), *would* (59), and *could* (70).

Visual Skill-Building, Writing Words
♦ Have students find and write words inside *been*: the homophones *be* (21) and *bee*. Extend the words-in-words activity with *more* (63), *many* (55), *them* (52), *your* (40).

Alphabetical Order, Writing Words
♦ Introduce the game ABC Order (see ***Spelling Sourcebook 1*** page 86). Use *been* and selected review words.

76 *its*

Choral Reading, Writing Rhymes
♦ Write these rhymes on the chalkboard, underline *its*, and have students read them chorally:

The horse swished <u>its</u> tail while the cow read <u>its</u> mail,
The bear rubbed <u>its</u> chin while the frog shined <u>its</u> skin,
The bird checked <u>its</u> map while the cat took <u>its</u> nap.

Ask students to create more stanzas:

The (animal/verb) its (noun) while the (animal/verb) its (rhyming noun).

Homophone Usage, Contractions, Writing Sentences
♦ Introduce the homophone of *its*, the word *it's*. Have students use the homophones in oral and written sentences to differentiate them. Define the terms *contraction* and *apostrophe*. Explain that *it's* is a contraction. Show how *is* contractions can be made with *that* (9), *what* (32), *there* (37), and *how* (49). Have students use the contractions in written sentences. Make a chart with context sentences for *its* and *it's*. Post the chart for easy reference as students write.

77 *who*

Book Tie-In, Writing Predictions
♦ Use *WHOO-OO Is It?* (Megan McDonald, Orchard, 1992), in which Mother Owl is troubled by a mysterious noise only to discover that it is the first owlet emerging from its shell. Before the ending is read, have students write predictions for what they think the strange noise might be.

Writing Riddles, Reading
♦ Ask students to write "Who Is It?" riddles using people well-known to all students. Have students write three clues, each followed by "Who is it?" Then let students take turns reading their riddles, one clue at a time, as the class tries to guess who the person is.

Book Tie-In
NA Follett
♦ Use *Horton Hears a Who* (Dr. Seuss, Random House, 1954), which tells in rhyming text how Horton the elephant saves the Whos of Whoville. Ask a student to prepare this classic tale for reading to the class.

78 *now*

Book Tie-In
♦ Use *Now One Foot, Now the Other* (Tomie dePaola, Putnam, 1981), in which Bobby helps his grandfather walk again following a stroke.

Visual Skill-Building, Writing Words, Writing Sentences
♦ Play the Word Look-Alike game. Ask students to circle the words in each row that are like the underlined word. Then they turn the paper over, picture the underlined word, and write it.

<u>now</u>	new	mow	now	not	won	own	now	row	now
<u>its</u>	if	it	it's	in	its	sit	his	its	fit
<u>like</u>	look	bike	like	lake	lock	like	kind	time	like

Next, have students write each of the underlined words in a sentence.

Sound-Symbol Awareness,
Writing Sentences

Write *now* on the chalkboard. Ask students to follow these directions to write new and review words:

Change one letter of *now* to make *not* (30).
Change one letter of *now* to make *new*.
Add one letter to *now* to make *know*.
Change one letter of *now* to make *cow, wow,* and *how* (49).

Have students write a sentence for each word they made.

79 *people*

Visual Skill-Building,
Writing Words

Write *people* on the chalkboard, and draw an outline around the word to accentuate its shape. Provide students with graph paper (or use the blackline master on page 108 of *Spelling Sourcebook 1*). Have students write *people* in the boxes and outline its shape (see Letter Grid Games on page 88 of *Spelling Sourcebook 1*). Expand the activity to include selected review words.

Reading Biographies

✓ a picture book series

Introduce students to interesting people through simplified biographies. Examples include *The One Bad Thing About Father* (F. N. Monjo, Harper, 1987) about Theodore Roosevelt, *A Picture Book of Eleanor Roosevelt* (David Adler, Holiday, 1991), or books in the *Great African American Series* (Enslow, 1991). Begin an ongoing collection of newspaper and magazine stories about people who have made contributions to our lives.

80 *my*

Sound-Symbol Awareness,
Vocabulary Skills, Writing
Rhymes, Choral Reading

Write *_y* on the chalkboard. Have students add beginning letters to make new words (*by, cry, dry, fry, fly, pry, sky, spy, sly, shy, try*). If rhyming words are suggested that do not follow the same spelling pattern, write them in a separate list (*pie*). Discuss unfamiliar words. Have students write rhymes using the patterned rhyming words and read them chorally.

Writing Exclamations

Introduce *my* as an exclamation (*My!*). Help students write sentences using *my* as an exclamation, such as *My! It's hot!*

81 *made* NA Follett

Book Tie-In, Writing Stories,
Creating a Book

Use *I Made a Mistake* (Miriam Nerlove, Scribners, 1986), in which the rhyming text relates nonsensical mistakes. Then have students write a story about a mistake they made. Compile the stories into class-made or student-made books (see Creating Classroom Books, page 138).

Other Word Forms,
Writing Sentences

Review common other word forms of *made*: *make* (72), *makes, making, maker*. Have students use the other word forms in oral and written sentences.

Homophone Usage, Book Tie-In,
Multiple Meanings

Introduce the homophone of *made*, the word *maid*. Then introduce the *Amelia Bedelia* books (Peggy Parish) about a literal-minded maid who tries hard to please her employers, Mr. and Mrs. Rogers. If the Rogers ask Amelia to *make* a bed, she builds a bed!

Word Analysis, Writing
Sentences

Write *made* on the chalkboard. Then write *mad*. Discuss the role of the silent *e*: It gives the letter *a* a long vowel sound. Show the examples *hop/hope, car/care, can/cane, do/doe, at/ate, bit/bite, pin/pine, fin/fine,* and *not/note*. Have students write sentences using the word pairs.

Please list ALL

82 *over*

Book Tie-In ✦ Use *Over, Under and Through and Other Spacial Concepts* (Tana Hoban, Macmillan, 1973) to reinforce *over*.

Antonyms ✦ Introduce the antonym of *over*, the word *under*.

Idiomatic Usage, Writing Explanations ✦ Ask students to explain in writing what they think it means to say each of these expressions (then discuss):

> to pull the wool over someone's eyes
> to turn over a new leaf
> to cry over spilled milk
> over and done with
> to go over like a lead balloon

Book Tie-In, Compound Words, Vocabulary Skills, Prefix Practice ✦ Use *All Aboard Overnight: A Book of Compound Words* (Betsy Maestro, Clarion, 1992) to prepare students to brainstorm for compound words that use *over* (*overnight, overalls, overboard, overcoat, overcome, overdo, overdue, overeat, overflow, overhand, overhead, overlap, overlook, overpass, overrule, overseas, overtime, overturn*). Discuss unfamiliar words. Introduce the term *prefix*. In these words, *over* could be called a prefix.

83 *did*

Predicting Spellings, Vocabulary Skills ✦ Write *did* on the chalkboard. Ask students to predict the spellings of *hid, bid, kid, lid, rid, dig, dim, dip, dish, drift,* and *dad*. Discuss unfamiliar words.

Other Word Forms, Writing Sentences ✦ Review common other word forms of *did: do* (45), *does, doing, doer, done, didn't, doesn't, don't*. Have students use the other word forms in oral and written sentences.

Creating a Book ✦ Create a "Did You Know?" class-made book of trivia facts. Ask each student to write one entry for the book (see page 138, Creating Classroom Books).

Palindromes ✦ Some words are spelled the same forward as backward. They are called palindromes. *Did* is a palindrome. Ask students to identify other palindromes. Choices may include *dad, mom, pop, peep, sis, bib, deed, noon, Anna,* and *Bob*.

84 *down*

NA Follett

Book Tie-In, Antonyms ✦ Review the concept of opposites with *Traffic: A Book of Opposites* (Betsy and Giulio Maestro, Crown, 1991). Then review the antonym of *down*, the word *up* (50).

Sound-Symbol Awareness ✦ Write *down* and *now* (78) on the chalkboard. Have students collect more words with *ow* as in *down* and *now* (*how* [49]), *town, brown, frown, crowd, flower, shower, power*).

Idiomatic Usage, Writing Explanations ✦ Ask students to explain in writing what they think it means to say each of these expressions (then discuss):

to back down	to be run down
to buckle down	to scale down
to put down	to talk down
down to earth	to lay down the law
to go down in history	Simmer down.

85 *only*

Sound-Symbol Awareness ✦ Write *only* and *many* (55) on the chalkboard. Ask students to listen for the long *e* sound they hear at the end of the word and to note that the sound is spelled with the letter *y*. Then collect other words in which the final *y* makes the long *e* sound (*very, any, every, country, city, story, money, family, daddy, puppy, tiny, baby, pretty, sunny, funny*).

Idiomatic Usage, Writing Explanations ✦ Ask students to explain in writing what they think it means to say each of these expressions (then discuss):

  Beauty is only skin deep.
  You're only as pretty as you act.
  You're only young once.

Writing Words ✦ Play the All-Play Spelling Bee (see **Spelling Sourcebook 1**, page 86). Use *only* and selected review words.

86 *way*
       NA Follett

Book Tie-In, Writing Stories ✦ Use *Pookins Gets Her Way* (Helen Lester, Houghton, 1987), the story of the lesson Pookins learns about demanding her own way. Follow up with students writing a story about a time they wanted to get their own way but didn't.

Book Tie-In, Writing Predictions
NA Follett ✦ Use *On Our Way to Market* (Dayle Ann Dodds, Simon, 1991), a rhyming, cumulative tale. Ask students to write a prediction of what obstacle may befall the farm boy on his next trip to market.

Sound-Symbol Awareness, Writing Sentences ✦ Write *way* on the chalkboard. Ask students to follow these directions to write new and review words:

  Change one letter of *way* to make *pay, day, may, say, hay, bay, ray*.
  Change one letter of *way* to make *why*.
  Change one letter of *way* to make *was* (13).
  Add one letter to *way* to make *ways*.
  Change one letter of *way* to make the name of a month. (*May*)
Have students write a sentence for each word they made.

Idiomatic Usage, Writing Explanations ✦ Ask students to explain in writing what they think it means to say each of these expressions (then discuss):

  by the way   No way.
  to have it both ways   to learn the hard way
  to have the right-of-way to take something the wrong way

Homophone Usage, Writing Sentences ✦ Introduce the homophone of *way*, the word *weigh*. Have students use the homophones in oral and written sentences to differentiate them.

87 *find*
   NA Follett

Book Tie-In, Visual Skill-Building, Research and Writing, Public Speaking ✦ Use *Find Demi's Sea Creatures* (Demi, Grosset, 1991), in which readers search to find large and small creatures hidden on the pages amid a sea of art. Follow up by having students research selected animals in the book, many of which are endangered. Ask students to report their findings orally and in writing.

Other Word Forms, Writing Sentences ✦ Introduce common other word forms of *find*: *finds, finding, finder, found*. Have students use the other word forms in oral and written sentences.

Creating a Word Puzzle, Other Word Forms ✦ Have students make a word search puzzle using *find* and its other word forms (see Letter Grid Games, **Spelling Sourcebook 1**, page 88).

Antonyms	✦ Introduce the antonym of *find*, the word *lose*, and the antonym of *found*, the word *lost*.
Book Tie-In, Writing a Story Ending	✦√ Use *Christmas in July* (Arthur Yorinks, HarperCollins, 1991), in which the dry cleaners cannot find Santa's pants. Have students write their solution to this problem before reading about Santa's attempts to solve it.
Homophone Usage, Writing Sentences	✦ Introduce the homophone of *find*, the word *fined*. Have students use the homophones in oral and written sentences to differentiate them. Review previously introduced homophones, especially *to* (5) and *two* (65) (*too* will be introduced at 112), and *there* (37) and *their* (42).

88 *use*

Homograph Usage	✦ *Use* is a homograph. A homograph is a word that has two pronunciations and meanings, but only one spelling. Discuss the homograph *use* with students (*use*, "to consume"; *use*, "purpose"). Explore the two pronunciations and meanings for other homographs. Choices may include *wind, read, close,* and *does*.
Other Word Forms, Writing Sentences	✦ Introduce common other word forms of *use*: *uses, used, using, useful, useless, usable*. Have students use the other word forms in oral and written sentences.
Prefix Practice, Book Tie-In, Writing Sentences	✦ Write the word *reuse* on the chalkboard. Review the term *prefix* introduced with *over* (82). Explain that *re* can be added to some words to change their meaning. Then read *Aunt Ippy's Museum of Junk* (Rodney Greenblat, HarperCollins, 1991), about an eccentric auntie who is a master of waste management and *reuses* everything. . . or puts it in her junk museum. Expand the lesson by adding *re* to *do* (45), *make* (72), *made* (81), and *did* (83). Note that *re* means "again." Have students write sentences using the words with the *re* prefix.

NA Follett

89 *may*

Sound-Symbol Awareness, Writing Rhymes, Reading	✦ Write *way* (86) on the chalkboard, and review *ay* words. Then have students write rhymes using the patterned rhyming words and read them to the class.
Sound-Symbol Awareness, Writing Sentences	✦ Write *may* on the chalkboard. Ask students to follow these directions to write new words: Capitalize one letter of *may* to make the name of a month. (May) Change *may* to make *stay*. Change *may* to make *mad*. Add letters to *may* to make *maybe*. Have students write a sentence for each word they made.

90 *water*

Book Tie-Ins, Writing a Summary, Writing Reasons	✦ Use *Follow the Water From Brook to Ocean* (Arthur Dorros, HarperCollins, 1991) to trace water from snow to the ocean. Then have students use a map to trace this sequence in a geographic area. Next have students write a summary of the route of the water. Then read *Water* (Alfred Leutscher, Dial, 1983) and have students list reasons why water is important. *NA Follett*

Other Word Forms, Suffix Practice, Spelling Rules, Writing Sentences

◆ Introduce common other word forms of *water*: *waters, watered, watering, watery*. Then write *watering* on the chalkboard, and underline the *ing*. Ask students to add the *ing* suffix to *do* (45), *will* (46), *see* (68), *find* (87). Point out that the final *e* is dropped before the *ing* is added to *like* (66), *time* (69), *make* (72), *use* (88). Review this spelling rule with students (see **Spelling Sourcebook 1**, page 85). Have students use the other word forms in oral and written sentences.

91 *long*

Book Tie-In, Writing Descriptions, Art

◆ Introduce *long, longer,* and *longest*. Then introduce *The Longest Float in the Parade* (Carol Carrick, Greenwillow, 1982). Follow up with students describing in writing and illustrating their long float parade entry.

Idiomatic Usage, Writing Explanations

◆ Ask students to explain in writing what they think it means to say each of these expressions (then discuss):

long ago	so long
in the long run	before long
to make a long story short	Long time no see.
He who laughs last, laughs longest.	

Visual Skill-Building, Writing Words

◆ Write *long* on the chalkboard, and draw an outline around the word to accentuate its shape. Provide students with graph paper (or use the blackline master on page 108 of **Spelling Sourcebook 1**). Have students write *long* in the boxes and outline its shape (see Letter Grid Games on page 88 of **Spelling Sourcebook 1**). Expand the activity to include selected review words.

92 *little*

Writing a List, Book Tie-In, Writing Stories

◆ Ask students to list stories that feature the word *little*. Examples may include *Little Red Riding Hood, The Three Little Pigs, The Little Red Hen, Chicken Little, The Little Engine That Could,* and *Little Toot*. Read *Little Fur Family* (Margaret Wise Brown, HarperCollins, 1992 . . . a reissue of the 1946 classic book). Follow up with students writing stories that feature a little character.

Antonyms

◆ Introduce the antonym of *little*, the word *big*.

Synonyms

◆ Introduce the word *synonym*. Brainstorm for synonyms of *little*. Choices may include *small, tiny, minute, teeny, itsy-bitsy, petite*. Contrast the words *synonym* and *antonym*.

Making Comparisons

◆ Write *long* (91), *longer, longest, little, littler,* and *littlest* on the chalkboard. Have students practice making comparisons using the words.

93 *very*

Book Tie-Ins, Writing Stories

◆ Use Eric Carle's books *The Very Busy Spider* (Putnam, 1985) and *The Very Hungry Caterpillar* (Putnam, 1969), *The Very Noisy Girl* (Elizabeth Winthrop, Holiday, 1991), or *A Very Young Gardener* (Jill Krementz, Dial, 1991) as a model for students to develop their own "Very _____" stories.

Sound-Symbol Awareness

◆ Review *y* making the long *e* sound at the end of a word (see *only*, [85]).

Writing Words

◆ Play Mystery Word (see **Spelling Sourcebook 1**, page 89). Use *very* and selected review words.

LIST WHATEVER VERSIONS ARE AVAILABLE!

Homophone Usage, Writing Sentences
◆ Introduce the homophone of *very*, the word *vary*. Have students use the homophones in oral and written sentences to differentiate them. Review previously introduced homophones, especially *to* (5) and *two* (65) (*too* will be introduced at 112), and *there* (37) and *their* (42).

94 *after*

Antonyms
◆ Introduce the antonym of *after*, the word *before*.

Compound Words, Writing Speculations
◆ Review the compound word *into* (61). Write *noon* on the chalkboard. Ask students to add *noon* to *after* to make the compound word *afternoon*. Have students write what they would do if their favorite TV star came to pick them up one afternoon after school. What would they do that afternoon together?

Idiomatic Usage, Writing Explanations
◆ Ask students to explain in writing what they think it means to say each of these expressions (then discuss):

time after time
keep after someone
look after someone

Alphabetical Order, Writing Words
◆ Have students put each set of words in alphabetical order:

some	little	people	many	were
after	first	after	could	after
who	after	other	after	your

Then play ABC Order (see ***Spelling Sourcebook 1***, page 86).

95 *words*

NA Follett

Book Tie-Ins, Creating a Book
◆ For books on words, use *Richard Scarry's Best Word Book Ever* (Richard Scarry, Western, 1963), a unique picture dictionary; *Merry-Go-Round: A Book About Nouns* (Ruth Heller, Putnam, 1990), a rhyming text with brilliantly colored illustrations; Heller's earlier book on verbs, *Kites Sail High: A Book About Verbs* (Grosset, 1988); and *Sparkle and Spin: A Book About Words* (Ann and Paul Rand, Abrams, 1991), an inventive look at words. Then create a class-made book of words (see page 138, Creating Classroom Books).

Writing a List, Public Speaking
◆ Ask students to make a list of words they think have pleasant sounds, such as *shadow, melody*, or *Coeur d'Alene, Idaho*. Then have students report orally to the class the words and sounds that are most appealing to them.

Eponyms, Book Tie-In
◆ Explore eponyms, words that come from the names of people or places. Use *Guppies in Tuxedos: Funny Eponyms* (Marvin Terban, Ticknor, 1988).

96 *called*

Word Analysis
◆ Write *called* on the chalkboard, and underline the double letters. Have students collect words with double letters. Put the words on a bulletin board, adding more words as students discover them. Include *all* (33), *will* (46), *see* (68), *been* (75), and *little* (92).

Other Word Forms, Writing Sentences
◆ Introduce common other word forms of *called*: call, calls, calling, caller. Have students use the other word forms in oral and written sentences.

Synonyms, Writing Sentences
◆ Review the term *synonym,* introduced with *little* (92). Ask students to brainstorm for synonyms of *called* using this sentence: "He _____ for help!" Choices may include *shouted, cried*, and *yelled*.

Writing Words	◆ Play Bingo (see **Spelling Sourcebook 1**, page 87). Use *called* and selected review words.

97 *just*

Book Tie-In, Writing Stories	◆ Use *Just Awful* (Alma Whitney, Harper, 1985), about a boy who feels "just awful" when he cuts his finger and visits the school nurse for the first time. In the end, all turns out well. Ask students to write a story about their "just awful" event that ended well.
Multiple Meanings, Writing Sentences	◆ Discuss these meanings of *just*: I have just one left. (only) It's just beautiful. (very) The judge is just. (fair) Ask students to write a sentence using each of the meanings.
Writing Words	◆ Have students play Connect the Dots (see **Spelling Sourcebook 1**, page 87). Use *just* and selected review words.

98 *where*

Book Tie-In, Writing Captions	◆ Use *All About Where* (Tana Hoban, Greenwillow, 1991) to have students write captions for the illustrations in the book.
Book Tie-Ins, Writing Descriptions	◆ Use *Where's Our Mama?* (Diane Goode, Dutton, 1991), a story that follows the adventures of two lost children in Paris trying to find their mother. Follow up by asking students to describe in writing a time when they were lost. Companion book: *Laney's Lost Momma* (Diane J. Hamm, Whitman, 1991).
Writing Words and Phrases	◆ Ask students to find and write examples of words and phrases in stories that tell *where*. Examples might include "at the seashore," "on the table," or "in the city." Write these on a chart titled "Where."
Visual Skill-Building	◆ Have students find words inside *where* (*he, her, here*).
Usage, Writing Sentences	◆ Some students may confuse the sound-alike words *where* and *wear*. Use the words in oral and written sentences to differentiate them.

99 *most*

Sound-Symbol Awareness	◆ Write *most* on the chalkboard, and underline the *st*. Give students these clues to guess new and review words that end with *st*: the opposite of *last* (*first*, [74]), the opposite of *slow* (*fast*), where Little Red Riding Hood met the wolf (*forest*), the price (*cost*), the morning meal (*breakfast*), the opposite of *most* (*least*). Next, give students clues to guess these words that begin with *st*: *stars, story, string, street, store, stop, step, stairs*.
Writing Questions and Answers	◆ Play Questions and Answers (see **Spelling Sourcebook 1**, page 90). Use *most* and selected review words.
Antonyms	◆ Introduce the antonym of *most*, the word *least*.

100 *know*

Book Tie-In	◆ Read and sing together using *I Know an Old Lady Who Swallowed a Fly* (Nadine Westcott, Little, 1980).

Homophone Usage, Writing Sentences	◆ Review the homophone for *know*, the word *no* (71). Have students use the homophones in oral and written sentences to differentiate them. Review previously introduced homophones, especially *to* (5) and *two* (65), and *there* (37) and *their* (42).
Word Analysis	◆ Write *know* on the chalkboard and ask students to identify the silent letters. Underline the *no* inside *know*. Expand the lesson to identification of other words with silent letters. Choices may include *have* (25), *two* (65), and *people* (79).
Other Word Forms, Vocabulary Skills, Writing Sentences	◆ Introduce common other word forms of *know: knows, knew, knowing, known, knowledge*. Discuss unfamiliar words. Have students use the other word forms in oral and written sentences.
Homophone Usage, Book Tie-Ins, Writing a List, Research and Writing	◆ Write *knows* and *nose* on the chalkboard. Discuss the homophones and write, *Who knows the nose?* Then use *Breathtaking Noses* (Hana Machotka, Morrow, 1992), which uses a guessing-game format to introduce a variety of animal noses. Follow up the reading by making a list of animals with distinctive noses. Answers might include elephants, anteaters, pigs, and hippos. Then ask students to write what purpose a nose serves. The book *Your Nose and Ears* (Joan Iveson-Iveson, Watts, 1985) can provide a resource for the research.

101 *get*

Predicting Spellings	◆ Write *get* on the chalkboard. Ask students to predict the spellings of *bet, jet, let, met, net, pet, set, wet, yet, got, gets, forget,* and *forgot.*
Other Word Forms, Spelling Rules, Writing Sentences	◆ Introduce common other word forms of *get: gets, got, gotten, getting*. Note that the *t* of *get* is doubled before the ending *ing*. Introduce this spelling rule to students (see ***Spelling Sourcebook 1***, page 85). Have students apply the rule to *get, let, sit, put, dig,* and *run*. Have students write sentences using the *ing* words.
Idiomatic Usage, Writing Explanations	◆ Ask students to explain in writing what they think it means to say each of these expressions (then discuss): to get butterflies in your stomach to get up on the wrong side of the bed to get in people's hair
Sorting Words	◆ Have students play Word Sorts (see ***Spelling Sourcebook 1***, page 92) using these words: *get, gets, jet, pet, got, getting, let, wet.*

102 *through*

Homophone Usage, Writing Sentences, Writing Words	◆ Introduce the homophone of *through*, the word *threw*. Have students write the homophones in sentences to differentiate them. Have students play Mystery Words (see ***Spelling Sourcebook 1***, page 89) to reinforce homophones.
Multiple Meanings, Writing Sentences	◆ Discuss meanings of *through*: Go *through* the door. I am *through* with my work. Review words that can mean more than one thing: *can* (38), *will* (46), *out* (51), *over* (82), *down* (84), *long* (91), *just* (97). Ask students to write the words in sentences to illustrate the different meanings.

103 *back*

Word Analysis, Predicting Spellings, Vocabulary Skills
◆ Have students write *back* and underline the *ck*. Then write _*ck* on the chalkboard and ask students to predict the spellings of *track, pack, quack, sack, stack, shack, tack, black, crack, duck, truck, luck, chick, kick, lick, pick, quick, sick, tick, check, neck, deck, peck, clock, dock, lock, rock,* and *sock*. Discuss unfamiliar words.

Idiomatic Usage, Writing Explanations
◆ Ask students to explain in writing what they think it means to say each of these expressions (then discuss):

back east	back and forth
to think back	a back order
to back out	to be laid back
back-to-back	to go back on your word

Antonyms
◆ Introduce antonyms of *back*, the words *front* and *forth*.

Other Word Forms, Vocabulary Skills, Writing Sentences
◆ Introduce common other word forms of *back: backs, backed, backing, backward(s)*. Discuss unfamiliar words. Have students write the other word forms in sentences.

104 *much*

Book Tie-In, Writing Predictions
✓◆ Use *How Much Is a Million?* (David Schwartz, Lothrop, 1985), which offers easy-to-understand comparisons of large numbers of things. Before reading each section of the book, ask students to write predictions: "How much time would it take to count from one to one million?"

Word Analysis, Sound-Symbol Awareness, Writing Sentences
◆ Write *much* on the chalkboard, and underline the *ch*. Give students these clues to guess words that end with *ch*: Halloween lady in black (*witch*), having much money (*rich*), helps you start a fire (*match*), wear it to tell time (*watch*). Give students clues to guess words that begin with *ch*: opposite of adults (*children*), to make different (*change*), to pick out (*choose*), for sitting (*chair*). Can students think of a word that begins and ends with *ch*?(*church*) Have students write the *ch* words in sentences.

Creating a Word Puzzle
◆ Have students make a word search puzzle using words with *ch* (see Letter Grid Games, ***Spelling Sourcebook 1***, page 88).

105 *go*

Book Tie-In, Writing a Story Ending
✓◆ Use *The Cows Are Going to Paris* (David Kirby and Allen Woodman, Caroline, 1991), in which country cows go to Paris and city people go to the pasture. Have students write an ending to the story before the ending is read.

Sound-Symbol Awareness, Writing Sentences
◆ Write *go* on the chalkboard. Ask students to follow these directions to write new and review words:

Add one letter to *go* to make *got*.
Change one letter of *go* to make *do* (45).
Add two letters to *go* to make *gold*.
Add two letters to *go* to make *goes*.
Change one letter of *go* to make *so* (57).

Have students write a sentence for each word they made.

Other Word Forms, Vocabulary Skills, Writing Sentences
◆ Introduce common other word forms of *go: goes, went, going, gone*. Have students write the other word forms in sentences.

Antonyms
✦ Introduce the antonyms of *go*, the words *come* and *stop*.

Idiomatic Usage,
Writing Explanations
✦ Ask students to explain in writing what they think it means to say each of these expressions (then discuss):

Go fly a kite!   on the go
going to the dogs   Go all out.
Go overboard.   touch and go

106 *good*

Synonyms, Writing Words
✦ Review synonyms of *little* (92) and *called* (96). Ask students to write synonyms of *good*.

Antonyms
✦ Introduce the antonym of *good*, the word *bad*.

Book Tie-In, Creating a Book
✦ Use *Perfect Pigs: An Introduction to Manners* (Marc Brown and Stephen Krensky, Little, 1983). Then create a "Good Manners at School" class-made book.

Word Analysis, Writing Words
✦ Note the double letters in *good*. Review words with double letters: *will* (46), *see* (68), *been* (75), *little* (92), *called* (96). Have students find and write more words with double letters.

Writing Comparisons
✦ Make comparisons for students, using *good*, *better*, and *best*. Extend the lesson to *long* (91) and *little* (92). Have students write comparisons using the three forms of each word.

107 *new*

Homophone Usage,
Writing Sentences
✦ Introduce the homophone of *new*, the word *knew*. Have students write the homophones in sentences to differentiate them. Review *through* (102) and *threw*; *to* (5) and *two* (65); *there* (37) and *their* (42).

Other Word Forms, Vocabulary
Skills, Writing Sentences
✦ Introduce common other word forms of *new*: *news, newer, newest, newness, newly*. Discuss unfamiliar words. Have students write the other word forms in sentences.

Antonyms
✦ Introduce the antonym of *new*, the word *old*.

Creating a Newspaper
✦ Add an *s + paper* to *new,* and explore the newspaper with students. Help them discover the different newspaper sections. Then develop a newspaper for parents with school news.

Prefix Practice, Vocabulary
Skills, Writing Sentences
✦ Review the *re* prefix introduced with *use* (88). Ask students to predict the meaning of *renew* and to check a dictionary for verification. Have students write other words with the *re* prefix: *do* (45), *make* (72), *made* (81), *did* (83), *called* (96). Then ask students to write the words in sentences.

108 *write*   NA Follett

Book Tie-In, Writing a List
✦ Discuss authors as writers. Use *A Writer* (M. B. Goffstein, Harper, 1984), which explains how a writer writes. Have students list their favorite authors and the books they wrote.   NA Follett

Book Tie-In,
Writing Predictions
✦ Discuss how writing began, with *Language and Writing* (Miriam Moss, Watts, 1988). Before the reading, ask students to write how they think writing started.

Homophone Usage,
Writing Sentences
✦ Introduce one homophone of *write*, the word *right*. Have students write the homophones in sentences to differentiate them.

Other Word Forms, Spelling
Rules, Vocabulary Skills,
Writing Sentences
✦ Introduce common other word forms of *write*: *writes, writing, wrote, written, writer*. Review the spelling rules for dropping the final silent *e* and doubling the consonant before adding a suffix (see *Spelling Sourcebook 1,* page 85). Discuss unfamiliar words. Have students write the other word forms in sentences.

Sound-Symbol Awareness,
Writing Sentences
✤ Write *write* on the chalkboard. Ask students to follow these directions to write new words:

Change one letter of *write* to make *white*.
Change one letter of *write* to make *wrote*.
Add one letter to *write* to make *writes*.
Add the *re* prefix to *write* to make *rewrite*.

Have students write a sentence for each word they made.

109 *our*

Homophone Usage,
Writing Sentences
✤ Introduce the homophone of *our*, the word *hour*. Have students write the homophones in sentences to differentiate them. Discuss *are* (15), emphasizing that it should not be misused in place of *our*.

Visual Skill-Building,
Writing Sentences
✤ Play the Word Look-Alike game. Ask students to circle the words in each row that are like the underlined word. Then they turn the paper over, picture the underlined word, and write it.

<u>our</u>	are	ore	out	our	hour	own	oar	our
<u>now</u>	new	how	cow	won	know	now	one	mow
<u>go</u>	to	go	no	do	got	go	so	go
<u>get</u>	yet	set	get	tag	gets	got	get	jet

Have students write each of the underlined words in a sentence.

110 *me*

Creating a Book
✤ Ask students to create an *About Me* book featuring their name, address, phone, family data, three things they like, and three things they don't like. Read aloud the "things I like" and "things I don't like" from each book, and have students guess which of their classmates was the author (see page 138, Creating Classroom Books).

Sound-Symbol Awareness,
Writing Sentences
✤ Write *me* on the chalkboard. Ask students to follow these directions to write new and review words:

Add two letters to *me* to make *time* (69).
Add two letters to *me* to make *some* (56).
Add two letters to *me* to make *same*, *name*, and *game*.
Change one letter of *me* to make *my* (80).
Add one letter to *me* to make *men*.

Have students write a sentence for each word they made.

Antonyms
✤ Review the antonym of *me*, the word *you* (8).

111 *man*

Spelling Rules
✤ Introduce the plural of *man*, the word *men*. Ask students how plurals of words are usually formed (add *s*). Then discuss how the plural of *man* is different. Introduce this spelling rule (see **Spelling Sourcebook 1**, page 85). Apply the rule to *woman/women*.

Antonyms
✤ Introduce the antonym of *man*, the word *woman*.

Predicting Spellings,
Vocabulary Skills
✤ Have students write *man*. Then ask students to predict the spellings of *fan, pan, pans, ran, tan, mat, mats, mad, map, maps, mash,* and *men*. Discuss unfamiliar words.

Writing Exclamations
✤ Introduce the exclamation *Man!* Review the exclamation *My!* (80). Have students write the exclamations in sentences, such as *Man! It's hot!*

112 *too*

Multiple Meanings

◆ Introduce the two meanings of *too*:

It is *too* late to play outdoors.
Mary can read. I can read, *too*.

Homophone Usage,
Writing Sentences

◆ Review the homophones *to* (5) and *two* (65). Have students write *to/too/two* in sentences to differentiate them. Post context sentences for these homophones on a classroom chart for easy reference. Add to the chart other homophones that present a challenge, such as *there* (37) and *their* (42). *They're* is word 1010 but may also be included.

Book Tie-In, Writing Stories

◆ Use *Earrings!* (Judith Viorst, Atheneum, 1990), the story of a struggle to prove you're not too young for earrings. Have students write about the "big" thing in their life that parents say they're too young for. Next, have students write about something they are too old for.

113 *any*

Visual Skill-Building,
Writing Words

◆ Review *many* (55). Have students find *any* inside *many*. Then write *any* and *many* on the chalkboard, and draw an outline around the words to accentuate their shape. Provide students with graph paper (or use the blackline master on page 108 of *Spelling Sourcebook 1*). Have students write *many* and *any* in the boxes and outline their shape (see Letter Grid Games on page 88 of *Spelling Sourcebook 1*). Expand the activity to include selected review words.

Alphabetical Order,
Writing Words

◆ Ask students to write these sets of review words in alphabetical order: *any/through/been, after/are/any, each/any/an, and/as/any*. Then play ABC Order (see *Spelling Sourcebook 1*, page 86) with *any* and selected review words.

114 *day*

Book Tie-In, Writing Stories,
Reading

◆ Use *The Day the Goose Got Loose* (Reeve Lindbergh, Dial, 1990), a story depicting the riot a loose goose caused. Use the story as a model for students to write about their eventful day: "The Day _____." Have students read their stories to the class.

Antonyms

◆ Introduce the antonym of *day*, the word *night*.

Idiomatic Usage,
Writing Explanations

◆ Ask students to explain in writing what they think it means to say each of these expressions (then discuss):

as different as night and day
Rome wasn't built in a day.
in this day and age
day in and day out
Save something for a rainy day.
That'll be the day.

Sound-Symbol Awareness,
Writing Rhymes, Reading

◆ Write _*ay* on the chalkboard. Review *way* (86) and *may* (89). Have students add beginning letters to make new words. Have students write rhymes using the patterned rhyming words and read them to the class.

115 *same*

Synonyms

◆ Review the term *synonym*. Ask students to name pairs of words that mean nearly the same thing (*creek/stream, everyone/everybody, sofa/davenport, ocean/sea, too/also, big/large, swim suit/bathing suit*).

Word Analysis, Writing Words	✦ Review final silent *e* with *same*. Ask students to write *are* (15), *have* (25), *one* (28), *were* (34), *there* (37), *some* (56), *these* (58), *more* (63), *like* (66), *time* (69), *make* (72), *people* (79), *made* (81), *use* (88), *little* (92), *where* (98), and *write* (108).
Sound-Symbol Awareness, Writing Sentences	✦ Write *same* on the chalkboard. Ask students to follow these directions to write new words:

Change one letter of *same* to make *game*.
Change one letter of *same* to make *sale*.
Remove two letters of *same* to make *am*.
Add one letter to *same* to make *shame*.
Change one letter of *same* to make *safe*.
Change one letter of *same* to make *save*.

Have students write a sentence for each word they made.

Antonyms	✦ Introduce the antonym of *same*, the word *different*.

116 *right*

Multiple Meanings, Writing Sentences	✦ Write on the chalkboard:

Turn right at the corner.
Your answer is right.

Review that some words have more than one meaning. Review *can* (38), *over* (82), *down* (84), *way* (86), *may* (89), *just* (97), *through* (102), and *back* (103). Ask students to write sentences that use different meanings of these words.

Idiomatic Usage, Writing Explanations	✦ Ask students to explain in writing what they think it means to say each of these expressions (then discuss):

Hang a right.	All right for you.
the right-of-way	to turn out all right
right off the bat	to go right through the roof
Right on!	right side up

Book Tie-In NA Follett	✦ Use *Right Now* (David Kherdian, Knopf, 1983), which develops the concepts of past, present, and future.
Sound-Symbol Awareness, Writing Words, Writing Word Clues	✦ Write *_ight* on the chalkboard. Have students write beginning letters to make new words. Then have students write a clue for each word and see if the class can use it to write the right word.
Antonyms	✦ Introduce antonyms of *right*, the words *left* and *wrong*.
Homophone Usage, Writing Sentences	✦ Review the homophone of *right*, the word *write* (108). Have students write the homophones in sentences to differentiate them.

117 *look*

Book Tie-Ins, Creating a Book NA Follett	✦ Use *The Turn About, Think About, Look About Book* and *The Look Again . . . and Again, and Again, and Again Book* (Beau Gardner, Lothrop, 1980 and 1983) to help students look at things carefully. Follow up by asking students to create *Look!* books (see page 138, Creating Classroom Books).
Book Tie-In	✦ Use *Come Look With Me: Animals in Art* (Gladys Blizzard, Thomasson-Grant, 1992) for an art-awareness lesson. Artists' paintings are presented with thought-provoking questions for students to answer.
Word Analysis, Writing Words	✦ Have students write *look* and underline the double letter. Ask students to write *all* (33), *will* (46), *see* (68), *been* (75), *little* (92), *called* (96), *good* (106), and *too* (112).

Other Word Forms, Writing Sentences
◆ Introduce common other word forms of *look: looks, looked, looking*. Have students write the other word forms in sentences.

Sound-Symbol Awareness, Writing Sentences
◆ Write *look* on the chalkboard. Ask students to follow these directions to write new and review words:

> Change *look* to make the opposite of *bad*. (*good* [106])
> Change one letter of *look* to make *lock*.
> Add one letter to *look* to make *looks*.
> Change one letter in *look* to make *book, cook, hook*.

Have students write a sentence for each word they made.

118 *think*

Book Tie-In, Solving Puzzles
NA Follett
◆ Use *Puzzlers* (Bill Oakes and Suse MacDonald, Dial, 1989), a visual perception picture book that challenges students to think. Have students write answers to selected puzzles.

Other Word Forms, Vocabulary Skills, Writing Sentences
◆ Introduce common other word forms of *think: thinks, thinker, thinking, thought*. Discuss unfamiliar words. Have students write the other word forms in sentences.

Word Analysis, Writing Tongue Twisters, Book Tie-In

NA Follett
◆ Review words with *th: the* (1), *that* (9), *with* (17), *they* (19), *this* (22), *there* (37), *their* (42), *them* (52), *then* (53), *other* (60), *than* (73), and *through* (102). Using the *th* words as a resource, have students write tongue twister sentences. Use *Timid Timothy's Tongue Twisters* (Dick Gackenbach, Holiday, 1986) for models and inspiration.

119 *also*

Synonyms
◆ Write *too* on the chalkboard. Use oral and written sentences to illustrate how *also* and one meaning of *too* are synonyms.

Writing Sentences
◆ Introduce the game Finish the Story (see **Spelling Sourcebook 1**, page 88) using *also* and selected review words.

Remember . . .

Develop spelling accountability as students write—see **Spelling Sourcebook 1**, Article 8, page 33. Spelling mastery is achieved ONLY when students can spell and use words consistently correctly in writing.

120 *around*

Predicting Spellings, Vocabulary Skills, Writing Rhymes
◆ Ask students to write *around* and underline *ound*. Then have students predict the spellings of *ground, bound, round, found, sound, hound, mound,* and *pound*. Discuss unfamiliar words. Have students write rhymes using the words.

Idiomatic Usage, Writing Explanations
◆ Ask students to explain in writing what they think it means to say each of these expressions (then discuss):

> She can wrap you around her little finger.
> Don't beat around the bush.
> What goes around comes around. (See literature entry below.)
> to boss around
> to horse around

Book Tie-In, Making Inferences
NA Follett
◆ Use *What Goes Around Comes Around* (Sally Ward, Doubleday, 1991) to illustrate the idiom. Following the reading, ask students to tell how the title of the book relates to its content.

121 *another*

Visual Skill-Building, Writing Words
Ask students to write words they find inside *another* (*a, an, no, the, other, he, her, not*). Extend the words-in-words activity to *around* (120), *think* (118), *know* (100), *where* (98), *down* (84), *been* (75), *many* (55). Then have students write words they find inside their reading and vocabulary words.

Compound Words, Predicting Spellings
Review compound words. Have students write *another* and underline the two word parts of the compound. Brainstorm for compound words. Have students predict the spellings of these compounds as they are written on the chalkboard: *into* (61), *birdhouse, airplane, sunset.*

Writing Words, Other Word Forms
Introduce Spelling Baseball (see ***Spelling Sourcebook 1***, page 91). Play the game with *another* and with selected review words and their other word forms.

122 *came*

Book Tie-In, Writing Predictions
NA Follet
Use *It Came From Outer Space* (Tony Bradman, Dial, 1992). Before the surprise ending of the story is read, have students write predictions about how they think it might end.

Predicting Spellings, Vocabulary Skills
Have students write *came*. Ask students to predict the spellings of *game, name, same* (115), *frame, flame, shame, tame, cake, cane, cape, care, case, cave,* and *became.* Discuss unfamiliar words.

Other Word Forms, Vocabulary Skills, Writing Sentences
Introduce common other word forms of *came: come, coming, comes.* Discuss unfamiliar words. Have students write the other word forms in sentences.

Antonyms, Writing Words
Introduce the antonym of *came*, the word *went*. Review *more* (63)/*less; little* (92)/*big; after* (94)/*before; most* (99)/*least; go* (105)/*stop, come; good* (106)/*bad; new* (107)/*old; man* (111)/*woman; day* (114)/*night; same* (115)/*different;* and *right* (116)/*left, wrong.* Say one word of each pair and ask students to write the antonym.

123 *come*

Other Word Forms, Writing Sentences
Review common other word forms of *come: came* (122), *comes, coming.* Have students write the other word forms in sentences.

Antonyms
Review the antonym of *come*, the word *go* (105).

Visual Skill-Building, Writing Sentences
Play the Word Look-Alike game. Ask students to circle the words in each row that are like the underlined word. Then they turn the paper over, picture the underlined word, and write it.

<u>come</u>	came	cone	cane	name	same	come	code
<u>think</u>	thank	think	thing	thick	think	talk	link
<u>look</u>	like	took	clock	look	tool	lock	cool
<u>where</u>	what	when	whose	where	here	when	we're

Have students write each of the underlined words in a sentence.

124 *work*

Book Tie-In, Making a Chart, Comparing and Contrasting
Use *Frederick* (Leo Lionni, Pantheon, 1966) to discuss work we do to prepare for winter. Then read a version of *The Ant and the Grasshopper.* Make a chart with students, showing the similarities and differences between the two tales. Then have students write about one thing in the two stories that is the same and one thing that is different.

Antonyms ◆ Introduce the antonym of *work*, the word *play*.

Creating a Book ◆ Discuss careers. Create class-made or student-made books about the work people do in a school, grocery store, tv station, post office, etc.

Visual Skill-Building, ◆ Write *work* on the chalkboard, and draw an outline around the word to
Writing Words accentuate its shape. Provide students with graph paper (or use the blackline master on page 108 of *Spelling Sourcebook 1*). Have students write *work* in the boxes and outline its shape (see Letter Grid Games on page 88 of *Spelling Sourcebook 1*). Expand the activity to include selected review words. Then have students make word shapes for review words, exchange papers with a partner, and see if the partner can write the words.

Other Word Forms, Vocabulary ◆ Introduce common other word forms of *work: works, worked, working, worker.*
Skills, Writing Sentences Discuss unfamiliar words. Have students write the other word forms in sentences.

Compound Words, Book Tie-In ◆ Discuss *workout, workshop, workhorse, workbench, workbook, workweek.* Then use *Snowy* (Berlie Doherty, Dial, 1993), the story of Rachel and her pet workhorse.

Idiomatic Usage, ◆ Ask students to explain in writing what they think it means to say each of these
Writing Explanations expressions (then discuss):

> All work and no play makes Jack a dull boy.
> all in a day's work
> Work your way up.

125 *three*

Writing Stories ◆ Review *one* (28) and *two* (65). Ask students to think of stories that feature the number *three* ("The Three Billy Goats Gruff," "The Three Bears," and "The Three Pigs"). Ask students to write their own stories of "three."

Book Tie-In, Comparing ✔ ◆ Use *The Three Little Pigs and the Big Bad Wolf* (Glen Rounds, Holiday, 1992), a
and Contrasting clever version of this classic tale. Provide students with other versions to compare and contrast.

Making a Chart ◆ Introduce number words *four* through *ten*, and review *first* through *tenth*, which were introduced with *first* (74). Have students make a 1–10 number chart using this format:

> 1 • one first
> 2 •• two second

Sound-Symbol Awareness, ◆ Write *three* on the chalkboard. Ask students to follow these directions to write
Writing Sentences new and review words:

> Remove one letter from *three* to make *tree*.
> Remove *th* from *three*. Then add one letter to make *free*.
> Remove two letters from *three* to make *the* (1).
> Remove *ee* from *three*. Add four letters to make *through* (102).

Have students write a sentence for each word they made.

126 *must*

Predicting Spellings ◆ Have students write *must*. Then ask them to predict the spellings of *most* (99), *much* (104), *mist, mast, dust, just* (97), *rust, trust,* and *mud*.

Writing a List ✦ Ask students to write one "Must Do" list of things they must do at school and one for home.

Sorting Words ✦ Have students play Word Sorts (see **Spelling Sourcebook 1**, page 92) using these words: *most* (99), *made* (81), *just* (97), *much* (104), *first* (74), *many* (55).

127 *because*

Book Tie-In, Writing Explanations ✦ Use *Because of Lozo Brown* (Larry King, Viking, 1988), a story about conquering a fear. Follow up with students explaining how they solved a problem of being afraid.

Book Tie-In, Predicting Spellings, Writing Stories ✓✦ Use *Animals Should Definitely Not Wear Clothing* (Judi Barrett, Macmillan, 1970), in which *because* is repeated in the story refrain. Begin by brainstorming for animals that may be in the book. Write the animals on the chalkboard, asking students to predict spellings. Next, read 3–4 pages of the book. Then have students use the chalkboard list of animals to write their own story following the "because" pattern in the book.

Visual Skill-Building, Writing Words ✦ Ask students to write words they find inside *because* (*be, cause, use, us*). Expand the activity by having students find words inside selected review words.

128 *does*

Homograph Usage, Writing Sentences ✦ *Does* is a homograph, a word that has two pronunciations and meanings but only one spelling. Discuss *does* with students. Review the homograph *use* (88). Ask students to write sentences using *does* and *use* and to read the sentences orally to reinforce the different pronunciations of the homographs.

Other Word Forms, Writing Sentences ✦ Introduce common other word forms of *does: do, did, doing, doer*. Have students write the other word forms in sentences.

129 *part*

Sound-Symbol Awareness, Writing Sentences ✦ Write *part* on the chalkboard. Ask students to follow these directions to write new words:

> Change one letter of *part* to make *past*.
> Change one letter of *part* to make *port*.
> Add one letter to *part* to make *party*.
> Add three letters to *part* to make *partner*.
> Remove the *p* from *part*. Then add two letters to make *start*.

Have students write a sentence for each word they made.

Other Word Forms, Vocabulary Skills, Writing Sentences ✦ Introduce common other word forms of *part: parts, parted, parting, partly*. Discuss unfamiliar words. Have students write the other word forms in sentences.

Multiple Meanings, Writing Sentences ✦ Brainstorm for meanings of *part*. Then have students check a dictionary for verification. Ask students to write sentences to illustrate the different meanings.

130 *even*

Multiple Meanings, Writing Sentences ✦ Have students use the dictionary to explore meanings for *even*. Then ask them to write the different meanings in sentences.

Writing Number Words ✦ Ask students to write the words for the even numbers 2–10.

Antonyms
◈ Introduce one antonym of *even*, the word *odd*.

Suffix Practice,
Writing Sentences
◈ Introduce the *ly* suffix. Illustrate its use with *even*, *part* (129), *like* (66), *time* (69), *most* (99), *over* (82), *new* (107), and *man* (111). Discuss how the use and meaning of the words change when the suffix is added. Have students use the *ly* words in written sentences.

131 *place*

Book Tie-In,
Writing Descriptions
◈ Use *I Know a Place* (Karen Ackerman, Houghton, 1992), about a child's special place. Follow up with students writing a description of their special place.

Creating a Book
◈ Guide students to create a class-made book of places in the community that are important to children: places to eat, places to play, places to shop, historical places. Make copies of the book. Share the books with Realtors or the Chamber of Commerce to help community visitors or new residents (see page 138, Creating Classroom Books).

Other Word Forms, Vocabulary
Skills, Writing Sentences
◈ Introduce common other word forms of *place*: *places, placed, placing, placement*. Discuss unfamiliar words. Have students write the other word forms in sentences.

Predicting Spellings,
Vocabulary Skills
◈ Have students write *place*. Then ask them to predict the spellings for *plate, ace, lace, plane, places, pace, lace, face, race*, and *trace*. Discuss unfamiliar words.

Prefix Practice, Book Tie-In
◈ Review the *re* prefix by writing *replace* on the chalkboard and asking students to brainstorm for words that use the *re* prefix: *use* (88), *make* (72), *write* (108), *new* (107), *called* (96), *made* (81), *do* (45). Use *Dinosaurs to the Rescue!: A Guide to Protecting Our Planet* (Laurie and Marc Brown, Joy Street, 1992), which introduces words related to environmental protection: *reduce, reuse, recycle*.

132 *well*

Multiple Meanings,
Writing Sentences
◈ Brainstorm for meanings of *well*. Then have students check a dictionary for verification. Ask students to write sentences to illustrate the different meanings.

Book Tie-In, Making a Poster
◈ Use *The Elephant in the Well* (Marie Hall Ets, Viking, 1972), a cumulative tale that shows how being small isn't correlated to being useless. Ask students to create a poster that tells about something helpful they did.

Word Analysis
◈ Review words with double letters. Include *been* (75), *called* (96), *little* (92), *good* (106), *too* (112), *look* (117), *three* (125).

Sound-Symbol Awareness,
Writing Rhymes, Reading
◈ Write _*ell* on the chalkboard. Have students add beginning letters to make new words. Then ask students to make rhymes using the patterned rhyming words and read them to the class.

133 *such*

Sound-Symbol Awareness,
Predicting Spellings
◈ Have students write *much* (104) and *such*. Brainstorm for words that begin or end with *ch*. Ask students to predict the spellings of the words as they are written. If *tch* ending spellings are suggested, write them in a separate category. Explain that the same sound is spelled with *tch* or *ch*.

Sorting Words
◈ Have students play Word Sorts (see **Spelling Sourcebook 1**, page 92) using these words: *such, much* (104), *some* (56), *each* (47), *which* (41), *lunch, state, same* (115).

Visual Skill-Building,
Writing Sentences

Play the Word Look-Alike game. Ask students to circle the words in each row that are like the underlined word. Then they turn the paper over, picture the underlined word, and write it.

<u>such</u>   much   suns   said   such   sack   sock   such
<u>three</u>   there   those   three   these   three   their   free
<u>well</u>   all   wheel   wall   will   wool   well   sell

Have students write each of the underlined words in a sentence.

134 *here*

Visual Skill-Building

Ask students to write words they find inside *here* (*he, her*). Then have students write a sentence that uses all three words.

Antonyms

Review the antonym of *here*, the word *there* (37). Note that *here* is inside *there*.

Homophone Usage, Writing
Words, Writing Speculations

Introduce the homophone of *here*, the word *hear*. Ask students to choose among *there, their, they're, here,* and *hear* to complete these sentences:

T_____ dogs are barking. (Their)
T_____ barking very loud. (They're)
I can h_____ the barking from h_____. (hear, here)
I don't know why t_____ barking. (they're)
I'll go over t_____ . (there)
I'll find out why t_____ dogs are barking. (their)

Then have students speculate in writing why the dogs were barking.

135 *take*

Book Tie-In, Writing a List

Use *"Take Care of Things," Edward Said* (Helen Buckley, Lothrop, 1991), in which a younger sibling feels lonely when an older child goes off to school. Follow up with students listing things various family members "take care of" at home.

Predicting Spellings,
Vocabulary Skills

Have students write *make* (72) and *take*. Then ask students to predict the spellings of *bake, cake, fake, stake, flake, lake, quake, rake, shake, wake, tape,* and *tame.* Discuss unfamiliar words.

Writing Subtraction Problems

Ask students to write math subtraction problems for another classmate to do:
Take three from eight to make _____ (five).

Antonyms

Introduce the antonym of *take*, the word *give.*

Other Word Forms, Spelling
Rules, Writing Sentences

Introduce common other word forms of *take: takes, took, taking, taken, taker.* Review the spelling rule for dropping the final *e* before adding *ing* (see **Spelling Sourcebook 1**, page 85) Have students write the other word forms in sentences.

Book Tie-In, Writing Advice

Read *Take a Nap, Harry* (Mary Chalmers, Harper, 1991), about Harry who isn't sleepy for his nap. Ask students to write "tips" for getting a young child to take a nap.

136 *why*

Book Tie-Ins, Writing a
Pourquoi Story

Use *Why Rat Comes First: A Story of the Chinese Zodiac* (Clara Yen, Children's Book Press, 1991); *Why Mosquitoes Buzz in People's Ears* (Verna Aardema, Dial, 1975), the 1976 Caldecott book; and *Why the Sun and Moon Live in the Sky* (Dayrell Elphinstone, Houghton, 1968) for *why,* or pourquoi, stories. Then ask students to write a short pourquoi story.

Creating a Riddle Book
◆ Engage students in "Why . . . Because" riddles. Use *Remember the A La Mode* (Charles Keller, Prentice-Hall, 1983):"Why is a river rich? Because it has two banks." Assemble a class-made book of *Why . . . Because* riddles collected or created by students (see page 138, Creating Classroom Books).

Sound-Symbol Awareness, Writing Sentences
◆ Have students write words that begin with *wh*. Include *what* (32), *when* (35), *which* (41), and *where* (98). Have students play Sentence Puzzles (see *Spelling Sourcebook 1*, page 91) using the *wh* words.

137 *help*

Creating a Personal Telephone Directory, Writing Guidelines
◆ Ask students to compile a telephone directory titled *Help*, listing emergency numbers of relatives, friends, and neighbors. Discuss use of the 911 emergency number. Then have students write guidelines for effective use of 911.

Writing Stories
◆ Brainstorm for stories in which helpfulness is a theme: "The Elves and the Shoemaker," "The Lion and the Mouse," *Clifford's Good Deeds* (Norman Bridwell, Scholastic, 1976). Then ask students to write a story about a time when someone helped them in a big way.

Other Word Forms, Vocabulary Skills, Writing Sentences
◆ Introduce common other word forms of *help: helps, helped, helping, helper, helpful, helpfully, helpfulness, helpless, helplessly, helplessness*. Discuss unfamiliar words. Have students write the other word forms in sentences.

Suffix Practice, Writing Sentences, Book Tie-In
◆ Discuss the *er* suffix (*helper*). Ask students to add the suffix to *time* (69), *make* (72), *find* (87), *use* (88), *call* (*called* [96]), *think* (118), and *work* (124). Have students use the *er* words in sentences. Then read *Who Is the Boss?* (Josse Goffin, Clarion, ✔ 1992), which features more *er* words, including *taller, nicer, stronger, faster*. Point out to students the two meanings for the *er* suffix: "someone who" and "more."

138 *put*

Idiomatic Usage, Writing Explanations
◆ Ask students to explain in writing what they think it means to say each of these expressions (then discuss):

putting on the dog	to put all your eggs in one basket
to put a bee in someone's bonnet	to put two and two together

Visual Skill-Building, Writing Words
◆ Write *put* on the chalkboard, and draw an outline around the word to accentuate its shape. Provide students with graph paper (or use the blackline master on page 108 of *Spelling Sourcebook 1*). Have students write *put* in the boxes and outline its shape (see Letter Grid Games on page 88 of *Spelling Sourcebook 1*). Expand the activity to include selected review words. Then have students make word shapes for review words, exchange papers with a partner, and see if the partner can write the words.

Other Word Forms, Spelling Rules, Writing a List
◆ Introduce common other word forms of *put: puts, putting*. Review the spelling rule for doubling the final consonant before adding *ing* (see *Spelling Sourcebook 1*, page 85). Review *get* (101). Have students compile a list of words that double the final consonant before the *ing* suffix is added.

139 *different* ✔   2 variations

Book Tie-In, Contrasting
◆ Use *The Ugly Duckling* (Lilian Moore, Scholastic, 1987) to introduce the concept of "being different." Have students contrast in writing and art how the Ugly Duckling was different from others at the beginning, as well as at the end of the story.

Antonyms ✦ Review the antonym of *different*, the word *same* (115). Review other opposites with their partners, including *back* (103), *go* (105), *good* (106), *new* (107), *man* (111), *day* (114), *right* (116), *work* (124), *even* (130), *here* (134), and *take* (135).

Analogies, Writing Sentences ✦ Introduce analogies. The analogies can be completed using the bank of words generated in the preceding antonym activity. Complete the analogies together.

    good is to bad as same is to _____ (different)

    right is to write as hear is to _____ (here)

    day is to night as play is to _____ (work)

    get is to set as make is to _____ (take)

    three is to odd as four is to _____ (even)

Then have students write the answer words in sentences.

140 *away*

Book Tie-In, Writing Stories ✔ Use *I'm Flying* (Alan Wade, Knopf, 1990), a picture story of weather balloons flying away with the young hero's math book, toothbrush, and other items he's eager to see disappear. Ask students to write a story about what they would like to send up, up, and away in a balloon.

Writing Predictions, Book Tie-In ✦ What does the family cat, Slobcat, do at home when the family is away? Have students write predictions. Then read *Slobcat* (Paul Geraghty, Macmillan, 1991) to find out that the cat is not the sleepy slob the family thinks he is and has an adventurous life when they're away.

Writing Words ✦ Have students play Connect the Dots (see *Spelling Sourcebook 1*, page 87) using *away* and selected review words.

141 *again*

Prefix Practice, Writing a List, Writing Reasons ✦ Review the *re* prefix, noting that it means "again." Some stories are so good, they can be *reread* many times. Ask students to list books that they would like to hear again and tell why each is worth rereading. Select from the students' lists of stories for repeat readings.

Word Analysis ✦ Write _*g*_ _*n* on the chalkboard. Ask students to fill in the vowels to make *again*. Extend the fill-in activity to *could* (70), *people* (79), *through* (102), *around* (120), *because* (127), *does* (128), *our* (109), *about* (48), *would* (59), *said* (43). Have students fill in the vowels and then write the whole word.

Writing Words ✦ Have students play Red and Green (see *Spelling Sourcebook 1*, page 90) using *again* and selected review words.

142 *off*

Antonyms, Book Tie-In
NA Follett
✦ Review the antonym of *off*, the word *on* (14). Review opposite concepts with *A Rainbow Balloon: A Book of Concepts* (Ann Lenssen, Cobblehill, 1992), which also introduces the process of preparing a hot-air balloon for ascension.

Word Analysis ✦ Review words with double letters. Include *been* (75), *little* (92), and *different* (139).

Sound-Symbol Awareness, Writing Sentences ✦ Write *off* on the chalkboard. Have students follow the directions to make new and review words:

    Change two letters of *off* to make *odd*.

    Change two letters of *off* to make *old*.

    Change two letters of *off* to make *own*.

    Take one letter away from *off* to make *of* (2).

Have students write a sentence for each word they made.

143 *went*

Sound-Symbol Awareness, Writing Rhymes, Reading
◆ Write _ent on the chalkboard. Have students add beginning letters to make new words (*bent, cent, dent, gent, rent, sent, tent, vent, scent, spent*). Have students make rhymes using the patterned rhyming words and read them to the class.

Antonyms
◆ Review the antonym of *went*, the word *came* (122).

Visual Skill-Building, Writing Sentences
◆ Play the Word Look-Alike game. Ask students to circle the words in each row that are like the underlined word. Then they turn the paper over, picture the underlined word, and write it.

went	want	west	rent	went	were	went	when
off	of	odd	off	for	too	elf	for
put	pat	put	top	pot	put	pit	but
here	where	her	here	hear	were	here	there

Have students write each of the underlined words in a sentence.

144 *old*   Na Follett

Book Tie-Ins, Writing a Letter
◆ Use *Old, Older, Oldest* (Leonore Klein, Hastings, 1983), a book that helps students understand age and life spans. Follow up by using the book *Annie and the Old One* (Miska Miles, Little, 1971) to develop appreciation for the elderly. ✓ Ask students to write a letter to someone they know who is old and special.

Usage, Writing Sentences
◆ Discuss the comparative and superlative forms of *old (older, oldest)* and of these review words: *good* (106), *new* (107), *little* (92). Have students write the words in sentences.

Sound-Symbol Awareness, Writing Sentences
◆ Write *old* on the chalkboard. Ask students to follow these directions to make new words:
  Add one letter to *old* to make *gold, told, sold.*
  Add two letters to *old* to make *older.*
  Change one letter of *old* to make *odd.*
Have students write a sentence for each word they made.

Antonyms
◆ Review the antonym of *old*, the word *new* (107).

145 *number*

Book Tie-In, Writing Math Problems
◆ Use *Anno's Math Games* (Anno Mitsumasa, Philomel, 1989), about using number sense for solving mathematical problems. Then have students write number problems to challenge their classmates.

Writing Number Words, Dictation
◆ Ask student partners to test each other on writing the number words *one–ten* (*one* [28], *two* [65], and *three* [125] are review words). Then dictate the following controlled-vocabulary sentences to students:
  Three people work here.   I want another one.
  I can write ten number words.   She would like two of these.

Other Word Forms, Vocabulary Skills, Writing Sentences
◆ Introduce common other word forms of *number: numbers, numbered, numbering.* Discuss unfamiliar words. Have students write the other word forms in sentences.

146 *great*

Book Tie-In, Writing Reasons
◆ Use *The Great Alexander the Great* (Joe Lasker, Viking, 1983), a picture biography. Ask students to write reasons why Alexander was considered great.

Book Tie-In, Writing a *News Story*	Read *Samuel Todd's Book of Great Inventions* (E. L. Konigsburg, Atheneum/Karl, 1991) for information about belt loops, Velcro, and other great inventions. Then ask students to think of something great they would like to invent and create a news story announcing the great invention.
Multiple Meanings, Writing Sentences	Discuss the different meanings of *great*. Ask students to use dictionaries as a resource. Have them write sentences using the different meanings.
Other Word Forms, Vocabulary Skills, Writing Sentences	Introduce common other word forms of *great: greater, greatest, greatly, greatness*. Discuss unfamiliar words. Have students write the other word forms in sentences.

147 *tell*

Book Tie-In, Writing a Story Ending, Reading	Use *Don't Tell the Whole World* (Joanna Cole, Crowell, 1990), the silly story of Emma who never intends to *tell* when someone says, "Don't tell!" Before the ending is read, have students write endings and read them to the class.
Book Tie-In, Writing a Telephone Message	Use *The Blabbermouths* (Gerda Mantinband, Greenwillow, 1992), a humorous version of the classic story that develops when one person tells a secret, who tells it to another, who tells it to another. Follow up by playing "telephone." Have one student write a message, then whisper it to another student, who whispers it to another. The last student to hear the message writes what was heard. Then compare the original message and the last one.
Other Word Forms, Vocabulary Skills, Writing Sentences	Introduce common other word forms of *tell: tells, told, telling*. Discuss unfamiliar words. Have students write the other word forms in sentences.
Idiomatic Usage, Writing Explanations	Have students explain in writing what they think it means to say each of these expressions (then discuss):

        to tell on someone   to tell someone off

        Time will tell.   to tell time

148 *men*

Spelling Rules	Have students write *man* (111) and its plural, *men*. Review this spelling rule (see *Spelling Sourcebook 1*, page 85). Ask students to brainstorm for other words that change their spellings in the plural form (*foot/feet, woman/women, mouse/mice, child/children*).
Sound-Symbol Awareness, Writing Sentences	Write *men* on the chalkboard. Ask students to follow these directions to write new and review words:

        Remove one letter of *men* to make *me* (110).

        Change *men* to make *when* (35).

        Add one letter to *men* to make *mean*.

        Change one letter of *men* to make a number word. (*ten*)

        Change one letter of *men* to make a bear's home. (*den*)

Have students write a sentence for each word they made.

Antonyms	Introduce the antonym of *men*, the word *women*.

149 *say*

Book Tie-In, Writing Words	Use *Easy as Pie: A Guessing Game of Sayings* (Marcia & Michael Folsom, Ticknor, 1985). Have students write what they think might be the last word in the book's alphabetized sayings . . . then turn the page to compare their word choices with the answer.

Other Word Forms, Vocabulary Skills, Writing Sentences

◆ Introduce common other word forms of *say: says, said* (43), *saying*. Have students write the other word forms in sentences.

Sound-Symbol Awareness, Writing Tongue Twisters

◆ Ask students to make a list of *s* and *sh* words to use for writing tongue twisters. Include *said* (43), *she* (54), *some* (56), *so* (57), *see* (68), *same* (115), and *such* (133). Then have students write tongue twisters.

Sound-Symbol Awareness, Sorting Words

◆ Have students write *say* and underline *ay*. Then have students compile a list of words with *ay*. Ask students to listen to the long *a* sound in the words. Then have them collect more words with the long *a* sound and sort them into categories to note the most frequent spellings for long *a* (most common: *ay* [*say*], *ai* [*train*], a-consonant-*e* [*same*]). Have one category for "other" to accommodate less common spellings.

150 *small*

Book Tie-Ins, Comparing and Contrasting, Making a Chart, Writing Stories

◆ Use *The Lion and the Rat: A Fable By La Fontaine* (Watts, 1963) to point out that *small* does not mean "lesser than." Compare and contrast this tale with the classic fable *The Lion and the Mouse*. Chart the similarities and differences between the tales. Another folk tale that celebrates being small is *The Vingananee and the Tree Toad: A Liberian Tale* (Verna Aardema, Warne, 1983). Following the readings, ask students to write a story in which the smallest character is the champion.

Other Word Forms, Writing Comparisons

◆ Introduce common other word forms of *small: smaller, smallest*. Have students write comparisons using the words.

Synonyms

◆ Ask students to make a list of synonyms for *small (tiny, little* [92], *itsy-bitsy, teeny, minute, petite)*.

Grade 3 begins

151 *every*

Compound Words, Writing Sentences

◆ Review compound words. Introduce the compounds *everyone, everybody, everywhere, everything*. Have students write the words and underline *every* in each of the compounds. Then they write the compounds in sentences.

Visual Skill-Building, Predicting Spellings

◆ Point out *ever* inside of *every*. Ask students to predict the spelling of the compound word *forever*. Then show *very* inside *every*.

Idiomatic Usage, Writing Explanations

◆ Have students explain in writing what they think it means to say each of these expressions (then discuss):

Every cloud has a silver lining.
Every minute counts.
every now and then

House on Maple Street
Homeplace (Pinckney)   *NA*

152 *found*

Antonyms, Book Tie-In, Creating a Bulletin, Writing Descriptions

◆ Introduce the antonym of *found*, the word *lost*. Then use the story *Lost and Found* (Jill Walsh, Andre Deutsch, 1985), which examines the articles children lose in their times and find from children of centuries past. Follow up by asking students to create a Lost and Found Bulletin listing and describing things in the school Lost and Found.

Sound -Symbol Awareness, Vocabulary Skills

◆ Write *_ound* on the chalkboard. Have students add beginning letters to write new words (*bound, found, hound, mound, pound, round, sound, ground*). Discuss unfamiliar words.

Lost   Paul: Brett Johnson

Book Tie-In, Writing Stories	Use *The Last Time I Saw Harris* (Frank Remkiewicz, Lothrop, 1991), in which Edmund and his chauffeur conduct a worldwide search for Harris the parrot. Follow up by asking students to write a story about a time they lost something and found it.
Other Word Forms, Vocabulary Skills, Writing Sentences	Review common other word forms of *found*: *find* (87), *finds, finding, finder*. Discuss unfamiliar words. Have students write the other word forms in sentences.

153 *still*

Multiple Meanings, Writing Sentences	Brainstorm with students for meanings of *still*. Then have them check a dictionary for verification. Ask students to write sentences to illustrate the different meanings.
Book Tie-In, Writing a Sequel	Use *Wriggly Pig* (Jon Blake, Tambourine, 1992), about a young pig-child who cannot sit still. Have students write a sequel to the story describing Wriggly Pig in another humorous situation.
Predicting Spellings, Vocabulary Skills	Have students write *still*. Then ask students to predict the spellings of *fill, chill, drill, stall, stiff, stuff, stick, shrill*, and *frill*. Discuss unfamiliar words.
Word Analysis, Creating a Word Puzzle, Visual Skill-Building	Note the double letters in *still*. Have students write review words with double letters: *been* (75), *little* (92), *called* (96), *good* (106), *too* (112), *look* (117), *different* (139). Have students make a word-search puzzle using *still* and other words that have double letters (see Letter Grid Games, **Spelling Sourcebook 1**, page 88).

154 *between*

Sound-Symbol Awareness, Sorting Words	Have students write *between* and underline the parts of the word in which they hear long *e*. Then have students compile a list of long *e* words. Ask students to sort the words into categories to illustrate the most frequent spellings for long *e* (most common: *ee [see], e [be], ea [eat], e*-consonant-*e [these]*). Have one category for "other" to accommodate less common spellings.
Idiomatic Usage, Writing Explanations	Ask students to explain in writing what they think it means to say each of these expressions (then discuss):

        Read between the lines.

        few and far between

        between you and me

        a go-between (See literature entry below.)

Book Tie-In, Writing Explanations	Use *The Go-Between* (Amy Hest, Four Winds, 1992), an intergenerational story. Have students explain how Lexi is the "go-between."
Word Analysis, Predicting Spellings	Have students brainstorm for more words that begin with the first syllable *be*. Then make a cumulative list on the chalkboard, having students predict spellings as the words are written (*because* [127], *begin, began, believe, before, become, below*).

155 *name*

Book Tie-Ins, Research and Writing, Creating a Book	Use *Tikki Tikki Tembo* (Arlene Mosel, Henry Holt, 1968), a Chinese tale explaining why Chinese children aren't given long names. Then have students do research to find students in their school with the longest and the shortest name. They may continue the survey to discover students with rhyming names, most common first/last name, students named after someone or something, etc. Summarize the survey results into a class-made book (see page 138, Creating Classroom Books). Companion book: *Chrysanthemum* (Kevin Henkes, Greenwillow, 1991), about a girl named for the flower.

E818 Pet   paper

Book Tie-In, Writing Jokes, *Reading*	✓ *What's Your Name?* (Scott Peterson, Lerner, 1987) is a joke book about names. After the reading, have students write their own name jokes and read them to the class.
Idiomatic Usage, *Writing Explanations*	◆ Ask students to explain in writing what they think it means to say each of these expressions (then discuss): to make a name for yourself Your name is mud. to be on a first name basis
Visual Skill-Building, *Writing Sentences*	◆ Play the Word Look-Alike game. Ask students to circle the words in each row that are like the underlined word. Then they turn the paper over, picture the underlined word, and write it.

<u>name</u> same mane name mare name mean mate
<u>found</u> sound found down round bound find hound
<u>small</u> smell smart snail malls small sell spill

Have students write each of the underlined words in a sentence.

Other Word Forms, Vocabulary *Skills, Writing Sentences*	◆ Introduce common other word forms of *name: names, named, naming, namely, nameless.* Discuss unfamiliar words. Have students write the other word forms in sentences.

156 *should*

Word Analysis, *Writing Explanations*	◆ Have students write *would* (59), *could* (70), and *should*. Then have students explain in writing what is the same and what is different about the words.
Writing Questions and Answers, *Creating a Book*	◆ Create an advice column. First, have students write a "What should I do?" question for the advice column. Collect the questions and redistribute them. Have students answer the question they get: "You should . . ." Compile the questions and answers into a class-made advice book (see page 138, Creating Classroom Books).
Writing Words	◆ Have students play the All-Play Spelling Bee (see **Spelling Sourcebook 1**, page 86). Include *should* and selected review words.

157 *home*   Prof. 810.8

Book Tie-In, Creating a Book	✓ Use *Home: A Collaboration of Thirty Distinguished Authors and Illustrators of Children's Books to Aid the Homeless* (edited by Michael Rosen, HarperCollins, 1992), which features the theme of "home" to benefit those without one. Follow up with students creating class-made or student-made books on this theme.
Suffix Practice	◆ Introduce the suffix *less* with *homeless.* Add *less* to *use* (88), *help* (137), *time* (169), and *name* (155). Conclude that the *less* suffix means "without".
Book Tie-In, Writing *Descriptions, Art* N/A	◆ Use *The Children's Book of Houses and Homes* (Carol Bowyer, Usborne, 1978) for drawings of homes around the globe. Follow up with students drawing and describing their own "dream home."
Idiomatic Usage, Writing *Explanations*	◆ Ask students to explain in writing what they think it means to say each of these expressions (then discuss): People in glass houses shouldn't throw stones. to make yourself at home. Bring home the bacon. Charity begins at home. till the cows come home

Other Word Forms, Vocabulary Skills, Writing Sentences	◆ Introduce common other word forms of *home: homes, homey, homeless*. Discuss unfamiliar words. Have students write the other word forms in sentences.
	◆ Reinforce final silent *e* words: *home, people* (79), *use* (88), *little* (92), *where* (98), *write* (108), *because* (127), and *place* (131).

158 *big*   ~~E 921 Crews~~

Book Tie-In, Comparing and Contrasting	◆ Use *Bigmama's* (Donald Crews, Greenwillow, 1991), a tale of Crews' childhood summers in Florida with his grandma, Bigmama. Ask students to interview an older friend or relative about childhood activities. Then have students compare and contrast those activities with the activities they often do.
Book Tie-Ins, Contrasting	◆ Study BIG animals. Include whales (biggest animals), elephants (biggest land animals), and dinosaurs (biggest reptiles of all time). Use books on dinosaurs and *Whales* (Gail Gibbons, Holiday, 1991), *Great Whales: The Gentle Giants* (Patricia Lauber, Holt, 1991), and *African Elephants: Giants of the Land* (Dorothy Patent, Holiday, 1991). Then have students contrast in writing the largest animals.
Suffix Practice	◆ Review *er/est* suffixes using *big* and *small* (150), *great* (146), *old* (144), *new* (107), *little* (92), and *long* (91).
Antonyms, Book Tie-In	◆ Review the antonym of *big*, the word *little* (92). Use *Big and Small, Short and Tall* (Lynne Cherry, Ticknor, 1986), which contrasts the biggest and smallest animals within a species.
Synonyms, Sequencing	◆ Have students make a list of synonyms for *big (huge, giant-sized, enormous, large, gigantic)*. Then have them try to sequence the synonyms from the smallest to the largest, based on connotations.

[handwritten left margin: 591.4 Jen   Big and Little NA   Steve Jenkins]

159 *give*

Multiple Meanings, Writing Sentences	◆ Brainstorm for meanings of *give*. Then have students check a dictionary for verification. Ask students to write sentences to illustrate the different meanings.
Idiomatic Usage, Writing Explanations	◆ Ask students to explain in writing what they think it means to say each of these expressions (then discuss):
	Give credit where credit is due.
	to give someone the cold shoulder
	to give your word
	to give someone a hand
	What gives?
	to give up
Other Word Forms, Vocabulary Skills, Writing Sentences, Spelling Rules	◆ Introduce common other word forms of *give: gives, giving, gave, given, giver*. Discuss unfamiliar words. Have students write the other word forms in sentences. Review the spelling rule for dropping the final *e* before adding a suffix beginning with a vowel (see ***Spelling Sourcebook 1***, page 85).
Antonyms	◆ Introduce antonyms of *give*, the words *take* and *receive*.
Book Tie-In, Creating a Greeting Card	◆ Use *The Present* (Michael Emberley, Little, 1991), about Arne's challenge to decide what to give his nephew for his birthday. Have students follow up the reading by creating a greeting card to accompany Arne's gift.

160 *air*   E 551.5 Bra

Book Tie-In, Art, Writing Words
√ Use *Air Is All Around You* (Franklyn Branley, Harper, 1986) for an introduction to the properties of air. Follow up by listing things that fly through the air. Have students draw, color, and cut out the shapes of things that fly. Assemble them on a bulletin board titled "Up in the Air" with each flying object labeled.

weather unit

Vocabulary Skills, Word Analysis, Writing Sentences
Introduce the word *error*, often confused with *air*. Expand the lesson to other confusing pairs of words: *are* (15) and *our* (109), *then* (53) and *than* (73). Have students use the words in oral and written sentences to differentiate them.

Homophone Usage, Writing Sentences
Introduce the homophone of *air*, the word *heir*. Have students write the homophones in sentences to differentiate them.

Compound Words, Writing Words
Introduce *airport*. Then ask students to find and write more compound words with *air* (*airmail, airline, aircraft, airbus, airstrip, airtight, airsick*). Discuss unfamiliar words.

161 *line*   E 516 Hob

Multiple Meanings, Writing Sentences
Brainstorm for meanings of *line*. Then have students check a dictionary for verification. Ask students to write sentences to illustrate different meanings.

Book Tie-In
√ Use *Spirals, Curves, Fanshapes, and Lines* (Tana Hoban, Greenwillow, 1992), which develops concepts through a child's eyes.

Other Word Forms, Spelling Rules, Vocabulary Skills, Writing Sentences
Introduce common other word forms of *line: lines, lined, lining, liner.* Review the spelling rule for dropping the final *e* before adding a suffix beginning with a vowel (see *Spelling Sourcebook 1,* page 85). Discuss unfamiliar words. Have students write the other word forms in sentences.

Idiomatic Usage, Writing Explanations
Ask students to explain in writing what they think it means to say each of these expressions (then discuss):

    to read between the lines.
    to swallow something hook, line, and sinker
    Toe the line.
    in the line of duty
    to drop someone a line

Sorting Words
Have students play Word Sorts (see *Spelling Sourcebook 1,* page 92) using these words: *line, like* (66), *home* (157), *long* (91), *little* (92), *write* (108), *give* (159).

162 *set*

Predicting Spellings
Have students write *set*. Then ask them to predict the spellings of *sit, sat, bet, get* (101), *jet, met, pet, let, wet, yet, send,* and *self.*

Other Word Forms, Writing Sentences
Introduce common other word forms of *set: sets, setting.* Discuss unfamiliar words. Have students write the other word forms in sentences.

Multiple Meanings, Word Analysis
Write *set* on the chalkboard. Discuss the different meanings and uses of *set.* Then have students check a dictionary for verification. Discuss the difference in meaning between *sit* and *set.* Review often-confused words (see *air* [160]).

Antonyms, Comparing and Contrasting
Introduce the antonym of *set*, the word *rise*. Ask students to write what is different between a *sunset* and a *sunrise* and then write what is the same about them.

163 *own*   DK

**Book Tie-In,
Writing Descriptions**

✓ Use *My Own Home* (Lyn Hoopes, HarperCollins, 1991), in which a little owl searches for a home. Discuss how everyone wants his or her own special place. Have students write a description of their real or make-believe own special place.

**Other Word Forms, Vocabulary
Skills, Writing Sentences**

Introduce common other word forms of *own: owns, owned, owning, owner.* Discuss unfamiliar words. Have students write the other word forms in sentences.

Writing Words

Play Race Track Spelling (see **Spelling Sourcebook 1**, page 90). Use *own* and selected review words.

164 *under*

Book Tie-In, Antonyms
N/A

Use *Nice or Nasty: A Book of Opposites* (Nick Butterworth and Mick Inkpen, Little, 1987). Review the antonym of *under*, the word *over* (82).

**Idiomatic Usage,
Writing Explanations**

Ask students to explain in writing what they think it means to say each of these expressions (then discuss):

to keep it under your hat
Don't let any grass grow under your feet.
to pull the rug out from under someone
water under the bridge
under the weather

**Prefix Practice, Vocabulary
Skills, Writing Sentences**

Show students how the word *under* can also be a prefix. Review *over* (82), which is both a word and a prefix. Discuss words with the *under* prefix (*undershirt, undertow, underwear, underline, underdog, underpass, underbrush, underprivileged, underage.*) Discuss unfamiliar words. Have students write the words in sentences.

165 *read*   E 811 Goo

**Book Tie-In, Writing a List,
Creating a Bibliography**

✓ Use *Good Books, Good Times!* (Lee Bennett Hopkins, Harper, 1990), a collection of poems on books and reading. Follow up by asking students to create a list of favorite books. Make a cumulative class list. Then have students vote to rate the top ten favorite books, and help them make a bibliography of these books.

Book Tie-In
N/A

Use *To Ride a Butterfly* (Nancy Larrick and Wendy Lamb, Bantam, 1991), a collection of readings contributed by fifty-two well-known authors and illustrators of children's books.

**Homophone Usage, Homograph
Usage, Writing Sentences,
Book Tie-In**

818 Ter

Introduce the homophone of *read*, the word *reed*. Then introduce the homograph *read*. Have students use the words in oral and written sentences to differentiate them. Use *The Dove Dove: Funny Homograph Riddles* (Marvin Terban, Ticknor, 1982). Review the homographs *use* (88) and *does* (128). Have students find and write more homographs (*wind, tear, present, close*).

**Other Word Forms, Vocabulary
Skills, Writing Sentences**

Introduce common other word forms of *read: reads, reading, reader.* Have students write the other word forms in sentences.

**Using Homophones and
Homographs**

Have students play Mystery Words (see **Spelling Sourcebook 1**, page 89) with homographs and homophones.

166 *last*

**Multiple Meanings,
Writing Sentences**

Brainstorm for meanings of *last*. Then have students check a dictionary for verification. Ask students to write sentences to illustrate the different meanings.

Other Word Forms, Vocabulary Skills, Writing Sentences	✦ Introduce common other word forms of *last: lasts, lasted, lasting*. Discuss unfamiliar words. Have students write the other word forms in sentences.
Sound-Symbol Awareness, Writing Sentences	✦ Write *last* on the chalkboard. Ask students to follow these directions to write new words:

> Change one letter of *last* to make *list*.
> Add one letter to *last* to make *blast*.
> Change one letter in *last* to make *fast, mast, past*.
> Change one letter in *last* to make *lost*.
> Add three letters to *last* to make *lasting*.

Have students write a sentence for each word they made.

Antonyms ✦ Review the antonym of *last*, the word *first* (74).

Visual Skill-Building, Writing Words ✦ Write *last* on the chalkboard, and draw an outline around the word to accentuate its shape. Provide students with graph paper (or use the blackline master on page 108 of *Spelling Sourcebook 1*). Have students write *last* in the boxes and outline its shape (see Letter Grid Games on page 88 of *Spelling Sourcebook 1*). Ask students to find other words that have the same shape as *last* (*find* [87], *back* [103], *look* [117]).

167 *never*

Antonyms ✦ Introduce the antonym of *never*, the word *always*.

Dictating and Writing ✦ Dictate these partial sentences for students to write and complete:

> I never can find my _____.   It is never right to _____
> I never like to _____.   I would never _____.
> Some people never _____.   I never know _____.

Analogies, Writing Sentences ✦ Review analogies (see 139). The analogies can be completed using words from the preceding dictation activity.

> fast is to slow as always is to _____ (never)
> see is to sea as wood is to _____ (would)
> day is to way as show is to _____ (know)
> their is to there as write is to _____ (right)
> big is to large as enjoy is to _____ (like)

Have students write the answer words in sentences.

Book Tie-In, Writing a Sequel ✦ Use *Never Grab A Deer By The Ear* (Colleen Bare, Cobblehill, 1993), a nature book, and *Never Satisfied* (Fulvio Testa, Henry Holt, 1988) about boys who want more adventure in their lives. Follow up with students writing sequels to the stories.

599.73 Bar (handwritten)

N/A (handwritten)

168 *us*

Sound-Symbol Awareness, Writing Sentences ✦ Write *us* on the chalkboard. Ask students to follow these directions to write new and review words:

> Change one letter of *us* to make *is* (7) and *as* (16).
> Add one letter to *us* to make *bus*.
> Add two letters to *us* to make *just* (97), *must* (126).
> Add one letter to *us* to make *use* (88).
> Add five letters to *us* to make *because* (127).

Ask students to write a sentence for each word they made.

Acronyms and Abbreviations

✦ Write US on the chalkboard and introduce US and USA as a shortcut for United States of America. Ask students to write what these letters are shortcuts for: TV (television), ABC (American Broadcasting System), NBC (National Broadcasting System), CBS (Columbia Broadcasting System), BLT (bacon, lettuce, and tomato), DJ (disc jockey), UFO (Unidentified Flying Object), CD (compact disc), ZIP (Zone Improvement Plan). Ask students to find and write more examples.

169 *left*

Multiple Meanings, Writing Sentences

✦ Brainstorm for meanings of *left*. Then have students check a dictionary for verification. Ask students to write sentences to illustrate the different meanings.

Antonyms

✦ Review the antonym of *left*, the word *right* (116).

Research and Writing, Public Speaking

✦ Have students find out about one of the following topics, tell about their findings in writing, and then present the information orally to the class:

- special products made for left-handed people
- the number of left-handed and right-handed people in their class/grade/school/family.
- challenges some left-handed people may have doing everyday things

170 *end*

Sound-Symbol Awareness, Vocabulary Skills, Writing Sentences

✦ Write _end on the chalkboard. Ask students to add beginning letters to make *bend, blend, lend, spend, trend, mend, send*. Discuss unfamiliar words. Have students write the words in sentences.

Other Word Forms, Vocabulary Skills, Writing Sentences

✦ Introduce common other word forms of *end: ends, ending, ended, endless*. Discuss unfamiliar words. Have students write the other word forms in sentences.

Antonyms

✦ Introduce the antonym of *end*, the word *begin*.

Idiomatic Usage, Writing Explanations

✦ Ask students to explain in writing what they think it means to say each of these expressions (then discuss):

You can't see the light at the end of the tunnel.
All's well that ends well.
to burn the candle at both ends
You can't see beyond the end of your nose.

Writing Story Endings

✦ Have students choose one of their favorite short stories and write a new ending for it.

171 *along*

Word Analysis

✦ Write *along* on the chalkboard, and underline the *ng*. Brainstorm for more words with *ng* (*long* [91], *young, bring, song, king*, or any word with the *ing* suffix).

Word Analysis, Vocabulary Skills, Writing Sentences

✦ Write on the chalkboard: She came <u>along</u> with me. She came <u>a long</u> way with me. Discuss the different meanings. Expand the lesson to *away* (140) and *a way*. Then ask students to write sentences using the words.

Word Analysis, Writing Sentences

✦ Have students collect *a_____* words (*along, about* [48], *around* [120], *away* [140], *again* [141], *alive, alone, asleep.*) Have students write the words in sentences.

Idiomatic Usage,
Writing Explanations

♦ Ask students to explain in writing what they think it means to say each of these expressions (then discuss):

along in years	to get along on a shoestring
to get along	to inch along

172 *while*

Sound-Symbol Awareness

♦ Write _ile on the chalkboard. Ask students to add beginning letters to make new words (*file, mile, pile, tile, smile*).

Visual Skill-Building,
Writing Sentences

♦ Play the Word Look-Alike game. Ask students to circle the words in each row that are like the underlined word. Then they turn the paper over, picture the underlined word, and write it.

<u>while</u>	where	when	which	while	mile	why	what
<u>read</u>	road	need	real	weed	read	reel	rain
<u>line</u>	loan	love	line	lone	line	lane	left

Have students write each of the underlined words in a sentence.

Writing Questions and Answers

♦ Review the *wh* words *what* (32), *when* (35), *which* (41), *where* (98). Have students play Questions and Answers using the *wh* words (see **Spelling Sourcebook 1**, page 90).

173 *might*

Multiple Meanings,
Writing Sentences

♦ Brainstorm for meanings of *might*. Then have students check a dictionary for verification. Ask students to write sentences to illustrate the different meanings.

Sound-Symbol Awareness,
Sorting Words

♦ Have students write *might* and underline *ight*. Then have students compile a list of long *i* words and sort them to note the most frequent spellings for long *i* (most common: *igh [might], y [my], i [mind], i*-consonant-*e [smile]*). Have one category for "other" to accommodate less common spellings.

Other Word Forms, Vocabulary
Skills, Spelling Rules,
Writing Sentences

♦ Introduce common other word forms of *might: mighty, mightier, mightiest*. Discuss unfamiliar words. Discuss the spelling rule that applies to adding a suffix to words ending in *y* (see **Spelling Sourcebook 1**, page 85). Have students write the other word forms in sentences.

Homophone Usage,
Writing Sentences

♦ Introduce the homophone of *might*, the word *mite*. Have students write the homophones in sentences to differentiate them.

Idiomatic Usage,
Writing Explanations

♦ Ask students to explain in writing what they think it means to say each of these expressions (then discuss):

The pen is mightier than the sword.
to act high and mighty

Book Tie-Ins, Writing
Descriptions, Writing a
Tall Tale

♦ Use *Paul Bunyan: A Tall Tale* (Steven Kellogg, Morrow, 1984) and *Fin M'Coul: The Giant of Knockmany Hill* (Tomie dePaola, Holiday, 1981), tales featuring a mighty character. Discuss mighty characters in folklore. Have students create a mighty character and write a description of the character. Then have them write a tall tale in which their character's might is featured.

[handwritten: E 398.2 Kel   E 398.2 DeP]

174 *next*

Book Tie-In, Writing a
Story Ending

♦ Use *Next Time, Take Care* (Ann Lindbergh, Harcourt, 1988), about Ralph who loses his hats. Before reading the story ending, have students write an ending.

[handwritten: N/A]

Sequencing, Writing Words,
Creating a Word Puzzle

✦ Play "What Comes Next?" Ask students to write three words that could come next:

> about been come different every
> (any words that would follow in alphabetical order)
> think thinking help helping work
> (*working*, then a verb and its *ing* form)
> little big old new day
> (*night*, then any pair of opposites)
> ten nine eight seven six
> (*five, four, three*)

Have students create their own "What Comes Next?" games to exchange and play with a partner.

175 *sound*

Book Tie-In, Onomatopoeia,
Predicting Spellings N/A

✦ Use *Zounds! The Kids' Guide to Sound Making* (Frederick Newman, Random, 1983), which teaches imitating the sounds of birds, animals, and musical instruments. Follow up by asking students to list words that sound like the sounds they refer to (*plop, thump, quack, hiss, zip, honk, crack, splash, buzz,* and *chirp.*) Write the words on the chalkboard and have students predict the spellings as they are written.

Book Tie-In, Choral Reading

✦ Use *Joyful Noise* (Paul Fleischman, HarperTrophy, 1988), a Newbery Medal winner good for reading chorally.

Multiple Meanings,
Writing Sentences

✦ Brainstorm for various meanings of *sound*. Then have students check a dictionary for verification. Ask students to write sentences to illustrate the different meanings.

Other Word Forms, Vocabulary
Skills, Writing Sentences

✦ Introduce common other word forms of *sound: sounds, sounded, sounding.* Discuss unfamiliar words. Have students write the other word forms in sentences.

Dictation and Writing

✦ Dictate these partial sentences for students to write and complete:

> I like the sound of _____.
> The sound of water is _____.
> Words with the long *a* sound _____.
> A big sound came from that little _____.

176 *below*

Antonyms

✦ Introduce the antonym of *below*, the word *above*.

Analogies, Alphabetical Order

✦ Ask students to complete these analogies with words that begin with the "be" syllable:

> good is to bad as above is to _____ (*below*)
> day is to night as after is to _____ (*before*)
> come is to become as side is to _____ (*beside*)
> found is to find as began is to _____ (*begin*)

Then have students write the answer words in alphabetical order.

Writing a Story Ending

✦ Play Finish the Story (see ***Spelling Sourcebook 1***, page 88). Use *below* and selected review words.

177 *saw*

E Seu

Book Tie-In,
Writing Descriptions

✦ Use *And to Think That I Saw It on Mulberry Street* (Dr. Seuss, 1937, Vanguard), one of the late doctor's classic rhymes. Follow up by asking students to write what they saw on Mulberry Street.

Multiple Meanings,
Writing Sentences

✦ Brainstorm for different meanings of *saw*. Then have students check a dictionary for verification. Review words that have more than one meaning (*can* [38], *down* [84], *way* [86], *may* [89], *long* [91], *just* [97], *through* [102], *back* [103], *too* [112], *right* [116], *part* [129], *even* [130], *place* [131], *well* [132], *great* [146], *still* [153], *home* [157], *line* [161], *set* [162], *last* [166], *left* [169], *might* [173]). Introduce Sentence Spelling (see ***Spelling Sourcebook 1,*** page 91) using words that have more than one meaning.

Other Word Forms,
Writing Sentences

✦ Review common other word forms of *saw: see, sees, seen, seeing.* Have students write the other word forms in sentences.

178 *something*

Visual Skill-Building

✦ Ask students to write words they find inside *something (some, thing, me, met, so, thin, in).*

Compound Words, Vocabulary
Skills, Writing Sentences

✦ Have students brainstorm for compound words that begin with *some (something, somewhere, sometime, sometimes, somebody)* and end with *some (lonesome, fearsome, tiresome).* Discuss unfamiliar words. Have students write the words in sentences.

179 *thought*

Sound-Symbol Awareness,
Vocabulary Skills,
Writing Sentences

✦ Write *_ought* on the chalkboard. Ask students to add *th, f, b,* and *br.* Explore words with the same, or nearly the same, vowel sound spelled in another way *(taught, cot, dot, got, hot, lot, pot, rot, tot).* Discuss unfamiliar words. Have students write the words in sentences.

Other Word Forms, Vocabulary
Skills, Writing Sentences

✦ Introduce common other word forms of *thought: think, thinks, thinking, thinker, thought, thoughtful, thoughtless, thoughtfully, thoughtlessly, thoughtfulness, thoughtlessness.* Discuss unfamiliar words. Have students write the other word forms in sentences.

Suffix Practice

✦ Review the *less* suffix introduced with *home* (157). Add the *less* suffix to *thought.* Have students brainstorm for more words to which the suffix can be added (*use* [88]), *end* [170], *help* [137], *rest, care*). Introduce the *ful* suffix. Add the suffix to *thought.* Have students brainstorm for more words to which the suffix *ful* can be added (*help* [37], *use* [88], *care, thank, wonder*).

Idiomatic Usage,
Writing Explanations

✦ Ask students to explain in writing what they think it means to say each of these expressions (then discuss):
    food for thought
    to have second thoughts
    to lose your train of thought

Remember . . .

Develop spelling accountability as students write—see *Spelling Sourcebook 1*, Article 8, page 33. Spelling mastery is achieved ONLY when students can spell and use words consistently correctly in writing.

180 *both*

Sound-Symbol Awareness, Writing Sentences

Write *both* on the chalkboard. Ask students to follow these directions to write new and review words:

Change two letters of *both* to make *with* (17).
Change one letter of *both* to make *bath*.
Add one letter to *both* to make *booth*.
Change *both* to make the opposite of *girl*. (*boy*)

Have students write a sentence for each word they made.

Research and Writing, Public Speaking

Have students find out about one of the following topics, tell about their findings in writing, and then present the information orally to the class:
- food that is both good for you and tastes good
- books that are both informational and fun to read

181 *few*

Predicting Spellings, Writing Sentences, Sound-Symbol Awareness

Ask students to write *few*. Then have them predict the spellings of *flew, blew, grew, drew, new* (107), *chew,* and *stew.* Have students write the words in sentences. Explore common spellings for the same vowel sound as the *ew* in *few* (*ue [blue], oo [boo], ui [suit]*).

Sorting Words

Have students play Word Sorts (see *Spelling Sourcebook 1,* page 92) using these words: *few, new* (107), *from* (23), *you* (8), *blue, for* (12).

182 *those*

Sound-Symbol Awareness, Sorting Words

Write *_ose* on the chalkboard. Ask students to add beginning letters to make new words and to listen to the long *o* sound in the words. Then have them collect more words with the long *o* sound to note the most frequent spellings for long *o* (most common: *o [no], o*-consonant-*e [those], ow [show], oa [coat], old [cold], oe [toe]*). Create a list of long *o* words. Have students write the words in categories sorted by the spelling for the long *o*. Have one category for "other" to accommodate less common spellings.

Antonyms

Review the antonym of *those,* the word *these* (58).

Writing Words

Play Spelling Baseball (see *Spelling Sourcebook 1,* page 91) using *those* and selected review words.

183 *always*

Visual Skill-Building, Writing Words, Word Analysis

Write *always* on the chalkboard, and draw an outline around the word to accentuate its shape. Provide students with graph paper (or use the blackline master on page 108 of *Spelling Sourcebook 1*). Have students write *always* in the boxes and outline its shape (see Letter Grid Games on page 88 of *Spelling Sourcebook 1*). Expand the activity by asking students to write more words that have one *l* letter (*would* [59], *like* [66], *people* [79], *only* [85], *long* [91], *look* [117], *also* [119], *old* [144], *should* [156], *line* [161], *last* [166], *left* [169], *along* [171], *while* [172], *below* [176]).

◆ ◆ ◆

E 782.40 Leo

Book Tie-In, Sorting N/A	◆ Use *Always Room for One More* (Sorche Nic Leodhas, Henry Holt, 1965), from the Scottish folk song. Follow up with students collecting and singing other folk songs and organizing them by country of origin.
Writing "Always True" Statements	◆ Have students write "Always True" statements, ideas that can never be false. Have students read aloud their "always true" statements to have classmates determine if they are always true: "Cars can go faster than bicycles." Always true? Not if the car is out of gas.
Antonyms	◆ Review the antonym of *always*, the word *never* (167). Then have students list antonym pairs in a timed five-minute write.

184 *show*

Multiple Meanings, Writing Sentences	◆ Brainstorm for meanings of *show*. Then have students check a dictionary for verification. Ask students to write sentences to illustrate the different meanings.
Book Tie-In, Writing a News Story N/A	◆ Use *Lenore's Big Break* (Susan Pearson, Viking, 1992), about a secretary who trains a flock of birds for a talent show . . . and wins! Have students write a news story about the event.
Sound-Symbol Awareness, Writing Words	◆ Write _ow on the chalkboard. Have students add beginning letters to make new words that rhyme with *show* (*grow, flow, know* [100]). Then have students write *now* (78) and brainstorm for words that contain an *ow* that sounds like the *ow* in *now* (*flower, brown, how*). Conclude that *ow* spells more than one sound in words.
Writing Descriptions, Public Speaking	◆ Have students write the names of their favorite three tv shows in order of preference with a brief description of each. Then they present their lists to the class and state reasons why they made their choices.
Public Speaking, Writing a Summary, Creating a Book	◆ Conduct an old-fashioned Show and Tell. Have students bring something to class to share. Following the sharing, have each student write a summary of his or her presentation to be included in class-made or student-made books that describe the Show and Tell entries (see page 138, Creating Classroom Books).

185 *large*

Book Tie-Ins, Predicting, Sequencing N/A	◆ Use *Giants of Land, Sea, and Air Past and Present* (David Peters, Knopf, 1986) ✓and *Little Giants* (Seymour Simon, Morrow, 1983) as resources on very large animals, to expand the study introduced with *big* (158). Before the reading, ask students to predict the book's content. Following the reading, ask students to sequence big beasts large-to-largest.
Book Tie-In, Writing Descriptions, Art N/A	◆ For humorous poetry about large, make-believe dinosaur animals (chickasaur, snakeydon), use *If Dinosaurs Were Cats and Dogs* (Colin McNaughton, Four Winds, 1991). Ask students to describe and illustrate their own make-believe dinosaurs. Display the animals on a bulletin board labeled with the animals' names and students' descriptions.
Sorting Words, Word Analysis	◆ Have students list words that are spelled with a *g*. Then sort the words into categories—those with hard *g* (*go*), soft *g* (*large*), ng (*long*), and "other" (*right*).
Antonyms	◆ Review the antonym of *large*, the word *small* (150).

186 *often*

Pronunciation	◆ Look up the pronunciation of *often* in a dictionary with students. *Often* is often mispronounced. Other words to reinforce for pronunciation include *probably, library,* and *February*.

Word Analysis,
Writing Sentences

◆ Note the silent *t* in *often*. Ask students to compile a list of words that have silent consonants (*know* [100], *through* [102], *should* [156], *climb, answer*). Have students write the words in sentences.

Antonyms, Writing a List

◆ Introduce the antonym of *often*, the word *seldom*. Have students list things they do *often* and things they do *seldom*.

187 *together*

Book Tie-In, Choral Reading

◆ Use *Side by Side: Poems to Read Together* (Lee Bennett Hopkins, Simon & Schuster, 1988). Have small groups of students prepare poems to read chorally to the class.

Visual Skill-Building,
Writing Words

◆ Have students write words they find inside *together* (*to, get, the, he*). Expand the activity to *something* (178), *great* (146), *because* (127), *know* (100), and words of the students' choice.

Writing Questions and Answers

◆ Play "Put Them Together." Have students write the question and the answer.
   What do you get when you put blue and yellow together?
   What do you get when you put three and two together?
   What do you get when you put peanut butter and bread together?
   What do you get when you put fire and paper together?

Antonyms

◆ Introduce the antonym of *together*, the word *apart*.

188 *asked*

Book Tie-In, Predicting,
Writing Book Titles

◆ Use *Everyone Asked About You* (Theodore Gross, Philomel, 1990), a rhyming picture book that tells who asked about Nora Blue when she stayed home from school. Before the reading, ask students to predict what the book is about. Following the reading, ask students to create other appropriate titles for the book.

Other Word Forms,
Writing Sentences

◆ Introduce common other word forms of *asked: ask, asks, asking*. Have students write the other word forms in sentences.

Suffix Practice, Word Analysis

◆ Have students write *ask*. Then make the word *asked* by adding the *ed* suffix. Expand the activity to other words that form the past tense by adding *ed*. Then have students write words that change the spelling of the base word in the past tense (*made* [81], *thought* [179], *came* [122], *went* [143], *found* [152], *saw* [177]).

189 *house*

Book Tie-In, Choral Reading

◆ Use *The House That Jack Built* (Jenny Stow, Dial, 1992). Have students read the rhyme chorally.

Book Tie-Ins, Career Awareness

◆ Use *This Is a House* (Colleen Bare, Cobblehill, 1992), *From Blueprint to House* (Franz Hogner, Carolrhoda, 1986), and *Houses* (Katherine Carter, Childrens, 1982) as resources to identify careers in home construction. First have students predict the jobs, then read. Make a class list of the jobs with the major skills needed to do each one.

Research and Writing,
Public Speaking

◆ Have students find out about one of the following topics, tell about their findings in writing, and then present the information orally to the class:
   • kinds of animal houses (nests, den, shell, hive)
   • kinds of people houses (igloo, lighthouse, condominium)
   • different kinds of bird nests and how birds make them

Compound Words, Vocabulary Skills, Writing Sentences

◆ Have students write compound words that contain *house* (*housebroken, housecleaning, houseboat, lighthouse, housefly, housecoat, housetop, housewife, housework, housemother, houselights, birdhouse, storehouse, outhouse, greenhouse, smokehouse, household, housekeeper*). Discuss unfamiliar words. Have students write the compound words in sentences.

Other Word Forms, Vocabulary Skills, Writing Sentences

◆ Introduce common other word forms of *house: houses, housing, housed.* Discuss unfamiliar words. Have students write the other word forms in sentences.

Idiomatic Usage, Writing Explanations

◆ Ask students to explain in writing what they think it means to say each of these expressions (then discuss):

on the house
bring the house down
like a house on fire

190 *don't*

Contractions, Predicting Spellings

◆ *Don't* is the first Core Word that is a contraction. Discuss the apostrophe, and list contractions on the chalkboard with the words that make them up *(don't—do not)*. Have students predict the spellings of the words as they are written.

Book Tie-In, Creating a Poster

◆✓ Use *Don't Forget the Bacon* (Pat Hutchins, Greenwillow, 1987), in which a boy mixes up the shopping list at the grocery store. Follow up with students making a "DON'T" poster reminding themselves of something they're not to forget.

Idiomatic Usage, Writing Explanations

◆ Ask students to explain in writing what they think it means to say each of these expressions (then discuss):

Don't hold your breath.
Don't count your chickens before they hatch.
Don't let me down.

191 *world*

Book Tie-Ins, Writing a News Story

◆ Use *The Biggest, Smallest, Fastest, Tallest Things You've Ever Heard of* (Robert Lopshire, Harper, 1980) and *Information Please Kids Almanac* (Alice Siegel, World Records Book, Houghton Mifflin, 1992) for world records. Follow up with students choosing one world record and writing a news story for the day the record was achieved.

ALT *biggest Jenkins*
E 591 *Jen*

Comparing and Contrasting, Writing Explanations

◆ Contrast a world map and a world globe. Have students summarize in writing the most important differences between the two and explain the disadvantages and advantages of each format.

Visual Skill-Building, Writing Sentences

◆ Play the Word Look-Alike game. Ask students to circle the words in each row that are like the underlined word. Then they turn the paper over, picture the underlined word, and write it.

<u>world</u>	would	word	world	work	world	wound
<u>house</u>	hose	house	mouse	blouse	house	houses
<u>those</u>	house	hose	there	these	those	threw
<u>thought</u>	through	though	thought	taught	though	ought
<u>form</u>	farm	from	form	horn	firm	harm
<u>want</u>	went	what	ward	word	want	tans
<u>saw</u>	sew	saw	was	sow	sea	saw

Have students write each of the underlined words in a sentence.

Idiomatic Usage,
Writing Explanations

❖ Ask students to explain in writing what they think it means to say each of these expressions (then discuss):

to be on top of the world	Set the world on fire.
not for the world	not a care in the world
out of this world	in a world of your own

192 *going*

Suffix Practice

❖ Have students write *go* and *going*. Expand the activity to *show* (184), *sound* (175), *end* (170), *last* (166), *read* (165), *number* (145), *help* (137), *part* (129), *work* (124), *look* (117).

Other Word Forms,
Writing Sentences

❖ Review common other word forms of *going: go* (105), *goes, gone*. Have students write the other word forms in sentences.

Idiomatic Usage,
Writing Explanations

❖ Have students explain in writing what they think it means to say each of these expressions (then discuss):

going to the dogs	going out of your way
going great guns	going in circles
going along for the ride	going all out

Antonyms

❖ Introduce the antonym of *going*, the word *coming*.

193 *want*

Word Analysis, Writing Words

❖ Write *w_nt* on the chalkboard. Ask students to add the vowel to make *want*. Play the vowel fill-in game with *world* (191), *house* (189), *often* (186), *thought* (179), *sound* (175), *because* (127), *people* (79), and *said* (43). Have students fill in the vowels and then write the whole word. Have students choose words to write on the chalkboard to continue the game.

Other Word Forms,
Writing Sentences

❖ Introduce common other word forms of *want: wants, wanted*. Have students write the other word forms in sentences.

Alphabetical Order

❖ Have students write each set of words in alphabetical order:

1. could, different, want, again
2. don't, between, every, want
3. air, world, want, very
4. because, most, much, through
5. little, other, great, always
6. both, been, who, first

Sound-Symbol Awareness,
Writing Sentences

❖ Write *want* on the chalkboard. Ask students to follow these directions to write new and review words:

Change one letter of *want* to make *went* (143).
Change two letters of *want* to make *wall*.
Remove one letter of *want* to make *ant*.
Add three letters to *want* to make *wanting*.

Have students write a sentence for each word they made.

194 *school*

Word Analysis,
Sound-Symbol Awareness

❖ Have students write *school* and underline the *oo*. Then brainstorm for more words that have *oo* (*look* [117], *too* [112], *good* [106], *moon, book*). Note the different sounds *oo* makes in words.

Book Tie-In,
Writing Speculations

❖ Use *King of the Playground* (Phyllis Naylor, Atheneum, 1992) to promote discussion of how to handle the school bully on the playground. Before reading the story ending, have students hypothesize in writing how Kevin's problem might be solved.

N/A

Book Tie-In, Writing Jokes, Creating a Book ✦ Use *School Daze* (Charles Keller, Prentice, 1979) for jokes about school. Follow up with students writing and collecting school jokes for a class-made book.

Book Tie-In, Writing Reasons ✦ Use *Morning, Noon, and Nighttime* (Lee Bennett Hopkins, Harper, 1980) for poetry about children during a normal school day. Have students choose their favorite poem and write why it is their favorite.

Writing Explanations ✦ Have students write how their school was named.

✓195 *important*   *E Bro*

Book Tie-In, Creating a Book ✦ Use *The Important Book* (Margaret Wise Brown, Harcourt, 1949), which asks "What is important about an apple?. . . the sky?" Use the book as a model for a class-made book (see page 138, Creating Classroom Books).

Dictating and Writing ✦ Dictate these partial sentences for students to write and complete:

School is important because _____.
Water is important because _____.
Air is important because _____.
I am important because _____.

196 *until*

Visual Skill-Building, Writing Words ✦ Write *until* on the chalkboard, and draw an outline around the word to accentuate its shape. Provide students with graph paper (or use the blackline master on page 108 of **Spelling Sourcebook 1**). Have students write *until* in the boxes and outline its shape (see Letter Grid Games on page 88 of **Spelling Sourcebook 1**).

Idiomatic Usage, Writing Explanations ✦ Ask students to explain in writing what they think it means to say each of these expressions (then discuss):

until the cows come home   until all hours

Book Tie-In, Writing Holiday Sayings *N/A* ✦ Introduce the shortcut word for *until*, *'til*. Use *Yours 'Til the Ice Cracks: A Book of Valentines* (Laura Geringer, HarperCollins, 1992) as a model for students to write whimsical Valentine's Day sayings.

197 *form*   *Water Dance Locker*

Book Tie-In, Writing a *N/A* *List, Comparing*   *water unit tie* ✦ Use *Water's Way* (Lisa Peters, Arcade, 1991) to explore the forms of water from clouds to steam to fog. Ask students to list the different forms of water before and after the reading. Then they write a comparison of their before-and-after knowledge.

Multiple Meanings, Writing Sentences ✦ Brainstorm for meanings of *form*. Then have students check a dictionary for verification. Review words that can be used in different ways: *show* (184), *saw* (177), *might* (173), *through* (102), *long* (91), *right* (116). Have students use the words in sentences to illustrate their different meanings.

Filling Out a Form ✦ Prepare a blackline master of a form for students to complete. Request information (name, address, phone, birth date, teacher's name, school). Provide assistance filling out the form. Emphasize legible writing and accuracy. Have students collect standard forms and discuss them (post office forms, library card application, school health information form).

Other Word Forms, Vocabulary Skills, Writing Sentences ✦ Introduce common other word forms of *form: forms, formed, forming.* Discuss unfamiliar words. Have students write the other word forms in sentences.

198 *food*

Book Tie-In, Writing a Menu ◆ Use *Eating the Plates: A Pilgrim Book of Food and Manners* (Lucille Penner, Macmillan, 1991), which explores how the Pilgrims obtained, stored, prepared, and ate their food. Have students follow up by creating a dinner menu for a Pilgrim meal.

394. 1 Pen

Eponyms, Creating a Book ◆ Use *Guppies in Tuxedos* (Marvin Terban, Ticknor, 1988) to introduce eponyms, or words that originated from names. Explore food eponyms (sandwich, hamburger, Graham crackers). Then have students create a class-made book of food eponyms.

eponyms
422 Ter

Book Tie-In, Creating a Book ◆ Use *Potluck* (Anne Shelby, Orchard/Jackson, 1992), a food alphabet book with entries such as "Otis offered onions." Use the book as a model for students' personal food alphabet books.

E She

Writing Recipes ◆ Ask students to write a recipe for a favorite food, and compile the results into a class-made book of favorite recipes.

Sorting Words ◆ Introduce the Mr. Pickyfood game (see *Spelling Sourcebook 1*, page 88).

199 *keep*

Sound-Symbol Awareness, Sorting Words, Book Tie-In, Writing Rhymes ◆ Write _eep on the chalkboard. Ask students to add beginning letters to make new words and to listen to the long *e* sound in the words. Then explore common letter combinations that make the long *e* sound (most common: *ee [see], e [me], ea [eat], e-consonant-e [these]*). Create a list of long *e* words. Have students write the words in categories sorted by the spelling for the long *e*. Have one category for "other" to accommodate less common spellings. Then have students note all the long *e* words in *Sheep in a Jeep* (Nancy Shaw, Houghton, 1986). Use the book as a model for students to write rhyming tales.

Other Word Forms, Book Tie-In, Writing a Want Ad ◆ Introduce common other word forms of *keep: keeps, keeping, kept, keeper, keepers*. Then use *Alvin the Zookeeper* (Ulf Lofgren, Carolrhoda, 1991). Follow up with students writing a want ad for a zookeeper.

E Lof

Sound-Symbol Awareness, Writing Sentences ◆ Write *keep* on the chalkboard. Ask students to follow these directions to write new words:

Change two letters of *keep* to make *seen*.
Change one letter of *keep* to make *deep, jeep, peep*.
Add letters to *keep* to make *keeping*.
Change *keep* to make *sleep*.

Have students write a sentence for each word they made.

200 *children*

Spelling Rules ◆ Have students write *children* and its singular *child*. Review this spelling rule (see *Spelling Sourcebook 1*, page 85).

Book Tie-In, Writing Reasons ◆ Use *Brothers and Sisters* (Maxine Rosenberg, Clarion, 1992), a story of a family told from the points of view of the oldest, middle, and youngest children. Have students write which position they would prefer to be and give reasons why.

Book Tie-In, Making Predictions ◆ Use *Kids* (Catherine and Laurence Anholt, Candlewick, 1992), a rhyming text that describes kids and what they do. Before reading have students make written predictions of what kinds of things the story-poem may include.

E Anh

Other Word Forms, Vocabulary Skills, Writing Sentences	◆ Introduce common other word forms of *children: child, childhood.* Discuss unfamiliar words. Have students write the other word forms in sentences.
Antonyms	◆ Introduce the antonym of *children,* the word *adults.*

201 *feet*

Book Tie-Ins, Writing Clues, Art	◆ Use *All Kinds of Feet* (Ron and Nancy Goor, Harper, 1984), an easy-to-read introduction to all kinds of animal feet and their uses. For more information, use *Some Feet Have Noses* (Anita Gustafson, Lothrop, 1982) and *Animal Tracks* (Arthur Dorros, Scholastic, 1991). Follow up with students drawing a footprint and below it writing clues to the identity of the animal.
Multiple Meanings, Writing Sentences	◆ Brainstorm for meanings of *feet.* Then have students check a dictionary for verification. Ask students to write sentences to illustrate the different meanings.
Homophone Usage, Writing Sentences	◆ Introduce the homophone of *feet,* the word *feat.* Have students use the homophones in oral and written sentences to differentiate them.
Idiomatic Usage, Writing Explanations	◆ Ask students to explain in writing what they think it means to say each of these expressions (then discuss): to get cold feet to land on both feet to stand on your own two feet
Spelling Rules	◆ Review the plural rule for *feet* (see ***Spelling Sourcebook 1,*** page 85). Then brainstorm for more words that follow the rule (*man* [111]/*men* [148], *woman/women, mouse/mice, child/children* [200]).

202 *land*

REF 910 Kno

Book Tie-Ins, Making a Map	◆ Use *Continents* (Dennis Fradin, Childrens, 1986) and *Geography From A to Z: A Picture Glossary* (Jack Knowlton, Harper, 1988) for an introduction to the earth's land masses. Follow up with a map-making activity in which students label the continents and oceans. Provide a spelling reference for appropriate words.
Other Word Forms, Vocabulary Skills, Writing Sentences	◆ Have students brainstorm for common other word forms of *land: lands, landed, landing.* Discuss unfamiliar words. Have students write the other word forms in sentences.
Sound-Symbol Awareness, Writing Sentences	◆ Ask students to write *land.* Then have them follow these directions to write new and review words: Change *land* to make *hand, band, grand, sand, stand.* Change *land* to make *lend.* Change two letters of *land* to make *last* (166). Have students write a sentence for each word they made.

203 *side*

Multiple Meanings, Writing Sentences	◆ Brainstorm for meanings of *side.* Then have students check a dictionary for verification. Ask students to write sentences to illustrate the different meanings.
Idiomatic Usage, Writing Explanations	◆ Ask students to explain in writing what they think it means to say each of these expressions (then discuss): to get up on the wrong side of the bed the wrong side of the tracks sunny side up

Homophone Usage, Writing Sentences	◆ Introduce the homophone for *side*, the word *sighed*. Have students write the homophones in sentences to differentiate them.
Other Word Forms, Vocabulary Skills, Writing Sentences	◆ Have students brainstorm for common other word forms of *side: sides, sided, siding, sideways*. Discuss unfamiliar words. Have students write the other word forms in sentences.

204 *without*

Compound Words, Word Analysis, Writing Sentences	◆ Have students write the compound word *without* and underline the two word parts. Then write *within* and have students predict its meaning. Have students write the words in sentences.
Compound Words, Writing Words	◆ Have students brainstorm for compound words. Include *into* (61) and *something* (178). Then play Spelling Baseball (see **Spelling Sourcebook 1**, page 91) using the compound words.
Writing Reasons	◆ Ask students to write about one electrical convenience they never want to do without. Have them provide reasons why.
Idiomatic Usage, Writing Explanations	◆ Ask students to explain in writing what they think it means to say each of these expressions (then discuss):

without fail
up a creek without a paddle
without batting an eye

Suffix Practice, Writing Explanations	◆ Review *help* (137), *home* (157), *end* (170), *thought* (179). Then have students add the *less* suffix to each word and explain in writing what the suffix means (without).

205 *boy*

Antonyms	◆ Introduce the antonym of *boy*, the word *girl*.
Listening, Public Speaking, Creating a Book	◆ Invite a Boy Scout or Girl Scout Leader to talk to the class. Explore Boy and Girl Scout Handbooks and the Bear Cub Scoutbook and Brownie Scoutbook. Ask active club members to "show and tell" what they do in the scouts. Help interested students become members. Summarize the information gathered on scouting in a class-made book (see page 138, Creating Classroom Books).
Book Tie-Ins, Writing Stories	◆ Use *The Boy Who Held Back the Sea* (Lenny Hort, Dial, 1987), a retelling of the story of the Dutch boy who saved Holland; *The Boy Who Wouldn't Talk* (Lois Bouchard, Doubleday, 1969), the tale of Carlos, who decides not to talk because of his confusion with the Spanish and English languages; and the classic fable, *The Boy Who Cried Wolf*. Then have students write a story, "The Boy Who . . ."
Writing Exclamations	◆ Have students use *boy* as an exclamation in written sentences.

206 *once*

Book Tie-In, Writing Tall Tales	◆ Use *Once, Said Darlene* (Steven Kellogg, Dutton, 1979), about a girl who tells too many tall tales. Follow up with students writing another of Darlene's tall tales, beginning with "Once upon a time."
Idiomatic Usage, Writing Explanations	◆ Ask students to explain in writing what they think it means to say each of these expressions (then discuss):

all at once
once and for all
once in a blue moon (See literature entry below.)
every once in a while

Book Tie-In, Making a Poster ◆ Use *Once in A Blue Moon* (Nicola Morgan, Oxford, 1992), which introduces a series of sayings that Morgan interprets literally. Have students choose a favorite saying and create a poster that illustrates the saying literally.

Word Analysis, ◆ Contrast *once* and *ounce*. Have students write the words in sentences.
Writing Sentences

207 *animal*   E 811.008 Zoo

Book Tie-In, Writing a List, ✓ Use *A Zooful of Animals* (William Cole, selector, Houghton, 1992) for
Alphabetical Order   experiences with zoo animal poetry. Have students list animals that might be found in a zoo. Write the animal names on word cards and play ABC Order (see *Spelling Sourcebook 1*, page 86).   E 222 Jon

Book Tie-In, Writing Facts ✓ Use *Aardvarks, Disembark!* (Ann Jonas, Greenwillow, 1990), an informative introduction to 132 species of animals. It is organized into an ABC book that uses as its framework the biblical story, "Noah and the Flood." Have students write one new "animal fact" they learned as a result of their reading.

Book Tie-In, Writing a Letter, Use *Ben Finds a Friend* (Anne-Marie Chapouton, Putnam, 1986), about a boy
Writing Reasons   who cannot have a pet but dreams of having one. Follow up by having students think of a pet they'd like to have and then write a letter to their parents telling why they should be allowed to have it.

Sorting Words ◆ Play the Mr. Pickypet game (see *Spelling Sourcebook 1*, page 88).

208 *life*   591.92 Tay

Book Tie-Ins, Hypothesizing Use the two picture books *Desert Life* and *Pond Life* (Barbara Taylor, Houghton, 1992), from the *Look Closer* series, for an introduction to plant and animal life in these two environments. Follow up with the information students think Taylor might include in a *Forest Life* book.

Book Tie-In, Sequencing, Art N/A Use *A First Look at Caterpillars* (Millicent Selsam and Joyce Hunt, Walker, 1988) to introduce life cycles. Follow up with students making sequential drawings labeled to explain the life cycle of the butterfly.

Idiomatic Usage ◆ Ask students to explain in writing what they think it means to say each of these
Writing Explanations   expressions (then discuss):
all walks of life
to have the time of your life
life of the party
to lead the life of Riley
to lead a dog's life

Spelling Rules ◆ Introduce the plural rule that applies to *life* (see *Spelling Sourcebook 1*, page 85). Have students write *lives*. Brainstorm for other words that follow this rule (*wolf/wolves, half/halves, calf/calves, scarf/scarves, knife/knives*).

209 *enough*

Idiomatic Usage ◆ Ask students to explain in writing what they think it means to say each of these
Writing Explanations   expressions (then discuss):
enough is enough
Let well enough alone.
old enough to know better

Word Analysis, Writing Words ◆ Brainstorm with students for other words that have silent letters. Include *would* (59), *could* (70), *people* (79), *through* (102), *write* (108), *right* (116), *should* (156), *might* (173), *thought* (179). Then play Bingo (see **Spelling Sourcebook 1**, page 87) using words with silent letters.

210 *took*

Book Tie-In, Writing a Story Ending ◆ Write on the chalkboard: *Who took it?* Then use *It Was a Dark and Stormy Night* (Keith Mosley, Dial, 1991), a mystery in which a fine diamond is stolen. Stop at a strategic point in the reading and ask students to solve the mystery by writing an answer to the question.

Other Word Forms, Writing Sentences ◆ Review common other word forms of *took: take* (135), *taking, takes, taken, taker.* Have students write the other word forms in sentences.

Sound-Symbol Awareness, Writing Sentences ◆ Write *took* on the chalkboard. Ask students to follow these directions to write new and review words:
Change *took* to make *look* (117), *book, shook, hook, cook.*
Change *took* to make *tool.*
Change *took* to make *talk.*
Have students write a sentence for each word they made.

211 *four*

Book Tie-In, Writing Stories ◆ Use *Four on the Shore* (Edward Marshall, Dial, 1985), about three friends who try to get rid of the fourth friend, Willie, by telling scary stories. However, Willie tells the scariest story. Follow up with students writing a scary story.

Reader E Mar

Research and Writing, Art, Creating a Book ◆ Ask students to research the cause for celebration on the Fourth of July. Discuss the information collected. Then ask each student to select one feature of the holiday, illustrate it, and write about it. Compile the results into class-made or student-made books.

Homophone Usage, Writing Sentences ◆ Review the homophone of *four*, the word *for* (12). Have students use the homophones in written sentences to differentiate them. (*Fore* could also be introduced.)

Dictation and Writing ◆ Review the number words *one* through *ten*. Then dictate these partial sentences and have students complete them:

I have one _____.   I can see two _____.
I want three _____.   Some people have four _____.
I know five _____.   There are six _____.
There are more than seven _____. Once I saw eight _____.
I would like nine _____.   I can name ten _____.

212 *head*

E 398. 2 Knu

Book Tie-In, Writing Pourquoi Tales ◆ Use *Why the Crab Has No Head* (Barbara Knutson, Carolrhoda, 1987), as an example of a "pourquoi tale," which tells "why" something is. Collect and read other pourquoi stories. Then have students write their own pourquoi stories.

Book Tie-In, Writing Facts ◆ Use *Heads* (Ron and Nancy Goor, Macmillan, 1988) for a unique study of animal heads—ears, nose, eyes, and mouth. Following the reading, ask students to write one interesting fact they learned from the book.

599 Goo

Idiomatic Usage,
Writing Explanations

◆ Ask students to explain in writing what they think it means to say each of these expressions (then discuss):

to beat your head against the wall
Use your head.
to have eyes in the back of your head
to have your head in the clouds
to get a head start

Other Word Forms, Vocabulary
Skills, Writing Sentences

◆ Have students brainstorm for common other word forms of *head: heads, headed, heading, header.* Discuss unfamiliar words. Have students write the other word forms in sentences.

Antonyms, Writing Explanations

◆ Introduce the antonyms *heads* and *tails.* Ask students to write an explanation of the logic in *Heads I win, tails you lose.*

213 *above*

Writing Descriptions,
Book Tie-In

◆ Ask students to write what they think it would be like to fly high above their school. A young girl pretends that she and her grandmother are flying high above Manhattan in *Abuela* (Arthur Dorros, Dutton, 1991). This book cleverly weaves Spanish words into the text. *E Dor*

Antonyms

◆ Review the antonym of *above,* the word *below* (176).

Word Analysis, Writing Words

◆ Review words with final silent *e.* Include *life* (208), *house* (189), *large* (185), *while* (172), *place* (131), *because* (127), *write* (108), *little* (92), *people* (79), *there* (37). Have students play Connect the Dots (see ***Spelling Sourcebook 1,*** page 87) using the words with final silent *e.*

Sorting Words

◆ Have students play Word Sorts (see ***Spelling Sourcebook 1,*** page 92) using these words: *above, people* (79), *write* (108), *about* (48), *around* (120), *place* (131), *away* (140), *along* (171).

214 *kind*

Multiple Meanings, Writing
Sentences, Writing a List,
Writing Explanations,
Writing a Summary

◆ Brainstorm for meanings of *kind.* Then have students check a dictionary for verification. Ask students to write sentences to illustrate the different meanings. Then ask them to think of story characters who demonstrate *kindness.* Make a class list of the characters. Then ask students to choose one character and tell in writing how the character was kind. Then pursue the other meaning of *kind,* as in "What kind?" Have students make lists of things for which there are different kinds, such as soup, dogs, flowers, ice cream and then list the different kinds. Help students to conduct a poll to determine people's favorite kind within each category. Have students summarize the results of the polls in writing. *E Joh*

Book Tie-In, Writing
Descriptions

◆ Use *What Kind of Baby-Sitter Is This?* (Dolores Johnson, Macmillan, 1991), in which Kevin is surprised by his new baby-sitter, who watches baseball and collects baseball cards. Follow up with students describing the kind of baby-sitter they'd like best.

Sound-Symbol Awareness, Sorting Words
◆ Write _*ind* on the chalkboard. Ask students to add beginning letters to make rhyming words (*bind, find* [87], *hind, mind, rind, wind*). Have them listen to the long *i* sound in the words. Then explore other letter combinations that make the long *i* sound (most common: *y [my], igh [might], i*-consonant-*e [fine])*. Create a list of long *i* words. Have students write the words in categories sorted by the spelling for the long *i*. Have one category for "other" to accommodate less common spellings.

Other Word Forms, Vocabulary Skills, Writing Sentences
◆ Have students brainstorm for common other word forms of *kind: kinds, kinder, kindest, kindly, kindness*. Discuss unfamiliar words. Have students write the other word forms in sentences.

Prefix Practice, Vocabulary Skills, Writing Sentences
◆ Have students write *kind*. Then have them make the word into *unkind*. Discuss the *un* prefix. Then have them add the prefix to *wanted* (*want* [193]), *even* (130), *just* (97), *used* (*use* [88]), *like* (66), *willing* (*will* [46]), *do* (45). Discuss unfamiliar words. Have students write the words with the *un* prefix in sentences.

215 *began*

Other Word Forms, Vocabulary Skills, Writing Sentences
◆ Have students brainstorm for common other word forms of *began: begin, begins, begun, beginning, beginner*. Discuss unfamiliar words. Have students write the other word forms in sentences.

Writing Words
◆ Play the Write and Fold Relay (see *Spelling Sourcebook 1*, page 93) using *began* and selected review words.

Word Analysis, Writing Words
◆ Have students write *began* and underline the *be*. Then ask them to write other words that begin with the *be* syllable (*below* [176], *between* [154], *because* [127], *begin*).

216 *almost*

Visual Skill-Building, Writing Words, Word Analysis
◆ Write *almost* on the chalkboard, and draw an outline around the word to accentuate its shape. Provide students with graph paper (or use the blackline master on page 108 of *Spelling Sourcebook 1*). Have students write *almost* in the boxes and outline its shape (see Letter Grid Games on page 88 of *Spelling Sourcebook 1*). Expand the activity by asking students to think of other words that have one *l* letter (*would* [59], *people* [79], *only* [85], *also* [119], *should* [156], *along* [171], *while* [172], *below* [176], *always* [183], *until* [196], *animal* [207]).

Book Tie-In, Writing a List, Research and Writing
✓◆ Use *Almost the Real Thing: Simulation in Your High-Tech World* (Gloria Skurzynski, Bradbury, 1991), a book of simulation devices including wind tunnels, auto crash dummies, and weightlessness simulators, which will challenge curious minds. Follow up with students exploring and reporting in writing "almost real" everyday things. Include foods (imitation butter), clothing (fake fur), and toys (play cars, dolls).

217 *live*

Homograph Usage, Writing Answers
◆ Write these sentences on the chalkboard:
Where does the President of the United States live?
What live animals might you see at a shopping mall?
Which TV shows are broadcast live?
Where might you see does, bucks, and fawns?
What use is an umbrella?
Which brand of soap does your family use?

Discuss the meanings and pronunciations of the homographs *live, use* (88), and *does* (128). Have students write answers to the questions.

Other Word Forms, Vocabulary Skills, Writing Sentences
◆ Have students brainstorm for common other word forms of *live: lives, lived, living, lively, livable*. Discuss unfamiliar words. Have students write the other word forms in sentences.

Spelling Rules, Writing Words
◆ Review the plural rule that applies to *life* (208) (see **Spelling Sourcebook 1**, page 85). Have students write *lives*. Brainstorm for other words that follow this rule (*wolf/wolves, half/halves, calf/calves, scarf/scarves, knife/knives, wife/wives, elf/elves, leaf/leaves.*)

Book Tie-In, Making a Poster, Writing Explanations
N/A ◆ Use *Animal Homes and Societies* (Billy Goodman, Little, 1992) to help students learn about where and how various animals live. Follow up with students making a poster of one animal and its home with information about how the animal lives.

218 *page*

Sound-Symbol Awareness, Writing Words
◆ Ask students to listen to the sound of the *g* in *page*. Then brainstorm for other words in which the *g* makes the same sound (*large* [185], *change, village, huge, general, angel, danger, edge, charge*).

Other Word Forms, Vocabulary Skills, Writing Sentences
◆ Have students brainstorm for common other word forms of *page: pages, paged, paging, pager*. Discuss unfamiliar words. Have students write the other word forms in sentences.

Writing Words
◆ Play the All-Play Spelling Bee (see **Spelling Sourcebook 1**, page 86) using *page* and selected review words.

219 *got*

Book Tie-In, Making Inferences
N/A ◆ Use *I've Got Your Nose* (Nancy Bentley, Doubleday, 1991), in which a witch tries on various noses to replace the one she dislikes. Following the reading, asks students to write why they think the author chose this title for the book.

Other Word Forms, Writing Sentences, Spelling Rules
◆ Review common other word forms of *got: gets, get, gotten, getting*. Have students use the other word forms in written sentences. Review the spelling rule for doubling the final consonant before adding *ing* (see **Spelling Sourcebook 1**, page 85). Compile a list of words that double the final consonant before the *ing* suffix is added (*get* [101], *put* [138], *set* [162], *begin*).

Book Tie-In, Writing Speculations
N/A ◆ Have students write *got* and then *forgot*. Use *The Angel Who Forgot* (Elisa Bartone, Green Tiger, 1992), a story about regaining one's memory. Have students follow up by hypothesizing in writing what might happen if they got to school and realized that they forgot. . . their lunch, their homework, how to read, or how to spell words.

220 *earth*   E 333.7 Bro

Book Tie-In, Completing a Project, Writing a Summary
✓ ◆ Use *Dinosaurs to the Rescue!: A Guide to Protecting Our Planet* (Laurie and Marc Brown, Joy Street/Little, 1992) for child-centered suggestions for making our earth's environment healthy. Follow up with one of the projects suggested in the book. Then ask students to summarize the project in writing.

Book Tie-In, Writing Explanations
✓ ◆ Use *What Makes Day and Night?* (Franklyn Branley, Harper, 1986) for a simple explanation of the earth's rotation. Follow up by having students write the explanation in their own words.

E 525 Bra

Compound Words, Research and Writing, Public Speaking

◆ Write *earthworm* and *earthquake* on the chalkboard and underline the word parts of each compound. Suggest *Earthworms* (Chris Henwood, Watts, 1988) and *Earthquake* (Christopher Lampton, Millbrook, 1991) as resources for written and oral reports.

221 *need*

Writing a List, Book Tie-In, Writing a Sequel

◆ Ask students to make a list of things they might need when they go for a day to the beach: *I'll need _____.* Then read *Not the Piano, Mrs. Medley* (Evan Levine, Orchard/Jackson, 1991), which features Mrs. Medley, who returns home again and again to collect all sorts of odd things she thinks she and her grandson Max may need at the beach. But she forgets the most important thing of all—their bathing suits! Have students write a sequel in which Mrs. Medley and Max go camping.

Other Word Forms, Vocabulary Skills, Writing Sentences

◆ Have students brainstorm for common other word forms of *need*: *needs, needed, needing, needy, needier, neediest, needless, needlessly, needlessness, needful, needfulness, needfully.* Discuss unfamiliar words. Have students write the other word forms in sentences.

Sound-Symbol Awareness, Sorting Words

◆ Review the *ee* words *see* (68), *three* (125), *between* (154), *keep* (199), and *feet* (201). Ask students to listen to the long *e* sound in the words. Then have them collect more words with the long *e* sound and sort them to note the most frequent spelling for long *e* (*most common: ee [see], e [me], ea [eat], e-consonant-e [these]*). Ask students to find examples of each. Have one category for "other" to accommodate less common spellings.

222 *far*

Idiomatic Usage, Writing Explanations

◆ Ask students to explain in writing what they think it means to say each of these expressions (then discuss):

as far as anyone knows
to come from far and wide
far out
So far, so good.

Antonyms

◆ Introduce the antonym of *far*, the word *near*.

Sound-Symbol Awareness, Writing Sentences

◆ Have students write *far*. Then have them follow these directions to write new and review words:

Add one letter to *far* to make *fair*.
Change one letter of *far* to make *for* (12).
Change one letter of *far* to make *fir*—a *fir* tree.
Change one letter of *far* to make *fur*—a rabbit's white *fur*.

Have students write a sentence for each word they made.

Other Word Forms, Vocabulary Skills, Writing Sentences

◆ Have students brainstorm for common other word forms of *far*: *farther, farthest.* Discuss unfamiliar words. Have students write the other word forms in sentences.

223 *hand*

Book Tie-In, Hypothesizing, Writing Descriptions

 ◆ Use *The Wonder of Hands* (Edith Baer, Macmillan, 1992), which relates the power of hands to explore, create, and communicate. Have students hypothesize how life would have been different if human hands had not had a thumb. Then have students describe in writing a challenge they would have doing a particular thing without using their thumbs.

Multiple Meanings, Book Tie-In,
Writing a Summary,
Creating a Book

◆ Discuss the multiple meanings of *hand*. Then use *At Taylor's Place* (Sharon Denslow, Bradbury, 1990) as a catalyst to explore things made by hand. Have students interview people who make something by hand and summarize the interview in writing. Create class-made or student-made books about the artisans and their handmade items, titled *By Hand* (see page 138, Creating Classroom Books).

Book Tie-In, Compound Words,
Vocabulary Skills,
Writing Sentences

◆ Use *The Holiday Handwriting School* (Robin Pulver, Four Winds, 1991), about challenges that students' favorite holiday characters experience with handwriting skills. Brainstorm for more words that contain *hand* as part of a compound (*handmade, handshake, handcuff, handball, handbag, handbook*). Discuss unfamiliar words. Have students use the compound words in sentences.

Idiomatic Usage,
Writing Explanations

◆ Ask students to explain in writing what they think it means to say each of these expressions (then discuss):
   A bird in the hand is worth two in the bush.
   close at hand
   hand-me-downs
   on the other hand
   to wait on someone hand and foot
   to give someone a hand

Other Word Forms, Vocabulary
Skills, Writing Sentences

◆ Have students brainstorm for common other word forms of *hand: hands, handed, handing, handful, handfuls, handy*. Discuss unfamiliar words. Have students write the other word forms in sentences.

224 *high*

Book Tie-Ins, Career Awareness,
Research and Writing

◆ Use *A Day in the Life of a High-Iron Worker* (John H. Martin, Troll, 1985), an exciting description of the career of Robert Cameron, a worker on some of the highest buildings in the world. Also use *Skyscraper Going Up! A Pop-Up Book* (Vicki Cobb, Harper, 1987), which page-by-page constructs a skyscraper. Ask students to write about other careers that necessitate working up high.

Idiomatic Usage,
Writing Explanations

◆ Ask students to explain in writing what they think it means to say each of these expressions (then discuss):
   Get into high gear.
   to get the high sign
   It's high time.
   to act high and mighty

Homophone Usage

◆ Introduce the homophone of *high*, the greeting *hi*.

Antonyms

◆ Introduce the antonym of *high*, the word *low*.

Other Word Forms, Vocabulary
Skills, Writing Sentences

◆ Have students brainstorm for common other word forms of *high: higher, highest, highly, highness*. Discuss unfamiliar words. Have students use the other word forms in written sentences.

225 *year*

Predicting Spellings

◆ Write *year* on the chalkboard. Brainstorm for other ways to measure time. Choices may include *minutes, hours, months, seconds, weeks,* and *days* (114). Ask students to predict the spellings of the words as they are written on the chalkboard.

| Other Word Forms, Vocabulary Skills, Writing Sentences | ◆ Have students brainstorm for common other word forms of *year: years, yearly.* Discuss unfamiliar words. Have students write the other word forms in sentences. |

Book Tie-In, Journal Writing — N/A Use *Farm Boy's Year* (David McPhail, Atheneum, 1992), which uses journal entries to tell about the daily life of a New England boy in the late nineteenth century. Use the book's format to introduce journal writing. Have students begin writing a journal that highlights their daily life.

Wallingford unit

226 mother E Joo

Book Tie-Ins, Creating a Greeting Card — ✓ Use *Mama, Do You Love Me?* (Barbara Joosse, Chronicle, 1991), an Inuit mother-daughter picture story in which a young girl tests her mother's love. For N/A a mother-son story, use *Busy! Busy! Busy!* (Jonathan Shipton, Delacorte, 1991), in which a boy helps his harried mother through a difficult moment. Have students follow up the readings by creating a greeting card telling their mother or grandmother why she is special.

Other Word Forms, Vocabulary Skills, Writing Sentences — ◆ Have students brainstorm for common other word forms of *mother: mothers, mothered, motherly.* Discuss unfamiliar words. Have students write the other word forms in sentences.

Antonyms, Creating a Word Puzzle — ◆ Introduce the antonym of *mother*, the word *father.* Then brainstorm for other antonym pairs. Have students create a crossword puzzle with the antonym pairs using one partner in the puzzle and the other as the word clue (use the grid paper on page 108 of **Spelling Sourcebook 1**).

227 light   E 387.1   Gib

Multiple Meanings, Writing Sentences — ◆ Brainstorm for meanings of *light.* Then have students check a dictionary for verification. Ask students to write sentences to illustrate the different meanings.

Book Tie-In, Compound Words, Predicting Spellings — ✓ Use *Beacons of Light: Lighthouses* (Gail Gibbons, Morrow, 1990), in which the purpose and history of a variety of lighthouses are shared. Have students write *lighthouse* and underline the two word parts. Then ask students to predict the spellings and meanings of *lighthearted, lightheaded, lightship,* and *lightweight.*

Antonyms, Writing Words — ◆ Review selected antonyms. Then use *Is It Light? Is It Dark?* (Mary Langford, Knopf, 1991). As the book is read, ask students to write the antonym partner in each antonym pair. For example, read, "Is it square? No it's _____." After students write *round*, show them the answer and the spelling in the book.

Idiomatic Usage, Writing Explanations — ◆ Ask students to explain in writing what they think it means to say each of these expressions (then discuss):

> as light as a feather
> to see the light
> out like a light
> see the light at the end of a tunnel
> to get the green light

Other Word Forms, Vocabulary Skills, Writing Sentences — ◆ Have students brainstorm for common other word forms of *light: lighter, lightest, lit, lightly, lighting, lightness, lighten, lightened.* Discuss unfamiliar words. Have students write the other word forms in sentences.

Word Analysis — ◆ Discuss the differences in spelling and meaning of *lighting, lightening, and lightning.*

228 *country*

Book Tie-Ins, Sequencing N/A Use *Forest, Village, Town, City* (Dan Beekman, Harper, 1982), a story of the development of the country called America, from wilderness to metropolis. For Canadian students, develop the concept of *country* through *We Live in Canada* (Jack Brickenden, Watts, 1985). Then ask students to write a sequence of important events in the development of their country.

Writing a List, Book Tie-In, Writing Explanations Ask students to make a list of symbols that stand for their country. For American students, answers may include Uncle Sam, the bald eagle, the flag, the United States seal, and "The Star-Spangled Banner." Use the book *Kids' America* (Steven Caney, Workman, 1978), which includes American symbols and how they originated. Next have students create a new symbol for their country and explain in writing why it is an appropriate one.

Antonyms, Spelling Rules, Writing Words Introduce the antonym of *country*, the word *city*. Then introduce the plural rule that applies to *country* and *city* (see **Spelling Sourcebook 1**, page 85). Have students write *countries*. Brainstorm for other words that follow this rule *(baby/babies, lady/ladies, story/stories)*.

Book Tie-In, Writing Reasons, Comparing and Contrasting, Writing Stories Read a version of Aesop's *The Country Mouse and the City Mouse*. Then have students write which mouse they would prefer to be and why. Using more than one version of the fable, have students compare and contrast the versions. Then have students write another version.

E 398.24 Bre
E 398.2 Mck
E 398.24 Sum

229 *father*

Book Tie-In, Writing Stories Use *Dirty Dave* (Nette Hilton, Orchard Books/Watts, 1990), an intricately illustrated, humorous picture book about a trio of elegantly dressed outlaws—Dirty Dave, his sister, and mom. While they're out terrorizing, their talented father stays home and sews their elegant clothes! Follow up the reading by asking students to write about someone in their family who has a special talent.

Other Word Forms, Vocabulary Skills, Writing Sentences Have students brainstorm for common other word forms of *father: fathers, fathered, fatherly*. Discuss any unfamiliar meanings. Have students write the other word forms in sentences.

Antonyms Review the antonym of *father*, the word *mother* (226).

230 *let*

Other Word Forms, Spelling Rules Have students brainstorm for common other word forms of *let: lets, letting*. Review the spelling rule that applies to *letting* (see **Spelling Sourcebook 1**, page 85). Brainstorm for other words that double the final consonant before the *ing* suffix is added (*get* [101], *put* [138], *set* [16], *top, run, cut, sit, shop*).

Sound-Symbol Awareness, Writing Sentences Write *let* on the chalkboard. Ask students to follow these directions to write new and review words:

> Change *let* to make *set* (162).
> Change *let* to make *lot*. (Discuss the two words *a lot*.)
> Change *let* to make *lit*.
> Add three letters to *let* to make *letter*.
> Add one letter to *let* to make *left*.

Have students write a sentence for each word they made.

231 *night*

Book Tie-In,
Research and Writing
◆ Use *Animals of the Night* (Merry Banks, Scribner, 1990) as a catalyst for interested students to do further research on night, or nocturnal, animals and create a brief written report to share with classmates.

Book Tie-In, Writing Stories
◆ Poetry that focuses on nighttime and families in an African-American neighborhood can be enjoyed in *Night on Neighborhood Street* (Eloise Greenfield, Dial, 1991). Follow up by asking students to write about the night moods of their neighborhood.

Sound-Symbol Awareness,
Writing Rhymes
◆ Write _ight on the chalkboard. Ask students to add beginning letters to make rhyming words with the same spelling pattern (*might* [173], *light* [227], *tight, sight, right* [116], *fight, bright, flight, slight, fright*). Have students write rhymes using the words.

Other Word Forms, Vocabulary
Skills, Writing Sentences,
Suffix Practice
◆ Have students brainstorm for common other word forms of *night: nights, nightly*. Discuss unfamiliar words. Have students write the other word forms in sentences. Review the *ly* suffix by asking students to add *ly* to *father* (229), *mother* (226), *year* (225), *high* (224), *earth* (220), *live* (217), *kind* (214), *last* (166), *great* (146), *different* (139), *most* (99). Discuss unfamiliar words. Have students write the words in sentences.

232 *picture*

Writing Speculations
◆ Play the Picture Puzzle game. Ask each student to cut a full-page picture from a magazine, cut it into four equal parts, and put three of the parts into an envelope. Distribute the fourth picture parts among the students so that each has one. Then students use their picture part as a clue about the whole picture. Have students write what they think the whole picture shows. They then share the writing and compare the answer with the whole picture.

Word Analysis,
Writing Sentences
◆ Distinguish between *picture* and *pitcher*. Discuss other words that sound and look similar and may be confusing. Choices may include *set* (162) and *sit, are* (15) and *our* (109), *pin* and *pen*, *then* (53) and *than* (73), *once* (206) and *ounce*. Have students write the often-confused pairs of words in sentences to differentiate them.

Idiomatic Usage,
Writing Explanations
◆ Ask students to explain in writing what they think it means to say each of these expressions (then discuss):

as pretty as a picture
get the picture
picture perfect

Other Word Forms, Vocabulary
Skills, Writing Sentences
◆ Have students brainstorm for common other word forms of *picture: pictures, pictured, picturing, picturesque*. Discuss unfamiliar words. Have students write the other word forms in sentences.

Synonyms, Research and
Writing, Public Speaking
◆ Introduce a synonym of *pictures*, the word *illustrations*. Have students find out about the Caldecott Medal for books (annual award for outstanding children's book illustrations). Ask students to locate a Caldecott Medal book and find out about the illustrator. Then have students tell about the book and its illustrator in a brief written report and present the report orally to the class.

233 *being*

Book Tie-In Introduce *human being*. Then share *How People First Lived* (William Jaspersohn, Watts, 1985) to show students how early human beings discovered speech, the wheel, and fire.

Other Word Forms, Writing Sentences Review common other word forms of *being: is* (7), *was* (13), *were* (34), *been* (75), *be* (21). Have students write the other word forms in sentences.

Sorting Words Have students play Word Sorts (see **Spelling Sourcebook 1**, page 92) using these words: *being, because* (127), *something* (178), *between* (154), *below* (176), *going* (192), *began* (215).

234 *study*   usually gr. 5

Book Tie-In, Writing Stories Use *The Whipping Boy* (Sid Fleischman, Greenwillow, 1986), the 1987 Newbery Medal book. The story parallels Mark Twain's *The Prince and the Pauper*, but the confusion is not caused by the clothing but by the pauper's knowledge. The prince refuses to study, so remains illiterate, but the pauper grows literate through reading. Following the story, have students write about something they learned from reading a book.

Other Word Forms, Vocabulary Skills, Spelling Rules, Writing Words Have students brainstorm for common other word forms of *study: studies, studied, studying, student, students, studious.* Discuss unfamiliar words. Review the spelling rule that applies to *study* (see **Spelling Sourcebook 1**, page 85). Have students write *studies.* Brainstorm for other verbs that follow this rule. Choices may include *try, copy, hurry,* and *carry.*

Writing a List Have students compile a list of study habits that help students learn effectively.

235 *second*

Multiple Meanings, Writing Sentences Brainstorm for meanings of *second.* Then have students check a dictionary for verification. Ask students to write sentences to illustrate the different meanings.

Idiomatic Usage, Writing Explanations Ask students to explain in writing what they think it means to say each of these expressions (then discuss):

second fiddle
second hand
to get your second wind
in a split second
on second thought

Predicting Spellings Review *first* (74). Then have students name the words and predict the spellings of *third, fourth, fifth, sixth, seventh, eighth, ninth,* and *tenth.*

236 *soon*

Idiomatic Usage, Writing Explanations Ask students to explain in writing what they think it means to say each of these expressions (then discuss):

A fool and his money are soon parted.
no sooner said than done
sooner or later
the sooner the better

Other Word Forms, Vocabulary Skills, Writing Sentences Have students brainstorm for common other word forms of *soon: sooner, soonest.* Discuss unfamiliar words. Have students write the other word forms in sentences.

237 *story*

Book Tie-In,
Research and Writing
◆ Use *A Story, a Story* (Gail Haley, Macmillan, 1970), the classic tale of how African "spider stories" began. As a class, make a list of different kinds of stories, such as fables, fairy tales, tall tales, pourquoi tales, noodlehead stories, and myths. Then help students to find a favorite example of each kind of story.

Book Tie-In,
Collecting Literature
◆ Use *Diane Goode's Book of Silly Stories and Songs* (Diane Goode, Dutton, 1992), seventeen folk tales and songs from around the world, to begin a collection of stories from around the world. Place a map on the classroom bulletin board; post a small construction paper book to represent each story from a different part of the world.

Book Tie-In, Writing Stories
◆ Use *Aunt Flossie's Hats and Crab Cakes Later* (Elizabeth Howard, Clarion, 1991), in which Aunt Flossie's great-great-nieces try on her many hats, each of which comes with a story. Follow up by asking students to bring interesting hats to class to generate creative stories.

Multiple Meanings,
Writing Sentences
◆ Brainstorm for meanings of *story*. Then have students check a dictionary for verification. Ask students to write sentences to illustrate the different meanings.

Writing Words, Spelling Rules
◆ Have students write *study* (234) and *studies, country* (228) and *countries,* and *story* and *stories.* Review the spelling rule that applies to these words (see *Spelling Sourcebook 1,* page 85). Have students brainstorm for more verbs and nouns that follow this rule (nouns: *city, family, baby*; verbs: *carry, fly, copy*).

238 *since*

Word Analysis, Writing a List
◆ Write *since* on the chalkboard, and underline the *ce.* Review *place* (131) and *once* (206). Then have students compile a list of words ending in *ce.* Choices may include *sentence, face, space, voice,* and *piece.* Have students underline the *ce* in each word.

239 *white*

Retelling a Story, Comparing
and Contrasting,
Writing Reasons
◆ Ask students to retell the story of Snow White. Then read one version of the folk tale, such as *Snow White* (Josephine Poole, Knopf, 1991). Then have students collect other versions to compare and contrast. Let students choose the version they like best and write why they made that choice.

Writing Color Words
◆ Show students a box of crayons. Then have students list color words they predict are included in the crayon box. Next, compare the crayon colors with the students' lists and have students check their spellings against the crayon labels.

Sound-Symbol Awareness,
Sorting Words
◆ Have students write *white.* Ask students to listen to the long *i* sound in the word. Then have them collect more words with the long *i* sound and sort them to note the most frequent spellings for long *i* (most common: *igh [might], y [my], ind [mind], i*-consonant-*e [smile]*). Have one category for "other" to accommodate less common spellings.

Other Word Forms, Vocabulary
Skills, Writing Sentences
◆ Have students brainstorm for common other word forms of *white: whiter, whitest, whiten.* Discuss unfamiliar words. Have students write the other word forms in sentences.

. Antonyms
◆ Introduce the antonym of the color *white,* the word *black.*

Remember . . .

Develop spelling accountability as students write—see *Spelling Sourcebook 1*, Article 8, page 33. Spelling mastery is achieved ONLY when students can spell and use words consistently correctly in writing.

240 *ever*

Sound-Symbol Awareness,
Writing Sentences,
Writing Reasons

◆ Ask students to write *ever*. Then have them follow these directions to write new and review words:

Add one letter to *ever* to make *never* (167).

Add a word to *ever* to make *forever* (*for* [12]).

Add a letter to *ever* to make *lever*. (Have students demonstrate what a lever is.)

Add two letters to *ever* to make *clever*. (Have students write the name of a clever story character and tell why he or she was clever.)

Add one letter to *ever* to make *every* (151).

Add a word to *every* to make *everywhere* (*where* [98]).

Have students write a sentence for each word they made.

Book Tie-In, Writing a Sequel

◆ Use *The Frog Prince Continued* (Jon Scieszka, Viking, 1991), in which the Prince and Princess find out the truth about life "happily ever after." Have students write a brief sequel following the reading.

241 *paper*

Book Tie-In, Writing a List

◆ Use *Paper Through the Ages* (Sharon Cosner, Carolrhoda, 1984) as an interesting introduction to paper and other writing surfaces. Have students follow up the reading by listing objects a writer might use to write on paper (*pencil, pen, paint brush, chalk, crayon*).

Book Tie-In, Writing Directions

◆ Students can have fun with paper-folding crafts with *Easy Origami* (Dokuohtei Nakano, Viking, 1986), which features over fifty projects. Have students write the directions to one easy folding craft.

Multiple Meanings,
Writing Sentences

◆ Brainstorm for meanings of *paper*. Then have students check a dictionary for verification. Ask students to write sentences to illustrate the different meanings.

Writing Speculations,
Comparing and Contrasting

◆ Charles Stillwell invented the brown paper bag in 1845 and a machine to make them in 1883. In the 1930s, a new kind of store became popular that made the paper bag a big success. Ask students to speculate in writing why the paper bag became so popular (when supermarkets came into being, the demand for paper bags grew) . Next, have students contrast and compare paper bags with options available today.

242 *hard*

Multiple Meanings,
Writing Explanations

◆ Brainstorm for meanings of *hard*. Then have students check a dictionary for verification. Next, ask students to write about something that was initially hard for them to do, but they learned to do it. After sharing these writing pieces, note with students that many things are initially difficult to do but can be mastered with determination and practice.

Idiomatic Usage,
Writing Explanations

◆ Ask students to explain in writing what they think it means to say each of these expressions (then discuss):

as hard as nails
cold, hard cash
to give someone a hard time
hard-and-fast rule
hard feelings
to learn the hard way

Antonyms

◆ Introduce antonyms of *hard*, the words *soft* and *easy*.

Other Word Forms, Vocabulary
Skills, Writing Sentences

◆ Have students brainstorm for common other word forms of *hard: harder, hardest, harden, hardly*. Discuss unfamiliar words. Have students write the other word forms in sentences.

243 *near*

Sound-Symbol Awareness,
Writing Words

◆ Write _*ear* on the chalkboard. Ask students to add beginning letters to make new words that rhyme with *near (hear, fear, dear, gear, rear, shear, tear, year)*. Then have students find and write *ear* words that do not rhyme with *near (bear, tear, pear, wear)*.

Antonyms

◆ Review the antonym of *near*, the word *far* (222).

Other Word Forms, Vocabulary
Skills, Writing Sentences,
Writing Words

◆ Have students brainstorm for common other word forms of *near: nears, neared, nearing, nearer, nearest, nearly*. Discuss unfamiliar words. Have students write the other word forms in sentences. Then introduce the game All in the Family (see **Spelling Sourcebook 1**, page 86). Use the other word forms of *near* and selected review words in the game.

244 *sentence*

Book Tie-In, Writing Sentences

◆ √Use *Aster Aardvark's Alphabet Adventures* (Steven Kellogg, Morrow, 1987) to introduce students to the longest, most exciting, compound-complex sentences they've ever read! Then have students write compound-complex sentences.

Multiple Meanings,
Writing Sentences

◆ Brainstorm for meanings of *sentence*. Then have students check a dictionary for verification. Ask students to write sentences to illustrate the different meanings.

245 *better*

Idiomatic Usage,
Writing Explanations

◆ Ask students to explain in writing what they think it means to say each of these expressions (then discuss):

Better late than never.
Better safe than sorry.
to build a better mousetrap

Sound-Symbol Awareness,
Answering Questions,
Writing Sentences

◆ Ask students to write *better*. Then have them follow these directions to write new words and to give answers to the questions:

Change *better* to make *letter*. (Can you think of two meanings for *letter*?)
Change *better* to make *bitter*. (What tastes bitter?)
Change *better* to make *batter*. (Can you think of two meanings for *batter*?)
Change *better* to make *setter*. (What is an Irish Setter?)

Have students write a sentence for each word they made.

246 *best*

Book Tie-Ins, Writing Lists ✦ Use *Best Friends: Poems* (Lee Bennett Hopkins ed., Watts, 1986), a collection of short poems about close friendships, and *Your Best Friend, Kate* (Pat Brisson, Bradbury, 1989). Then ask students to list the things best friends do for each other to stay best friends.

Idiomatic Usage, Writing Explanations ✦ Ask students to explain in writing what they think it means to say each of these expressions (then discuss):

> to put your best foot forward
> to wear your Sunday best
> all for the best

Sound-Symbol Awareness, Writing Sentences ✦ Ask students to write *best*. Then have them follow these directions to write new words:

> Change *best* to make *test, nest, pest, rest, west.*
> Change *best* to make *bent.*
> Change *best* to make *bet.*

Have students write a sentence for each word they made.

247 *across*

Word Analysis, Writing Sentences ✦ Ask students to use *across* and *a cross* in sentences. Then expand the lesson to *around* (120) and *a round*, *away* (140) and *a way*, *along* (171) and *a long*.

Writing Words ✦ Play Race Track Spelling (see *Spelling Sourcebook 1*, page 90) using *across* and selected review words.

248 *during*

Dictation and Writing ✦ Dictate these partial sentences and have students complete them:

> During the day, I always _____.
> During the night, I never _____.
> During school, children should _____.
> During my life, it is important to me to _____.

249 *today*

Word Analysis, Compound Words, Writing Words ✦ Have students write *today* and *tonight* and underline the two word parts. Then have students brainstorm for more compound words that use *day* or *night* (231). Choices may include *daybreak, daydream, daylight, daytime, nightgown, nightmare, nightshirt,* and *nighttime.*

Abbreviations, Writing Dates and Times ✦ Introduce these abbreviations to students: *A.M./a.m./AM* (time from midnight to noon) and *P.M./p.m./PM* (time from noon to midnight). Also list the days of the week and their abbreviations, and the months of the year and their abbreviations. Then have students practice writing given dates and times.

250 *however*

Word Analysis, Compound Words, Sorting Words ✦ Ask students to write *however* and underline the two word parts. The meaning of some compound words is a composite of its word parts; others do not get their meaning in this way. Ask students to use those criteria to categorize these compounds: *however, understand, baseball, newspaper, railroad, cannot, today* (249), *without* (249), *something* (178). Then have students find more compounds and write them in the correct category.

251 *sure*

Idiomatic Usage, Writing Explanations
◆ Ask students to explain in writing what they think it means to say each of these expressions (then discuss):

      sure-footed

      a sure thing

      for sure

Sound-Symbol Awareness, Writing Words
◆ Write these words on the chalkboard: *sure, special, machine, ocean, pressure, addition, show* (184). Ask students to listen for the *sh* sound in the words. Underline the letters that spell the *sh* sound. Then have students collect more words that have the *sh* sound to discover that a variety of letters can spell the sound but that the letter combination *sh* is the most common spelling. The second most common is *ti* as in *nation*. The *s* spelling, as in *sure* and *sugar* occurs only in those two words and their other word forms.

Other Word Forms, Vocabulary Skills, Writing Sentences
◆ Have students brainstorm for common other word forms of *sure: surely, sureness, surer, surest*. Discuss unfamiliar words. Have students write the other word forms in sentences.

252 *knew*

Homophone Usage, Writing Sentences, Research and Writing, Creating a Book
◆ Review the homophone of *knew*, the word *new* (107). Underline *new* inside *knew*. Have students use the homophones in written sentences to differentiate them. *Gnu*, the African antelope, could also be introduced. Have students research the animal and compile the results into a class-made book, *Things to Know about the Gnu* (see page 138, Creating Classroom Books).

Word Analysis, Writing Words
◆ Discuss the silent *k* of *knew*. Have students brainstorm for other words that begin with a silent *k*. Choices may include *know* (100), *knife*, and *knot*.

Other Word Forms, Vocabulary Skills, Writing Sentences
◆ Review common other word forms of *knew: know* (100), *knows, known, knowing, knowingly, knowledge*. Discuss unfamiliar words. Have students write the other word forms in sentences.

253 *it's*

Homophone Usage, Writing Words
◆ Discuss *it's* and *its* (76). Review the use of an apostrophe in a contraction. Review selected homophones, including *to* (5), *too* (65), *two* (112); *there* (37), *their* (42), *they're*; *through* (102), *threw*; *write* (108), *right* (116); *here* (134), *hear*; and *new* (107), *knew* (252). To reinforce homophones, play Mystery Words (see **Spelling Sourcebook 1**, page 89).

Book Tie-In, Writing Riddles
√ Use *Hey, Hay! A Wagonful of Funny Homonym Riddles* (Marvin Terban, Clarion, 1991), a collection of humorous brainteasers. Follow up with students writing their own silly riddles using homophones.

Book Tie-In, Writing Stories
N/A Use *It's Me, Hippo!* (Mike Thaler, Harper, 1983), a book of four short stories about a friendly hippo. Have students write another short story about this hippo.

Contractions, Writing Words
◆ Have students brainstorm for more contractions that employ *is (he's, she's, what's, that's, who's, there's, here's, one's)*. Have students write the contractions and the words that make it up.

254 *try*

Spelling Rules, Suffix Practice

Review the spelling rule for adding suffixes to words ending in *y* (see **Spelling Sourcebook 1**, page 85). Then ask students to add the *s*, *ed*, and *ing* suffixes to *try*, *cry*, *dry*, *fry*, and *pry*.

Idiomatic Usage, Writing Explanations

Ask students to explain in writing what they think it means to say each of these expressions (then discuss):

try out for something

try out something

try on something

try something

Other Word Forms, Vocabulary Skills, Writing Sentences

Have students brainstorm for common other word forms of *try: tries, tried, trying*. Discuss unfamiliar words. Have students write the other word forms in sentences.

255 *told*

Sound-Symbol Awareness, Sorting Words

Write *_old* on the chalkboard. Ask students to add beginning letters to make new words and to listen to the long *o* sound in the words. Then have them collect more words with the long *o* sound to note the most frequent spellings for long *o* (most common: *o [no]*, *o-consonant-e [those]*, *ow [show]*, *oa [coat]*, *old [cold]*, *oe [toe]*). Create a list of long *o* words. Have students write the words in categories sorted by the spelling for the long *o*. Have one category for "other" to accommodate less common spellings

Homophone Usage, Writing Sentences

Introduce the homophone of *told*, the word *tolled*. Have students use the homophones in written sentences to differentiate them.

Other Word Forms, Vocabulary Skills, Writing Sentences

Review common other word forms of *told: tell (147), tells, telling, teller*. Discuss unfamiliar words. Have students write the other word forms in sentences.

256 *young*

Antonyms, Writing Advantages, Comparing and Contrasting

Review the antonym of *young*, the word *old* (144). Then ask students to write the advantages of being young instead of old and the advantages of being old instead of young.

Other Word Forms, Vocabulary Skills, Writing Sentences

Have students brainstorm for common other word forms of *young: younger, youngest, youngster*. Discuss unfamiliar words. Have students write the other word forms in sentences.

Visual Skill-Building

Have students write *young* and underline *you* inside.

257 *sun*

Book Tie-In

N/A Use *The Story of Light* (Susan Roth, Reteller, Morrow, 1990), a Cherokee myth that tells how Spider brings a spark of light from the sun back to the shadowed side of the world. Review *light* (227) and *story* (237) with this lesson.

Homophone Usage, Writing Sentences

Introduce the homophone of *sun*, the word *son*. Have students use the homophones in written sentences to differentiate them.

Other Word Forms, Vocabulary Skills, Writing Sentences

Have students brainstorm for common other word forms of *sun: suns, sunned, sunning, sunny, sunnier, sunniest*. Discuss unfamiliar words. Have students write the other word forms in sentences.

258 *thing*

Book Tie-Ins, Creating a Book
◆ Use *Things to Know Before Going to Camp* and *Things To Know About Going to the Dentist* (Lisa Marsoli, Silver, 1985), two books in the *Things to Know* series. Ask students to use these books as a model for their own *Things to Know* books (see page 138, Creating Classroom Books).

Idiomatic Usage, Writing Explanations
◆ Ask students to explain in writing what they think it means to say each of these expressions (then discuss):

Do your own thing.
to be in the swing (or swim) of things
Of all things!
the in thing to do

Sound-Symbol Awareness, Writing Sentences
◆ Ask students to write *thing*. Then have them follow these directions to write new and review words:

Change *thing* to make *think* (118).
Change *thing* to make *bring, sing, ring, wing*.
Change *thing* to make *thin*.
Change *thing* to make *thick*.

Have students write a sentence for each word they made.

Anagrams, Writing Words
◆ Ask students to rearrange the letters of *thing* to make a word that has a long *i* sound (*night*). Have students find and write more anagrams (*was/saw, evil/live, tears/rates, nameless/salesmen*).

259 *whole*

Homophone Usage, Writing Words
◆ Write on the chalkboard: *The whole class saw the hole on the playground.* Discuss the homophones *whole* and *hole*. Then ask students to write a sentence using both homophones. Select review homophones and expand the lesson by asking students to use both homophone partners in the same sentence.

Book Tie-In, Research and Writing, Comparing and Contrasting
◆ Use *Seven Blind Mice* (Ed Young, Philomel, 1992) to illustrate the importance of looking at the *whole* situation before making a decision. The Indian fable of the blind men exploring an elephant has been revised for a new generation of readers. Ask students to research the original version and then compare and contrast the two.

Idiomatic Usage, Writing Explanations
◆ Ask students to explain in writing what they think it means to say each of these expressions (then discuss):

the whole ball of wax
on the whole
to go whole hog

Other Word Forms, Vocabulary Skills, Writing Sentences
◆ Have students brainstorm for common other word forms of *whole: wholes, wholly, wholesome*. Discuss unfamiliar words. Have students write the other word forms in sentences.

260 *hear*

Writing Reasons, Creating a Book, Book Tie-Ins
◆ What are the most beautiful sounds? Ask students to write sentences with this frame: *I like to hear _____ because _____*. Compile the results into class-made or student-made books. Discuss and have students write about the challenges of people who cannot hear. Use *What Is the Sign for Friend?* (Judith

N/A

Greenberg, Watts, 1985), about Shane, who communicates through signing. A beginning book of instructions for signing is *Handtalk* (Remy Charlip and Mary ✓ Beth Ancona, Macmillan, 1974). Also, *Mandy* (Barbara Booth, Lothrop, 1991) N/A is a sensitive story about a young deaf girl.

Homophone Usage,
Writing Sentences
◆ Review the homophone of *hear*, the word *here* (37). Have students use the homophones in written sentences to differentiate them.

Other Word Forms, Vocabulary
Skills, Writing Sentences
◆ Have students brainstorm for common other word forms of *hear: heard, hearing*. Have students write the other word forms in sentences.

261 *example*

Word Analysis, Writing Words
◆ Have students write *example*. Note the final silent *e*. Then dictate previously introduced words with final silent *e* for students to write: *whole, sure, sentence, white, since, life, side, page, picture, live, above, once, house, large, those, while, line, give, home, name, take, here, place, because, come, came, same, write, where, little, use, made, people, make, time, like, more, these, some, there, were, one, have, are*. Have students create an ongoing list of other words with final silent *e*.

Alphabetical Order
◆ Have students write these words in alphabetical order: *each* (47), *even* (130), *every* (151), *end* (170), *enough* (209), *earth* (220), *ever* (240), *example*.

Writing Words
◆ Play Spelling Baseball (see **Spelling Sourcebook 1**, page 91) using review words that either begin or end with *e*.

262 *heard*

Homophone Usage,
Writing Sentences
◆ Introduce the homophone of *heard*, the word *herd*. Have students use the homophones in written sentences to differentiate them.

Other Word Forms, Vocabulary
Skills, Writing Sentences
◆ Review common other word forms of *heard: hear* (260), *hears, hearing*. Have students write the other word forms in sentences.

Analogies, Writing Words
◆ Review analogies (see 139, 167). Then have students write these analogies and complete them with the appropriate word:

　　hard is to soft as old is to ＿＿＿＿＿＿ (young [256])
　　it's is to its as hole is to ＿＿＿＿＿＿ (whole [259])
　　try is to tried as tell is to ＿＿＿＿＿＿ (told [255])
　　younger is to youngest as better is to ＿＿＿＿＿＿ (best [246])
　　know is to knew as hear is to ＿＿＿＿＿＿ (heard)

263 *several*

Antonyms
◆ Review the antonym of *several*, the word *few* (181) (or its synonym, *many* [55]) .

Writing Words
◆ Have students brainstorm for words that relate to "how many or how much." Choices may include *some* (56), *many* (55), *few* (181), *much* (104), *one* (28), *two* (65), *three* (125), *four* (211), *ten, fifty, dozen*, and *a lot*. Emphasize that *a lot* is always written as two words.

264 *change* ✓

Book Tie-In,
Writing Explanations
◆ Guide students through *Insect Metamorphosis: From Egg to Adult* (Ron and Nancy Goor, Atheneum, 1990), a superbly illustrated story of butterfly life cycle changes. Review the sequential steps of metamorphosis (*life* [208]). Then have students explain the transformation in their own words.

Research and Writing, Book Tie-In	◆ Have students research the behavior and physiology of a chameleon's color change. Use *Chameleons: Dragons in the Trees* (James Martin, Crown, 1991). Have students write answers to the questions, "How does a chameleon change color?" and "Why does a chameleon change color?"
Book Tie-In, Writing Explanations, Speculating, Writing Descriptions	*Changes* (Anthony Browne, Knopf, 1991) shows changes in nature (plants, animals, insects, birds) through colorful photographs and text. Follow up with students writing about how they have changed from infancy until now. Then have them speculate about changes they can anticipate making over the next seven years. Have students describe themselves and their lives fifteen years from now.
Idiomatic Usage, Writing Explanations	◆ Ask students to explain in writing what they think it means to say each of these expressions (then discuss):

to change horses in midstream
for something to change hands
to change your tune

Other Word Forms, Vocabulary Skills, Writing Sentences	◆ Have students brainstorm for common other word forms for *change: changes, changed, changing, changeable, changeless, changer*. Discuss unfamiliar words. Then reinforce the other word forms of *change* and selected review words with the game All in the Family (see **Spelling Sourcebook 1**, page 86).
Multiple Meanings, Writing Sentences, Book Tie-In	◆ Brainstorm for meanings of *change*. Then have students check a dictionary for verification. Ask students to write sentences to illustrate the different meanings.
	Have students read *Amelia Bedelia* (Peggy Parish, Harper, 1963) to see how she "changed" the towels for her employers, Mr. and Mrs. Rogers. Then have students write another Amelia Bedelia story in which she misinterprets words that have more than one meaning.

265 *answer*

Antonyms	◆ Introduce the antonym of *answer*, the word *question*.
Book Tie-In, Creating a Book	◆ Suggest books that pose and answer a question: *Why Did the Dinosaurs Disappear? Questions About Life in the Past* (Philip Whitfield, Viking, 1991), *Where Do Cats Live?* (Ron Hirschi, Walker, 1991), *How Much Is a Million?* (David Schwartz, Scholastic, 1986). Then have students ask and answer a question of their choice to bind into a student-made book.
Writing Questions and Answers	◆ Play Questions and Answers (see **Spelling Sourcebook 1**, page 90).

266 *room*

Book Tie-Ins, Writing a List	Use *The Day That Henry Cleaned His Room* (Sarah Wilson, Simon, 1990), about the carloads of junk Henry shovels out of his room. Before the reading, have students make a list of the weird things Henry may discover during his annual room cleaning. Another room-cleaning story to complement this lesson is *Eeps, Creeps, It's My Room* (Martha Hickman, Abingdon, 1984).
Book Tie-In, Writing Reasons	◆ For a poetry collection about a variety of rooms, use *Roomrimes: Poems* (Sylvia Cassedy, Crowell, 1987). Have students decide which is their favorite room in their house and write why.
Other Word Forms, Vocabulary Skills, Writing Sentences	◆ Have students brainstorm for common other word forms for *room: rooms, roomy, roomier, roomiest, roomful*. Discuss unfamiliar words. Have students write the other word forms in sentences.

267 *sea*

Homophone Usage,
Writing Sentences
◆ Review the homophone of *sea*, the word *see*. Have students use the homophones in written sentences to differentiate them.

Book Tie-Ins
◆ Use *Armien's Fishing Trip* (Catherine Stock, Morrow, 1990), a sea adventure set near the South African town of Kalk Bay. Brainstorm for other books with a sea setting. One choice might be *Sam, Bangs, and Moonshine* (Evaline Ness, Henry Holt, 1966), with its Caldecott Medal–winning illustrations of the sea.

Research and Writing
◆ Provide students with world maps and have them find and write the names of seas. Then have students research the seas and report the information in writing. Research questions could include:

> Which sea is land-locked—and for that reason sometimes called a lake? (Caspian Sea)
> Which sea is the largest? (Mediterranean Sea—includes the Black Sea and Sea of Azov.)
> Which sea is the deepest? (Caribbean Sea)
> Which sea is the closest to where you live?
> Which sea would you like to visit on a vacation? Why?

268 *against*

Idiomatic Usage,
Writing Explanations
◆ Ask students to explain in writing what they think it means to say each of these expressions (then discuss):

> against the clock
> to have the cards stacked against you
> to swim against the current
> to beat your head against a wall
> against all odds

Visual Skill-Building
◆ Have students find *again* (144) inside *against*.

Antonyms
◆ Review the antonym of *against*, the word *for* (12).

Writing Sentences
◆ Play Sentence Spelling (see **Spelling Sourcebook 1**, page 91) to reinforce dictation skills using *against* and selected review words.

269 *top*

Multiple Meanings,
Writing Sentences
◆ Brainstorm for meanings of *top*. Then have students check a dictionary for verification. Ask students to write sentences to illustrate the different meanings.

Idiomatic Usage,
Writing Explanations
◆ Ask students to explain in writing what they think it means to say each of these expressions (then discuss):

> to blow your top
> to be on top of the world
> at the top of your lungs

Other Word Forms, Writing
Descriptions, Spelling Rules,
Suffix Practice
◆ Have students brainstorm for common other word forms of *top: tops, topped, topping*. Ask students to describe in writing their favorite ice cream topping. Then review the spelling rule that applies to *topping* (see **Spelling Sourcebook 1**, page 85). Have students write other words that double the final consonant before the *ing* suffix (*get* [101], *put* [138], *set* [162], *let* [230], *run, cut, sit, stop, shop*).

270 *turned*

Other Word Forms, Vocabulary Skills, Writing Sentences

◆ Have students brainstorm for common other word forms of *turned: turn, turns, turning, turner*. Discuss unfamiliar words. Have students write the other word forms in sentences.

Prefix Practice, Answering Questions

◆ Review the *re* prefix. Then ask students to answer these questions:

What would happen if you returned your library book after the due date?

Why might it be necessary to restudy information for a test? (*study* [234])

What experience would you like to relive? (*live* [217])

What book would you like to reread? Why? (*read* [165])

Why do some fillings in teeth need to be replaced? (*place* [131])

Why do writers rewrite their stories? (*write* [108])

What things does your family reuse? (*use* [88])

What might you choose to rename your school? (*name* [155])

271 *learn*

Idiomatic Usage, Writing Explanations

◆ Ask students to explain in writing what they think it means to say each of these expressions (then discuss):

Live and learn.

to learn the ropes

to learn something by heart

Other Word Forms, Vocabulary Skills, Writing Sentences

◆ Have students brainstorm for common other word forms of *learn: learns, learned, learning, learner*. Discuss unfamiliar words. Have students write the other word forms in sentences.

Sound-Symbol Awareness

◆ Have students write *learn, turned* (270), *first* (74), *were* (34). Note the different spellings of the vowel sound.

Writing Explanations, Sequencing

◆ Have students use their own words to write the independent word-study steps to learn to spell a word (see ***Spelling Sourcebook 1***, page 27).

272 *point*

Idiomatic Usage, Writing Explanations

◆ Ask students to explain in writing what they think it means to say each of these expressions (then discuss):

to get to the point

beside the point

to make a point

to miss the point

Sound-Symbol Awareness, Sorting Words

◆ Write *point* and *boy* (205) on the chalkboard. Underline the *oy* and *oi*. Have students say the words and note the common vowel sound. Then they brainstorm for other words with this vowel sound and sort them by *oy* or *oi* spelling. Choices may include *enjoy, toy, noise, oil, join,* and *voice*.

Other Word Forms, Vocabulary Skills, Writing Sentences

◆ Have students brainstorm for common other word forms of *point: points, pointed, pointing, pointer, pointless*. Discuss unfamiliar words. Have students write the other word forms in sentences.

Word Analysis, Writing Words

◆ Write *p_ _nt* on the chalkboard. Ask students to fill in the vowels to make *point* and then to write the whole word. Extend the fill-in activity to include *learn* (271), *turned* (270), *against* (268), *several* (263), *heard* (262), *young* (256), *country* (228), *earth* (220), *enough* (209), *thought* (179), *people* (79), *through*

(102), *around* (120), *because* (127), *does* (128), *our* (109), *about* (48), *should* (156), *said* (43).

273 *city*

Spelling Rules, Writing Words ✦ Review the plural rule used to turn *country* (228) into *countries* (see **Spelling Sourcebook 1**, page 85). Have students write *cities*. Brainstorm for other words that follow this rule *(baby/babies, lady/ladies, study* (234)*/studies, story* (237)*/stories)*.

Writing Cities and States, Writing Speculations ✦ Ask students to use a map to find and write "unusual names for cities," such as Boring, Oregon. Note with students the comma written between city and state. Make a collection of these names. Then ask students to hypothesize in writing how each name may have originated.

Book Tie-In, Writing a List, Sound-Symbol Awareness ✦ Use *Magic Carpet* (Pat Brisson, Bradbury, 1991), which follows the travels of a magic carpet that stops only in cities that begin with the letter *S*. Prior to the reading, ask students to create a list of cities beginning with *S* that may be included in the story.

274 *play*

Multiple Meanings, Book Tie-Ins, Writing a Sequel, Writing Reasons ✦ Discuss meanings of *play*. Then introduce books that use *play* with different meanings: *Amazing Grace* (Mary Hoffman, Dial 1991), is about Grace, who is told she can't be Peter Pan in the school play because she is a girl and black. But Grace wins the part and executes it superbly! *Simon Says . . . Let's Play* (Sally Foster, Cobblehill/Dutton, 1990), a photographic survey of fun-to-play games complete with directions. Ask students to create a sequel book of additional games they like to play. *Join the Band!* (Marjorie Pillar, HarperCollins, 1992) is a photo essay of students who play instruments in the school band. Follow up by asking students to interview a person who plays an instrument to find out why he or she chose that instrument. Then they summarize the reasons in writing.

Book Tie-In, Creating a Class Play ✦ Use *Plays From Favorite Folk Tales: 25 One-Act Dramatizations of Stories Children Love* (Sylvia Kamerman ed., Plays, 1987) as a resource to put on a class play.

Idiomatic Usage, Writing Explanations ✦ Ask students to explain in writing what they think it means to say each of these expressions (then discuss):

All work and no play makes Jack a dull boy.
Play it safe.
to play a trick on someone
When the cat's away the mice will play.

Other Word Forms, Vocabulary Skills, Writing Sentences, Suffix Practice, Answering Questions ✦ Have students brainstorm for common other word forms of *play: plays, played, playing, player, playful.* Discuss unfamiliar words. Have students write the other word forms in sentences. Review the suffix *ful*. Then have students answer these questions:

What might a playful puppy do?
What might a thoughtful child do? (*thought* [179])
What might a helpful teacher do? (*help* [137])
What might a useful gift be? (*use* [88])

275 *toward*

Multiple Meanings, Writing Sentences
✦ Discuss *toward* and *towards*. Contrast the words with their antonyms *backward* and *backwards*. Note that these words are generally interchangeable. Have students use the words in sentences.

Writing Words
✦ Play the All-Play Spelling Bee (see **Spelling Sourcebook 1**, page 86) using *toward* and selected review words.

276 *five*

Book Tie-Ins, Comparing and Contrasting, Writing Stories
✦ Use *The Five Chinese Brothers* (Claire Bishop, Putnam, 1938), the classic tale of the identical brothers who each have a trait that saves the lives of all of them. Have students compare and contrast variants of this tale. Variants include *The Riddle of the Drum* (Mexico), *Rum Pum Pum* (India), and *The Fool of the World and the Flying Ship* (Russia). Then have them write their own version of the tale.

Book Tie-In, Making a Poster
✦ Use *Your Five Senses* (Ray Broekel, Childrens, 1984), an easy-to-read text with photographs and diagrams to explain hearing, smelling, touching, tasting, and seeing. Have students make a poster for each of the senses that includes one fact about that sense.

Writing Number Words
✦ Review the number words *one* through *ten*. Show the numeral and have students write the number word.

277 *himself*

Antonyms, Predicting Spellings, Compound Words
✦ Have students write *him* (67) and *her* (64). Then ask students to write *himself* and *herself* and underline the two word parts of each compound. Have students predict the spellings of *yourself* and *myself*. Review *into* (61), *something* (178), *without* (204), *today* (249), and *however* (250).

Compound Words, Writing Words
✦ Have students create a list of compound words. Then play Compound Bingo (see **Spelling Sourcebook 1**, page 87) using the compound words.

278 *usually*

Suffix Practice, Writing Words, Vocabulary Skills
✦ Have students write *usually* and underline the *ly*. Ask them to read the word without the *ly (usual).* Then have students add the *ly* suffix to *like* (66), *time* (69), *just* (97), *most* (99), *new* (107), *man* (111), *right* (116), *part* (129), *even* (130), *different* (139), *great* (146), *name* (155), *last* (166), *world* (191), *important* (195), *kind* (214), *live* (217), *high* (224), *year* (225), *mother* (226), *light* (227), *father* (229), *night* (231), *second* (235), *hard* (242), *near* (243), *sure* (251). Discuss unfamiliar meanings.

Prefix Practice, Answering Questions
✦ Have students write *usual* and *usually*. Then have them write the words with the *un* prefix (*unusual, unusually*). Ask students how the prefix changes the meaning. Then have them write answers to these questions:

When is a law unjust? (*just* [97])
Why do unthoughtful people have few friends? (*thought* [179])
When might you feel that food is unimportant to you? (*important* [195])
What is an example of an unkind remark? (*kind* [214])
What should you do if you're unsure of a spelling on a job application? (*sure* [251])
What kind of weather would be unusual for your area in winter?

Suffix and Prefix Practice
❖ Introduce Password (see ***Spelling Sourcebook 1***, page 89). Play the game using *ly* suffix words and *un* prefix words.

279 *money*

Book Tie-In, Comparing and Contrasting, Creating a Book
❖ Use *The Kids' Complete Guide to Money* (Kathy Kyte, Knopf, 1984) as a creative guide to earning, saving, and spending money. Follow up with students comparing and contrasting prices on items they often buy. Compile the results into a class-made shopping guidebook.

math tie

Book Tie-In, Writing Explanations
❖ To stimulate a discussion on values, introduce *The Money Tree* (Sarah Stewart, Farrar, 1991), in which a tree that produces dollar bills generates considerable community interest. Follow up with students writing about something money cannot buy and explaining why it has no price.

Idiomatic Usage, Writing Explanations
❖ Ask students to explain in writing what they think it means to say each of these expressions (then discuss):
  Money burns a hole in your pocket.
  to have money to burn
  to pour money down the drain
  Time is money.

280 *seen*

Homophone Usage, Writing Sentences
❖ Introduce the homophone of *seen*, the word *scene*. Have students use the homophones in written sentences to differentiate them.

Other Word Forms, Writing Sentences
❖ Review common other word forms of *seen*: *see* (68), *sees*, *seeing*, *saw*. Have students write the other word forms in sentences.

Sorting Words
❖ Have students play Word Sorts (see ***Spelling Sourcebook 1***, page 92) using these words: *think* (118), *seen*, *work* (124), *see* (68), *working*, *saw*, *thinking*, *seeing*, *worker*, *thought* (179).

281 *didn't*

Contractions, Writing Words
❖ Ask students to write *did* (83) and *not* (30). Then have them identify the letter for which the apostrophe in *didn't* stands (*o*). Review *don't* (190).

Book Tie-In, Informational Writing
❖ Write on the chalkboard: *I didn't know . . .* Then use *Whales* (Gail Gibbons, Holiday House, 1991). Follow up by having students write something they didn't know about whales before the reading.

282 *car*

Book Tie-In, Creating a Book
❖ Use *The A-to-Z Book of Cars* (Angela Royston, Barron's, 1991), a fascinating book of information and photographs, taking the car buff from Alpha Romeo to Zodiac Zephyr. Have students make a new A-to-Z book of their favorite cars.

Book Tie-In, Writing Explanations
❖ Use *Cars and How They Go* (Joanna Cole, Crowell, 1983) for students who are interested in how car engines work. Then have students write in their own words the purpose of selected car parts, such as a transmission.

Writing to Persuade, Art
❖ Have students collect new car brochures and study the language chosen to describe the cars. Then they create their own car and the brochure to advertise it.

Sound-Symbol Awareness, Writing Sentences
✦ Write *car* on the chalkboard. Ask students to follow these directions to write new words:

Add one letter to *car* to make *cart*.
Add two letters to *car* to make *chart*.
Add one letter to *car* to make *card*.
Change *car* to make *far, tar, bar, star*.

Have students write a sentence for each word they made.

283 *morning*

Antonyms
✦ Introduce the antonym of *morning*, the word *evening*.

Homophone Usage, Writing Sentences
✦ Introduce the homophone of *morning*, the word *mourning*. Have students write the homophones in sentences to differentiate them.

Dictation and Writing
✦ Dictate these partial sentences and have students complete them:

It's morning when _____.
Every morning I _____.
On a school day morning, I usually _____.
On a morning when I don't have school, I _____.

284 *I'm*

Contractions, Word Analysis, Writing Words
✦ Have students write the contraction *I'm*. Then brainstorm for ways writers and speakers take "shortcuts" in addition to contractions. Choices may include abbreviations, clipped words *(airplane/plane, bike/bicycle)*, initials or acronyms *(TV, BLT, ZIP code)*, blends *(smog, brunch)*. Have students write examples of each kind of shortcut word.

285 *body*

Book Tie-In, Making a Checklist
✦ Use *Why Does My Nose Run? and Other Questions Kids Ask About Their Bodies* (Nancy Baggett and Joanne Settel, Atheneum, 1985), which capitalizes on natural curiosities. Follow up with students creating a checklist of "tips" to keep their bodies safe and healthy using information they learned in the book.

Spelling Rules, Writing Words
✦ Review the plural rule used to turn *city* (273) into *cities* (see **Spelling Sourcebook 1**, page 85). Have students write *bodies*. Brainstorm for other words that follow this rule *(baby/babies, lady/ladies, country* [228]*/countries, study* [234]*/studies, story* [237]*/stories).*

286 *upon*

Compound Words, Writing Words
✦ Have students write the compound word *upon* and underline the two word parts. Review other compound words, including *into* (61), *something* (178), *without* (204), *today* (249), *however* (250), and *himself* (277). Have students write the compounds and underline the word parts.

Writing Stories
✦ Ask students to brainstorm for "all-time favorite" fairy tale characters. Choices may include the giant in "Jack in the Beanstalk," the wolf in "The Three Little Pigs," and "Little Red Riding Hood." Then have students write one fairy tale featuring several of the characters. The story should begin, "Once upon a time . . ."

287 *family*

Book Tie-In, Writing Jokes, Creating a Book ◆ Use *Oh Brother! and Other Family Jokes* (Charles Keller, Prentice, 1982) as a model for students to write their own family jokes. Compile the results into a class-made book (see page 138, Creating Classroom Books).

Book Tie-In, Writing Explanations ◆ Use *Your Family, My Family* (Joan Drescher, Walker, 1980) to explore various family arrangements. Follow up with students writing about one thing that makes their family unique.

Spelling Rules, Writing Plurals ◆ Review the plural rule for *family* (see **Spelling Sourcebook 1**, page 85). Have students write the plurals of *family, body* (285). Have students brainstorm for ways words are made plural. Then have them write examples.

288 *later*

Other Word Forms, Vocabulary Skills, Writing Sentences ◆ Have students brainstorm for common other word forms of *later: late, latest, lately, lateness*. Discuss unfamiliar words. Have students write the other word forms in sentences.

Writing Comparative Words, Writing Sentences ◆ Have students write comparison forms for *late (later, latest), sure* (251), *near* (243), *hard* (242), *white* (239), *light* (227), *high* (224), *kind* (214), *great* (146), *old* (144), *little* (92). Then have them write comparisons using selected comparatives.

289 *turn*

Multiple Meanings, Writing Sentences ◆ Brainstorm for meanings of *turn*. Then have students check a dictionary for verification. Ask students to write sentences to illustrate the different meanings.

Idiomatic Usage, Writing Explanations ◆ Ask students to explain in writing what it means to say each of these expressions (then discuss):

Turn over a new leaf.
out of turn
to turn out all right
to turn your nose up at something

Other Word Forms, Prefix Practice ◆ Review common other word forms of *turn: turned* (270), *turns, turning, turner*. Then review the *re* prefix by asking students to write *return*. The *re* prefix means "back" in *return, remove, recall*, and *repay*. However, it means "again" in most words, such as *use* (88), *new* (107), *write* (108), *place* (131), *name* (155), *live* (217), *told* (255), *learn* (271), *play* (274).

Book Tie-In, Writing Stories ◆ Write *turned* on the chalkboard and ask students to think of stories in which a character is magically turned into something else, such as in *Frog Medicine* N/A (Mark Teague, Scholastic, 1991). Then write *turns* on the chalkboard and ✓ discuss *taking turns*. Use *The Rat and The Tiger* (Keiko Kasza, Putnam, 1993), a story that features fairness and taking turns.

290 *move*

Book Tie-In, Writing Predictions ◆ ✓ Use *Ming Lo Moves the Mountain* (Arnold Lobel, Greenwillow, 1982), a humorous tale of a man's attempt to move a mountain away from his house. Before the reading, ask students to write predictions of why Ming wants to move the mountain.

Book Tie-In, *Writing Descriptions*	✦ Use *The Horse in the Attic* (Eleanor Clymer, Dell, 1983), about Caroline's move to a new house and the picture of the horse she discovers in the attic. Ask students who have moved from one house to another to describe their experience in writing.
Idiomatic Usage, *Writing Explanations*	✦ Ask students to explain in writing what they think it means to say each of these expressions (then discuss):

        to get a move on

        to move on

        to move up in the world

Other Word Forms, Vocabulary *Skills, Writing Sentences,* *Spelling Rules*	✦ Have students brainstorm for common other word forms of *move: moves, moved, moving, mover, movement*. Discuss unfamiliar words. Have students write the other word forms in sentences. Have students write *remove* and a definition for it. Review the spelling rule for adding suffixes to words that end in final silent *e* (see ***Spelling Sourcebook 1***, page 85).

End Grade 3

291 *face*

Book Tie-In, Writing Directions	✦ Use *Five Minute Faces* (Snazaroo, Random, 1992), a resource for painting many different faces—from a simple clown to elaborate decoration. There are large illustrations for each face-painting project. Once students have followed the directions to create these faces, have them create an original face-painting project with directions.
Reading, Writing a Summary	✦ Use issues of the thematic children's magazine, *Faces: The Magazine About People.* Have students read a short feature article and write a summary.
Sound-Symbol Awareness, *Sorting Words*	✦ Have students write *face*. Then have them compile a list of words with long *a* to note the most frequent spellings for the long *a* sound (most common: *ay [say]*, *ai [train]*, *a*-consonant-*e [same]*). Have students sort the words, with one category for "other" to accommodate less common spellings.
Idiomatic Usage, *Writing Explanations*	✦ Ask students to explain in writing what they think it means to say each of these expressions (then discuss):

        to face the music

        to fall flat on your face

        to keep a straight face

Other Word Forms, Vocabulary *Skills, Writing Sentences*	✦ Have students brainstorm for common other word forms of *face: faces, faced, facing*. Discuss unfamiliar words. Have students write the other word forms in sentences.

292 *door*

Book Tie-In, Writing Stories	✦ Use *Possum Come A-Knockin'* (Nancy Van Lann, Knopf, 1990), a rhythmic trickster tale told in dialect. Following the reading, have students write a funny tale about someone who "came a-knockin'" at the classroom door.
Book Tie-In, Writing a Sequel	✦ Use *Knock! Knock!* (Colin and Jacqui Hawkins, Aladdin, 1991) to have students guess what creature lurks behind the door. Then have students write a sequel.
Writing Explanations	✦ Ask students to explain in writing what a *door prize* is.

293 *cut*

Book Tie-In,
Informational Writing

◆ Use *Cuts, Breaks, Bruises, and Burns* (Joanna Cole, Crowell, 1985) as an introduction to simple injuries and what to do about them. Follow up with students writing about one of their injuries (including how it might have been avoided).

Idiomatic Usage,
Writing Explanations

◆ Ask students to explain in writing what they think it means to say each of these expressions (then discuss):

    to cut back
    Cut it out!
    to cut corners

Other Word Forms, Vocabulary
Skills, Writing Sentences,
Spelling Rules

◆ Have students brainstorm for common other word forms of *cut: cuts, cutting, cutter, cutters.* Discuss unfamiliar words. Have students write the other word forms in sentences. Review the suffix rule that applies to *cut* (see **Spelling Sourcebook 1**, page 85). Have students apply the rule to *top* (269), *put* (138), *set* (162), *shop, step, trip, sit,* and *star.*

294 *done*

Sound-Symbol Awareness,
Writing Sentences

◆ Ask students to write *done*. Then have them follow these directions to write new and review words:

    Change *done* to make a number word (*one* [28]).
    Change one letter of *done* to make *none*.
    Change one letter of *done* to make *bone* and *gone*. (Note with students
        the different vowel sounds.)
    Change *done* to make *don't* (190).
    Change *done* to make *dine*.

Have students write a sentence for each word they made.

Other Word Forms, Vocabulary
Skills, Writing Sentences

◆ Review common other word forms of *done: did* (83), *do* (45), *does* (128), *doing, didn't, doesn't, don't* (190), *doer*. Discuss unfamiliar words. Have students write the other word forms in sentences.

295 *group*

Other Word Forms, Vocabulary
Skills, Writing Sentences

◆ Have students brainstorm for common other word forms of *group: groups, grouped, grouping.* Discuss unfamiliar words. Have students write the other word forms in sentences.

Sound-Symbol Awareness,
Writing Words

◆ Review the inconsistency of the vowel pair *ou*, using *group, you* (8), *about* (48), *would* (59), *thought* (179), *enough* (209), and *young* (256). Then ask students to collect other words with *ou*.

Sorting Words

◆ Have students play Word Sorts (see **Spelling Sourcebook 1**, page 92) using these words: *group, grow, could* (70), *green, out* (51), *around* (120), *country* (228), *great* (146), *ground.*

296 *true*

Book Tie-In, Writing Stories

◆ Use *The True Story of the Three Little Pigs* (Jon Scieszka, Viking Kestrel, 1989), the "true" story of A. Wolf. Then have students create their own "true" stories of favorite fairy tale characters.

Other Word Forms, Vocabulary Skills, Writing Sentences, Prefix Practice

◆ Introduce the common other word forms of *true: truly, truer, truest, trueness, truth, truthful, truthfully, truthfulness.* Discuss unfamiliar words. Have students write the other word forms in sentences. Write *true* on the chalkboard and ask students to write the prefix that would turn it into a word that means "false" (*un*).

297 *half*

Spelling Rules, Writing Plurals

◆ Introduce the plural rule that applies to *half* (see **Spelling Sourcebook 1**, page 85). Have students write the plural of *half (halves).* Brainstorm for other words that follow this rule *(life* [208]*/lives, wolf/wolves, leaf/leaves, elf/elves, half/halves, calf/calves, scarf/scarves, knife/knives).*

Idiomatic Usage, Writing Explanations

◆ Ask students to explain in writing what they think it means to say each of these expressions (then discuss):
> Half a loaf is better than none.
> six of one and half a dozen of another
> to be half-hearted
> to have half a mind to do something

298 *red*

Book Tie-In, Comparing and Contrasting, Making a Chart

◆ Use *Lon Po Po: A Red-Riding Hood Story From China* (Ed Young, Philomel, 1989) to introduce a variation of the popular Red Riding Hood tale. Ask students to collect other versions for comparison and contrast. Have students chart the similarities and differences.

Book Tie-In, Research and Writing, Hypothesizing

◆ Use *The Raggedy Red Squirrel* (Hope Ryden, Lodestar, 1992), a wildlife essay on the squirrel's daily habits. Have students follow up by researching other kinds of squirrels. Have students hypothesize in writing what they think might happen if a squirrel lived in their classroom.

Idiomatic Usage, Writing Explanations

◆ Ask students to explain in writing what they think it means to say each of these expressions (then discuss):
> to see red
> to get the red-carpet treatment
> to have a red face

Other Word Forms, Vocabulary Skills, Writing Sentences

◆ Have students brainstorm for common other word forms of *red: redder, reddest, reddening, redden, reddened.* Discuss unfamiliar words. Have students write the other word forms in sentences.

Homophone Usage, Homograph Usage, Writing Sentences, Book Tie-In, Writing Riddles

◆ Review the homophone of *red*, the word *read*, and the homograph *read* (to read a book). Have students use the homophones and homographs in written sentences to differentiate them. Use *Hey, Hay!: A Wagonful of Funny Homonym Riddles* (Marvin Terban, Clarion, 1991) to encourage students to write their own silly riddles.

299 *fish*

Book Tie-In, Writing Riddles

◆ Use *Fishy Riddles* (Katy Hall and Lisa Eisenberg, Dial, 1983) as a model for students to write riddles about fish and ocean life.

Book Tie-In,
Writing a Story Ending

◆ Use *No Plain Pets!* (Marc Ian Barasch, HarperCollins, 1991), in which a young narrator looks at unusual pets but chooses a goldfish. Have students write a story ending before they hear this one read.

Art, Research and Writing,
Writing Descriptions

◆ Ask students what fish, besides goldfish, might make good pets. Create a construction paper fish tank for the bulletin board filled with students' colored illustrations and written descriptions of various fish pets. Then create a construction paper fry pan for the bulletin board, and have students illustrate and describe fish we may eat. Discuss the nutritional value of fish.

Other Word Forms, Vocabulary
Skills, Writing Sentences

◆ Have students brainstorm for common other word forms of *fish: fishes, fished, fishing, fisherman, fishermen, fishy, fishery.* Discuss unfamiliar words. Have students write the other word forms in sentences. Play All in the Family (see *Spelling Sourcebook 1*, page 86) to reinforce other word forms of *fish* and selected review words.

Spelling Rules, Writing Words

◆ Introduce the spelling rule for the plural of *fish (fish)* (see *Spelling Sourcebook 1*, page 85). Have students find and write other words that follow this spelling pattern *(sheep, moose, deer).*

Remember . . .

Develop spelling accountability as students write—see *Spelling Sourcebook 1*, Article 8, page 33. Spelling mastery is achieved ONLY when students can spell and use words consistently correctly in writing.

300 *plants*

Book Tie-In,
Comparing and Contrasting

◆ Use *Wonderful Pussy Willows* (Jerome Wexler, Dutton, 1992), an unusual photo essay of a plant that interests children. Before the reading have students write what they know about this plant. Following the reading have students turn their papers over and repeat the activity. Have students tell what they learned.

Book Tie-Ins, Writing a List

◆ Use *Johnny Appleseed* (Reeve Lindbergh, Joy Street/Little, 1990), a rhyming picture book about the folk hero. Follow through with a similar tale, *Cherry Tree* (Ruskin Bond, Caroline, 1991), an intergenerational tale of a young girl who plants a cherry pit that grows into a tree that mirrors her own growth. Follow up with students creating a list of plants or trees that produce food we eat. Begin with apple and cherry.

Other Word Forms, Vocabulary
Skills, Writing Sentences

◆ Have students brainstorm for common other word forms of *plants: plant, planted, planting, planter, plantation, plantations.* Discuss unfamiliar words. Have students write the other word forms in sentences.

301 *living*

Book Tie-In, Creating a Book

◆ Use *Living Dangerously: American Women Who Risked Their Lives for Adventure* (Doreen Rappaport, HarperCollins, 1991), about six women who broke new ground in climbing, flying, diving, running, exploring, and going over Niagara Falls in a barrel. Have students create comparable class-made or student-made books that feature adventurous men, women, and children who have set records by living dangerously.

Homograph Usage, Writing Sentences, Other Word Forms	✦ Have students write the homograph *live* (217) in sentences to illustrate its two different meanings and pronunciations. Then for each pronunciation, have students write the other word forms: *lives, lived, living, livable; lively, livelier, liveliest.* Discuss unfamiliar words. Have students write the other word forms in sentences.
Career Awareness, Book Tie-In, Writing a Summary, Public Speaking	✦ Making a living can be achieved in many interesting ways. Introduce students to the unusual career choices made by the eight individuals profiled in *You Call That a Farm? Raising Otters, Leeches, Weeds, and Other Unusual Things* (Sam and Beryl Epstein, Farrar, 1991). Follow up with students interviewing someone with a unique career. Have them summarize the interview in writing and in a talk to the class.
Antonyms	✦ Introduce the antonym of *living*, the word *dying.*
Spelling Rules, Suffix Practice, Writing Words	✦ Review the spelling rule for adding suffixes to words that end in final silent *e* (see *Spelling Sourcebook 1*, page 85). Include *live* (217), *move* (290), *change* (264), *line* (161), *write* (108), and *make* (72). Have students find and write more words that follow this spelling rule. Then they write the words with suffixes to illustrate the rule.

302 *black*

Book Tie-In, Creating a Book	✦ Use the 1991 Caldecott winner *Black and White* (David Macaulay, Houghton, 1990) to intrigue students with the artistic quality and with the four stories told through four quadrants on each page. Have students use this book as a model for writing their own four-story black and white book.
Antonyms	✦ Review the antonym of the color *black*, the word *white* (239).
Sound-Symbol Awareness, Writing Sentences	✦ Ask students to write *black*. Then have them follow these directions to write new and review words:

      Change *black* to make *back* (103).
      Change *black* to make *pack, quack, sack, tack.*
      Change *black* to make *brick.*
      Change *black* to make *blast.*
Have students write a sentence for each word they made.

Other Word Forms, Vocabulary Skills, Writing Sentences	✦ Have students brainstorm for common other word forms of *black: blacker, blackest, blacken.* Discuss unfamiliar words. Have students write the other word forms in sentences.

303 *eat*

Book Tie-Ins, Making a Poster	✦ Use *Bugs for Dinner? The Eating Habits of Neighborhood Creatures* and *What's For Lunch? The Eating Habits of Seashore Creatures* (Sam and Beryl Epstein, Macmillan, 1989 and 1985) as entertaining resources. Have each student select a creature from one of the books and create a poster featuring fascinating facts about what and how it eats.
Book Tie-In, Creating a Menu	✦ Use *How to Eat Fried Worms* (Thomas Rockwell, Watts, 1973), about Billy who bets his friends that he can eat 15 worms a day. Have students follow up the reading by creating worm menus for Billy that feature creative worm meals.
Other Word Forms, Vocabulary Skills, Writing Sentences	✦ Have students brainstorm for common other word forms of *eat: eats, eating, eaten, ate, eatery.* Discuss unfamiliar words. Have students write the other word forms in sentences.
Synonyms	✦ Have students write synonyms for *eat (gobble, snack, gnaw, consume, swallow).*

Research and Writing, Public Speaking	❖ Have students research one of the following topics, tell about their findings in writing, and then present the information orally to the class: restaurants in your community careers in the food industry how airline food is planned and prepared
Sorting Words	❖ Play the Mr. Pickyfood game (see *Spelling Sourcebook 1*, page 88).

304 *short*

Book Tie-Ins, Writing Short Stories, Creating a Book	❖ Introduce students to books of short stories. Examples could include *Rats on the Roof and Other Stories* (James Marshall, Dial, 1991), *A Trick of the Light: Stories to Read at Dusk* (Jackie Vivelo, Putnam, 1987), featuring nine eerie stories, and *Short Takes: A Short Story Collection for Young Readers* (Elizabeth Segel, Lothrop, 1986). Have students work in cooperative groups to create a book of original short stories.
Other Word Forms, Vocabulary Skills, Writing Sentences, Suffix Practice	❖ Have students brainstorm for common other word forms of *short: shorts, shorted, shorting, shortly, shortness, shorten.* Discuss unfamiliar words. Review the *ly* suffix and have students write sentences using these words plus *ly: short, true* (296), *near* (243), *hard* (242), *night* (231).
Idiomatic Usage, Writing Explanations	❖ Ask students to explain in writing what they think it means to say each of these expressions (then discuss): caught short to get the short end of the stick in short order to run short short and sweet

305 *United States*

Book Tie-In, Completing a Project	❖ Use *Kids' America* (Steven Caney, Workman, 1978), a collection of information and projects focusing on US food, holidays, music, schools, people, jobs, and hobbies. Have students complete a project suggested in the book.
Abbreviations	❖ Ask students how *United States* is abbreviated (US or USA). Then create a book of common abbreviations including the Post Office abbreviations for each of the states and Canadian provinces.
Book Tie-In, Research and Writing, Creating a Book	❖ Use *The Spice of America* (June Swanson, Carolrhoda, 1983), a book of unusual, factual stories about America's past. Have students research other interesting trivia to add to the collection and compile it into a class-made book.

306 *run*

Book Tie-In, Research and Writing	❖ Use *Jim Thorpe: Young Athlete* (Laurence Santrey, Troll, 1983) to introduce the great runner. Thorpe's Indian heritage is highlighted. Have interested students research current records for running and write a report on their findings.
Multiple Meanings, Writing Sentences	❖ Brainstorm for meanings of *run.* Then have students check a dictionary for verification. Ask students to write sentences to illustrate the different meanings. Review these words with multiple meanings: *side* (203), *kind* (214), *hand* (223), *light* (227), *country* (228), *second* (235), *paper* (241), *hard* (242), *room* (266), *top* (269), *point* (272), *play* (274), *turn* (289), *face* (291), *cut* (293), and *short* (304). Have students write the words in sentences to illustrate their different meanings.

Other Word Forms, Writing Sentences, Suffix Practice	✦ Have students brainstorm for common other word forms for *run: runs, running, ran, runner*. Have students write the other word forms in sentences. Review the spelling rule for adding suffixes that applies to *run* (see **Spelling Sourcebook 1**, page 85). Review adding suffixes to *cut* (293), *top* (269), *sun* (257), *let* (230), *set* (162), *put* (138), and *get* (101).
Idiomatic Usage, Writing Explanations	✦ Ask students to explain in writing what they think it means to say each of these expressions (then discuss):

> in the long run
> to be off to a running start
> to get the run-around
> to be run down
> to run something into the ground
> run-of-the-mill
> Still waters run deep.

307 *book*

Book Tie-In, Sequencing	✦ Use *How a Book is Made* (Aliki, Crowell, 1986) to show students the stages in publishing a book. Follow up with students identifying the steps and writing them in sequential order.
Writing a Letter	✦ Have students write a letter to the author of a favorite book. Letters can be sent to the authors in care of the publisher.
Analogies, Writing Sentences	✦ Review analogies (see 139, 167, 262). Introduce the use of colons to write analogies. Then have students write these analogies and complete them with the appropriate word:

> play : toy :: read : _____ (book)
> cut : cutting :: run : _____ (running)
> Alberta : Canada :: Utah : _____ (United States [305])
> sooner : later :: false : _____ (true [296])
> sun : son :: scene : _____ (seen [280])
> room : house :: page : _____ (book)
> nearly : near :: shortly : _____ (short [304])
> do not : don't :: did not : _____ (didn't [281])

Have students write the answer words in sentences.

Idiomatic Usage, Writing Explanations	✦ Ask students to explain in writing what they think it means to say each of these expressions (then discuss):

> by the book
> to hit the books
> one for the books
> to throw the book at someone

Research and Writing, Public Speaking	✦ Have students research one of the following topics, tell about their findings in writing, and then present the information orally to the class:

> Caldecott and Newbery Medal books
> the most popular children's books according to librarians and book sales
>   from book stores
> the career of a book editor

308 *gave*

Sound-Symbol Awareness, Writing Sentences
◆ Ask students to write *gave*. Then have them follow these directions to write new and review words:

Change *gave* to make *save, brave, pave, rave, wave, grave*.
Change *gave* to make *have* (25).
Change *gave* to make *game*.
Change *gave* to make *gate*.
Change *gave* to make *give* (159).

Have students write a sentence for each word they made.

Other Word Forms, Vocabulary Skills, Writing Sentences
◆ Review common other word forms of *gave: give* (159), *gives, giving, giver, given*. Discuss unfamiliar words. Have students write the other word forms in sentences.

Writing Words
◆ Have students play Connect the Dots (see **Spelling Sourcebook 1**, page 87) to reinforce *gave* and selected review words.

309 *order*

Multiple Meanings, Writing Sentences
◆ Brainstorm for meanings of *order*. Then have students check a dictionary for verification. Ask students to write sentences to illustrate the different meanings.

Book Tie-In, Sound-Symbol Awareness, Creating a Book
◆ Use *From Acorn to Zoo: And Everything in Between in Alphabetical Order* (Satoshi Kitamura, Farrar, 1992) for sentences that feature one letter of the alphabet: for *k*, "a kangaroo in a knotted apron fries an egg in the kitchen for a king and a koala." Have students use the book as a model for their own alphabetical book.

Other Word Forms, Vocabulary Skills, Writing Sentences
◆ Have students brainstorm for common other word forms of *order: orders, ordered, ordering, orderly, orderliness*. Discuss unfamiliar words. Have students write the other word forms in sentences.

Prefix Practice
◆ Review the *re* prefix. Have students write the prefix with *order, run* (306), *plant(s)* (300), *group* (295), *move* (290), and *turn* (289).

Filling Out an Order Form
◆ Have students bring mail-order catalogs to class and practice filling out an order form.

Idiomatic Usage, Writing Explanations
◆ Ask students to explain in writing what they think it means to say each of these expressions (then discuss):

something is on back order
to call the meeting to order
made to order
out of order
in apple-pie order

310 *open*

Antonyms
◆ Introduce the antonym of *open*, the word *close*.

Idiomatic Usage, Writing Explanations
◆ Ask students to explain in writing what they think it means to say each of these expressions (then discuss):

to open a can of worms
to open Pandora's box
to open your heart to someone
to open up to someone

Other Word Forms, Vocabulary Skills, Writing Sentences

✦ Have students brainstorm for common other word forms of *open: opens, opened, opening, openly, opener, openness*. Discuss unfamiliar words. Have students write the other word forms in sentences.

Hypothesizing, Writing Explanations

✦ The first can opener was invented by William Lyman in 1870, but the tin can has been used since 1810. Ask students to write how they think cans may have been opened before people had can openers. (with sharp tools)

Other Word Forms, Writing Words

✦ Have students play All in the Family using other word forms of *open* and selected review words (see **Spelling Sourcebook 1**, page 86).

311 *ground*

Research and Writing

✦ Have students research Ground Hog Day and explain in writing the superstition related to February 2.

Idiomatic Usage, Writing Explanations

✦ Ask students to explain in writing what they think it means to say each of these expressions (then discuss):

    to break new ground
    to cover a lot of ground
    to drive something into the ground
    to get in on the ground floor
    to hold your ground
    to lose ground

Multiple Meanings, Writing Sentences

✦ Brainstorm for meanings of *ground*. Then have students check a dictionary for verification. Ask students to write sentences to illustrate the different meanings.

Other Word Forms, Vocabulary Skills, Writing Sentences

✦ Have students brainstorm for common other word forms of *ground: grounds, grounded, grounding*. Discuss unfamiliar words. Have students write the other word forms in sentences.

Writing Words

✦ Have students play the All-Play Spelling Bee (see **Spelling Sourcebook 1**, page 86) using *ground* and selected review words.

312 *cold*

Book Tie-In, Informational Writing

✦ Use *Antarctica* (Helen Cowcher, Farrar, 1990), a superb picture book with brief text that will introduce students to Antarctica. Prior to the reading, ask students what they know about this continent. As a follow-up to the reading, ask students to write one thing they learned.

Book Tie-In, Writing Similes

✦ *BRRR!* (James Stevenson, Greenwillow, 1991) is a tall tale Grandpa tells to the children when they complain of the winter's cold. Follow up with students writing similes: as cold as _____ .

Antonyms

✦ Introduce the antonym of *cold*, the word *hot*.

Idiomatic Usage, Writing Explanations

✦ Ask students to explain in writing what they think it means to say each of these expressions (then discuss):

    to get cold feet
    to get the cold shoulder
    out cold
    to blow hot and cold
    to catch a cold

Other Word Forms, Vocabulary Skills, Writing Sentences
✦ Have students brainstorm for common other word forms of *cold: colds, colder, coldest, coldness, coldly.* Discuss unfamiliar words. Have students write the other word forms in sentences.

Research and Writing, Public Speaking
✦ Have students research one of the following topics, tell about their findings in writing, and then present the information orally to the class:

the newest technology in cold weather clothing

the meaning of *average daily temperature*

the coldest and hottest temperatures ever recorded in your state or province

313 *really*

Dictation and Writing
✦ Dictate these partial sentences and have students complete them:

One thing I do really well is _____ .

I have a really good time when _____ .

Once when it was really cold, _____ .

I'm really sure _____ .

I don't really like to _____ .

Word Analysis, Writing Words
✦ Write *r _ _ lly* on the chalkboard. Ask students to fill in the vowels to make *really* and then to write the whole word. Extend the fill-in activity to include *ground* (311), *true* (296) *turn* (289) *money* (279), *usually* (278), *learn* (271), *against* (268), *several* (263), *heard* (262), *young* (256), *country* (228), *earth* (220), *enough* (209), *thought* (179), *people* (79), *through* (102), *around* (120), *because* (127), and *does* (128). Then have students choose words to continue the game with a partner.

Other Word Forms, Vocabulary Skills, Writing Sentences
✦ Have students brainstorm for common other word forms of *really: real, reality, realize, realistic.* Discuss unfamiliar words. Have students write the other word forms in sentences.

314 *table*

Book Tie-In, Writing Advice, Creating a Book
✦ Use *From Hand to Mouth: Or How We Invented Knives, Forks, Spoons, and Chopsticks & the Table Manners to Go With Them* (James Giblin, Harper, 1987), a cross-cultural guide to table manners. Follow up by posing questions to students about table manners and asking them to respond as an advice columnist might. Compile the questions and answers into a class-made advice book.

Creating a Word Puzzle
✦ Have students create a word-search puzzle (see Letter Grid Games in **Spelling Sourcebook 1**, page 88) using *table* and selected review words. Students can exchange games and complete the puzzles.

315 *remember*

Book Tie-In, Writing an Epitaph
✦ Use *The Remembering Box* (Eth Clifford, Houghton, 1985), in which Joshua's grandmother makes him a "remembering box" shortly before she dies. Have students write an epitaph for Joshua's grandmother following the reading.

Other Word Forms, Vocabulary Skills, Writing Sentences
✦ Have students brainstorm for common other word forms of *remember: remembers, remembered, remembering, remembrance.* Discuss unfamiliar words. Have students write the other word forms in sentences.

Antonyms, Book Tie-In,
Writing a Story Ending

◆ Introduce the antonym of *remember*, the word *forget*. Use *Soap! Soap! Don't Forget The Soap!: An Appalachian Folktale* (Tom Birdseye, Holiday, 1993) featuring a boy with a bad memory. Have students write the story ending with the game Finish the Story to reinforce selected review words (see *Spelling Sourcebook 1*, page 88).

316 *tree*

Book Tie-In, Informational
Writing, Art

◆ Use *Tree of Life: The World of the African Baobab* (Barbara Bash, Sierra Club/Little, 1989) for an introduction to this amazing tree. Make a bulletin board baobab tree. Then ask students to write interesting facts about the tree to hang from its branches. This activity could be expanded to other trees indigenous to the area.

Book Tie-In,
Predicting

◆ A sensitive departure from traditional December holiday books is *Night Tree* (Eve Bunting, Harcourt, 1991), in which a family decorates a tree in the forest with food tidbits for the hungry animals. Prior to the reading, ask students to predict what foods might be included on a tree decorated for the forest animals' consumption.

Sound-Symbol Awareness,
Sorting Words

◆ Review the *ee* words *see* (68), *three* (125), *between* (154), *keep* (199), *feet* (201), and *seen* (280). Ask students to listen to the long *e* sound in the words. Then have them collect more words with the long *e* sound and sort them to note the most frequent spellings for long *e* (most common: *ee* [see], *e* [me], *ea* [eat], *e*-consonant-*e* [these]). Ask students to find examples of each. Have one category for "other" to accommodate less common spellings.

Research and Writing,
Public Speaking

◆ Have students research one of the following topics, tell about their findings in writing, and then present the information orally to the class:

how tree rings are formed within a tree trunk
the difference between deciduous and evergreen trees
kinds of flowering trees

317 *course*

Multiple Meanings,
Writing Sentences

◆ Brainstorm for meanings of *course*. Then have students check a dictionary for verification. Ask students to write sentences to illustrate the different meanings. Review these words with multiple meanings: *side* (203), *kind* (214), *hand* (223), *light* (227), *country* (228), *second* (235), *paper* (241), *hard* (242), *room* (266), *top* (269), *point* (272), *play* (274), *turn* (289), *face* (291), *cut* (293), *short* (304), *ground* (311), *order* (309), and *run* (306). Have students write the words in sentences to illustrate their different meanings.

Homophone Usage,
Writing Sentences

◆ Introduce the homophone of *course*, the word *coarse*. Discuss its meaning. Then have students use the homophones in written sentences to differentiate them.

Idiomatic Usage,
Writing Explanations

◆ Ask students to explain in writing what they think it means to say each of these expressions (then discuss):

as a matter of course
in due course
par for the course

318 *front*

Writing Newspaper Headlines

◆ Have students look at the front page of a newspaper and identify the information (name, date, city, table of contents, most important stories). Discuss headlines and their purpose (to create interest and attention for the story, to sell papers).

Then provide students with news stories clipped from a newspaper and have them write the front page headlines.

Antonyms ✦ Review the antonym of *front*, the word *back* (103).

Art, Writing Explanations ✦ Ask students to draw and label a map to explain a weather *front*.

Writing Words ✦ Have students play Password with *front* and selected review words (see **Spelling Sourcebook 1**, page 89).

319 *American*

Art, Writing Reasons, Research and Writing, Comparing and Contrasting ✦ Brainstorm for American symbols (Uncle Sam, eagle, US flag, Great Seal, etc.). Then ask each student to create a new American symbol and write why it's a good one. Have students research the symbols of countries such as *Canada*, and compare and contrast them with American symbols.

Analogies, Writing Sentences ✦ Review analogies (see 307) and the use of colons for words. Then have students write these analogies and complete them with the appropriate word:

Canada : Canadian :: America : _____ (American)
cold : hot :: back : _____ (front [318])
no : know :: coarse : _____ (course [317])
arm : body :: branch : _____ (tree [316]) or trunk)
close : open :: forget : _____ (remember [315])
fold : told :: fable : _____ (table [314])

Have students write the answer words in sentences.

Capitalization ✦ Discuss the capital *A* in *American*. Discuss capitals in *I* (24), *I'm* (284), *United States* (305), *Canada*, and *Canadian*.

320 *space*

Book Tie-In, Writing a Journal Entry ✦ *A Flight of Discovery Aboard the Space Shuttle* (Barbara Embury, Harper, 1990) uses dramatic pictures and text to describe what shuttle passengers see when they look back to Earth. Have students write a journal entry for one day in space aboard the shuttle.

Book Tie-In, Writing Predictions, Vocabulary Skills ✦ For a dictionary of space vocabulary, use *Space Words* (Seymour Simon, HarperCollins, 1991). The dictionary format includes illustrations and concise explanations. Before exploring the book, have students list those words they think will be included.

Sound-Symbol Awareness, Writing Sentences ✦ Ask students to write *space*. Then have them follow these directions to write new and review words:

Change *space* to make *face* (291), *race, grace, lace, place* (131).
Change *space* to make *spice*.
Change *space* to make *ace*.

Have students write a sentence for each word they made.

Other Word Forms, Vocabulary Skills, Writing Sentences ✦ Have students brainstorm for common other word forms of *space*: *spaces, spaced, spacing, spacious*. Discuss unfamiliar words. Have students write the other word forms in sentences.

Research and Writing, Public Speaking ✦ Have students research one of the following topics, tell about their findings in writing, and then present the information orally to the class:

Sally Ride
current NASA projects
the qualifications required of astronauts

321 *inside*

Antonyms ✧ Introduce the antonym of *inside*, the word *outside*.

Writing Predictions ✧ Ask each student to prepare a sealed bag containing a familiar mystery object. Play "What's Inside?" by asking students to feel the contents and write what they think the object inside might be. Then they compare the predictions with the actual contents of the bags.

Compound Words, ✧ Have students create a list of compound words. Then play Compound Bingo
Writing Words (see ***Spelling Sourcebook 1***, page 87) using the compound words.

322 *ago*

Word Analysis, ✧ Have students write *ago* and listen to the unaccented *a*. Review *a* _____
Alphabetical Order words. Include *about* (48), *around* (120), *away* (140), *along* (171), *above* (213), *across* (247), *against* (268), *American* (319). Have students write the words in alphabetical order.

Writing Sentences ✧ Have students play Sentence Puzzles using *ago* and selected review words (see ***Spelling Sourcebook 1***, page 91).

323 *sad*

Sequencing, ✧ Point out that some good stories make us feel sad. Ask students to rate their
Conducting a Survey favorite tearful tales on a scale of 1 to 10 tissues. How many are necessary for the reading? Create a bulletin board with the results of the survey.

Book Tie-Ins, Writing Stories ✧ Young readers learn from the experiences of others through books. The touching story of Robbie's sadness when his mother dies is found in *There Are Two Kinds of Terrible* (Peggy Mann, Doubleday, 1977). Also use *Mama's Going to Buy You a Mockingbird* (Jean Little, Viking, 1984), which also explores grief at death. Follow up by discussing the kinds of experiences that make people feel sad. Then have students write about one that happened to them.

Other Word Forms, Vocabulary ✧ Have students brainstorm for common other word forms of *sad: sadder, saddest,*
Skills, Suffix Practice, *sadden, sadly, sadness.* Discuss unfamiliar words. Have students write the other
Spelling Rules word forms in sentences. Review the spelling rule for doubling the consonant before adding a suffix (see ***Spelling Sourcebook 1***, page 85). Have students brainstorm for more words that follow this rule *(run* [306], *cut* [293], *top* [269], *sun* [257], *let* [230], *set* [162], *put* [138], *get* [101], *shop, drop, hit, ship, stop).* Then have students write the words with the suffixes.

Antonyms, ✧ Introduce the antonym of *sad*, the word *happy*. Then have students create a
Creating a Greeting Card greeting card to give to someone to make the person feel happy.

324 *early*

Word Analysis ✧ Have students write *early* and underline *ear*. Contrast the pronunciation of the letters in *ear* and *early*.

Antonyms ✧ Introduce the antonym of *early*, the word *late*.

Other Word Forms, ✧ Have students brainstorm for common other word forms of *early: earlier*
Writing Comparatives *earliest*. Review comparison usage with *sad* (323), *cold* (312), *later* (288), *sun* (257), *young* (256), *sure* (251), *good* (106), *better* (245), *best* (246), *hard* (242), *white* (239), *soon* (236), *light* (227), *high* (224), *large* (185), *great* (146), *new* (107), and *little* (92). Have students write the words in comparison sentences.

Idiomatic Usage,
Writing Explanations
	◆ Ask students to explain in writing what they think it means to say each of these expressions (then discuss):
	    bright and early
	    early on
	    Early to bed, early to rise, makes a man healthy, wealthy, and wise.
	    The early bird gets the worm.

325 *I'll*

Capitalization	◆ Have students write *I'll*. Discuss the capital *I* and capitalization rules. Review the use of capitals in *I* (24), *I'm* (284), *United States* (305), *American* (319), *Canada*, and *Canadian*. Ask students to find and write more words that should be capitalized.
Homophone Usage, *Writing Sentences*	◆ Introduce the homophones for *I'll*, the words *isle* and *aisle*. Discuss word meanings. Have students write the homophones in sentences to differentiate them.
Writing Words, *Homophone Usage*	◆ Have students play Mystery Words to reinforce usage of *I'll*, *aisle*, and *isle* and selected homophones (see **Spelling Sourcebook 1**, page 89).

326 *learned*

Other Word Forms, Spelling *Rules, Suffix Practice,* *Writing Sentences*	◆ Review the other word forms of *learned*: *learn* (271), *learns, learning, learner*. Review the spelling rule for the *er* suffix (see **Spelling Sourcebook 1**, page 85). Have students write the *er* suffix with *learn, open* (310), *run* (306), *cut* (293), *move* (290), *turn* (289), *play* (274), *point* (272), *keep* (199), *read* (165), *own* (163), *help* (137), *work* (124), *think* (118), *write* (108), and *time* (69). Have students write the words with the *er* suffixes in sentences.

Sound-Symbol Awareness,
Writing Sentences
	◆ Ask students to write *learned*. Then have them follow these directions to write new and review words:
	    Change *learned* to make *learn* (271).
	    Change *learned* to make *earned*.
	    Take one letter away from *learned* to make *leaned*.
	Have students write a sentence for each word they made.

327 *brought*

Sound-Symbol Awareness,
Writing Sentences
	◆ Ask students to write *brought*. Then have them follow these directions to write new and review words:
	    Change *brought* to make *bought*.
	    Change *brought* to make *ought*.
	    Change *brought* to make *thought* (179).
	Have students write a sentence for each word they made.

Word Analysis, Writing Words	◆ Have students brainstorm for words that are spelled with a silent *gh* (*through* [102], *right* [116], *might* [173], *thought* [179], *enough* [209], *high* [224], *light* [227], *night* [231]). Then have students write the words and underline the silent letters.
Other Word Forms, *Writing Sentences*	◆ Have students brainstorm for common other word forms of *brought*: *bring, brings, bringing*. Expand the lesson to other word forms of *thought* (179). Have students write the other word forms in sentences.

Dictation, Proofreading
✦ Have students play Sentence Spelling to reinforce dictation and proofreading skills (see **Spelling Sourcebook 1**, page 91).

328 *close*

Homophone Usage, Writing Sentences
✦ Introduce the homophone of *close*, the word *clothes*. Have students use the homophones in written sentences to differentiate them.

Homograph Usage, Writing Sentences
✦ Review homographs (*use* [88], *does* [128], *read* [165], *live* [217]). Then have students use *close* and other homograph partners in written sentences to differentiate them.

Antonyms
✦ Review one antonym of *close*, the word *open* (310); and another antonym, the word *far* (222).

Other Word Forms, Vocabulary Skills, Writing Sentences
✦ Introduce the other word forms for the two different forms of the homograph *close: closes, closed, closing; closer, closest, closely, closeness*. Discuss word meanings. Have students write the other word forms in sentences.

Idiomatic Usage, Writing Explanations
✦ Have students explain in writing what they think it means to say each of these expressions (then discuss):
  too close for comfort
  a close call
  to close down
  to draw to a close

329 *nothing*

Compound Words, Writing Words
✦ Have students write *nothing* and underline the two word parts of the compound. Have students brainstorm for more compound words (*into* [61], *something* [178], *without* [204], *today* [249], *however* [250], *himself* [277], *upon* [286], *inside* [321]).

Writing Questions and Answers
✦ Have students play Questions and Answers to reinforce in context *nothing* and selected review words (see **Spelling Sourcebook 1**, page 90).

330 *though*

Word Analysis, Writing Sentences, Writing Words
✦ Have students write the look-alike words *though, thought* (179), and *through* (102). Introduce *thorough*. Then have students write the words in sentences to differentiate among them.

Writing Explanations, Sound-Symbol Awareness
✦ The *ou* is the most variant vowel spelling pattern. Help students discover this with *though, through* (102), *would* (59), *our* (109), *four* (211), *country* (228), *group* (295), *enough* (209), and *brought* (327). Have students find and write more *ou* words. Then have students summarize in writing the variability of the *ou* in English spellings.

331 *idea*

Dictation and Writing
✦ Dictate these partial sentences and have students complete them:
  It would be a good idea to _____.
  One really bad idea I once had was _____.
  My idea of a great day is _____.
  I usually get my best ideas when _____.

Research and Writing, ✦ Have students research one of the following topics, tell about their findings in
Public Speaking writing, and then present the information orally to the class:
                    inventors and their ideas
                    the purpose of patents
                    contrasting of ideas for the solution to a current
                        newsworthy problem

332 *before*

Idiomatic Usage, ✦ Ask students to explain in writing what they think it means to say each of these
Writing Explanations expressions (then discuss):
                    Don't count your chickens before they hatch.
                    before long
                    to cast pearls before swine
                    to put the cart before the horse
                    to think twice before doing something

Antonyms ✦ Review the antonym of *before*, the word *after* (94).

Antonyms, Writing Words ✦ Have students play the All-Play Spelling Bee (see ***Spelling Sourcebook 1***, page
                86) with this variation: Use only antonyms and have the players write the
                antonym of the word that is said.

Hypothesizing, ✦ Have students hypothesize and report in writing:
Writing Predictions
                    What might happen if dessert was always served and eaten before the rest
                        of the meal?
                    What might happen if the car engine is started in the garage before the
                        garage door is opened?
                    What might happen if the movie projector at the cinema breaks before the
                        end of the movie?

333 *lived*

Other Word Forms, ✦ Review the other word forms of *lived*: *live* (217), *lives, living* (301), *livable*.
Spelling Rules   Review *life* (208) and *lives* and the spelling rule that applies to the words (see
                Spelling Sourcebook 1, page 85).

Antonyms ✦ Introduce the antonym of *lived*, the word *died*.

Hypothesizing, ✦ Have students choose a historical period. Then ask them to hypothesize in
Writing Descriptions writing what life might have been like if they had lived during that time.

Analogies, Writing Sentences ✦ Review analogies (see 307, 319) and the use of colons for words. Then have
                students write these analogies and complete them with the appropriate word:
                    give : giving :: live : _____ (living)
                    inside : outside :: after : _____ (before [332])
                    there : their :: aisle : _____ (I'll [325] or isle)
                    bring : brought :: learn : _____ (learned [326])
                    sad : happy :: late : _____ (early [324])
                    shut : close :: zero : _____ (nothing [329])
                Have students write the answer words in sentences.

334 *became*

Other Word Forms, Vocabulary ✦ Introduce the other word forms of *became: become, becomes, becoming*. Discuss
Skills, Writing Sentences unfamiliar words. Have students write the other word forms in sentences.

Writing Words ✦ Have students play Race Track Spelling using *became* and selected review words (see ***Spelling Sourcebook 1***, page 90).

Sound-Symbol Awareness, Writing Sentences ✦ Ask students to write *became*. Then have them follow these directions to write new and review words:

Change *became* to make *came* (122).
Change *became* to make *become*.
Change *became* to make *because* (127).

Have students write a sentence for each word they made.

335 *add*

Antonyms ✦ Introduce the antonym of *add*, the word *subtract*.

Other Word Forms, Vocabulary Skills, Writing Sentences ✦ Have students brainstorm for common other word forms of *add: added, adds, adding, addition, additional*. Discuss unfamiliar words. Have students write the other word forms in sentences.

Homophone Usage, Writing Sentences ✦ Introduce the homophone of *add*, the word *ad* (the clipped form of *advertisement*). Have students write the homophones in sentences to differentiate them.

Hypothesizing, Writing Predictions ✦ Have students hypothesize and report in writing:

What do you think might happen if you add freshwater fish to the saltwater aquarium?
What might the outcome be if you add red paint to a can of white paint? Yellow paint? Blue paint?

336 *become*

Other Word Forms, Writing Sentences ✦ Review the other word forms of *become: becomes, becoming, became* (334). Note the other word forms of *come*. Have students write the other word forms in sentences.

Writing the Past Tense ✦ Ask students to brainstorm for words that change their spellings in the past tense rather than add *ed* (*become/became* [334], *run* [306]/*ran*, *give* [159]/*gave* [308], *say* [149]/*said* [43], *find* [87]/*found* [152], *think* [118]/*thought* [179], *begin/began* [215], *come* [123]/*came* [122]).

337 *grow*

Book Tie-In, Comparing and Contrasting, Making a Chart ✦ Use *Eat the Fruit, Plant the Seed* (Millicent Selsam, Morrow, 1980) to help students learn how to grow such plants as avocados, citrus, and pumpkins. Follow up by having students collect different versions of the classic story "Jack and the Beanstalk" to compare and contrast. Have students create a chart of the differences.

Book Tie-In, Writing Reasons ✦ Use *Through Our Eyes: Poems and Pictures About Growing Up* (Lee Bennett Hopkins, selector, Little, 1992) to begin a collection of favorite poems and stories about the feelings and challenges of growing up. Have students decide what age would be their favorite age to be and write reasons why.

Other Word Forms, Vocabulary Skills, Homophone Usage, Writing Sentences ✦ Have students brainstorm for common other word forms of *grow: grows, grew, growing, grown, grower, growth*. Discuss the homophone *grown, groan*. Have students write the words in sentences.

Sound-Symbol Awareness,
Sorting Words

✦ Write _ow on the chalkboard. Ask students to add beginning letters to make new words that rhyme with *grow*. Have them listen to the long *o* sound in the words and then collect more words with the long *o* sound to note the most frequent spelling for long *o* (most common: *o [no], o*-consonant-*e [those], ow [show], oa [coat], o [cold], oe [toe]*). Create a list of long *o* words. Have students write the words in categories sorted by the spelling for the long *o*. Have one category for "other" to accommodate less common spellings.

338 *draw*

Book Tie-In

✦ Use *Draw!* (Kim Solga, North Light, 1991) to encourage kids to experiment with drawing.

Multiple Meanings,
Writing Sentences

✦ Have students brainstorm for different meanings of *draw*. Then have them check a dictionary for verification. Ask students to write sentences using the different meanings.

Other Word Forms, Vocabulary
Skills, Writing Sentences

✦ Have students brainstorm for common other word forms of *draw: draws, drew, drawing, drawn, drawer*. Discuss unfamiliar words. Have students write the other word forms in sentences.

Idiomatic Usage,
Writing Explanations

✦ Ask students to explain in writing what they think it means to say each of these expressions (then discuss):

back to the drawing board
to beat someone to the draw
to draw a blank
to draw blood
to draw to a close
to draw the line

339 *yet*

Sound-Symbol Awareness,
Writing Sentences

✦ Ask students to write *yet*. Then have them follow these directions to write new and review words:

Change *yet* to make *get* (101), *net, jet, pet, let* (230),
    set (162), *wet, fret*.
Change *yet* to make *yes*.
Change *yet* to make *yell*.
Have students write a sentence for each word they made.

340 *less*

Usage, Writing Sentences

✦ Introduce the use of *less* and *fewer (fewer:* can be counted/*less:* refers to quantity). Have students use the words in writing to differentiate them.

Other Word Forms, Vocabulary
Skills, Writing Sentences

✦ Have students brainstorm for common other word forms of *less: lesser, lessen, least*. Discuss unfamiliar words. Have students write the other word forms in sentences.

Antonyms,
Creating a Word Puzzle

✦ Introduce the antonym of *less*, the word *more* (63). Then review selected antonyms. Have students make a word search puzzle using antonym pairs. Have them hide one antonym partner in the puzzle and write the other as a clue (see Letter Grid Games, *Spelling Sourcebook 1*, page 88).

Idiomatic Usage,
Writing Explanations

Ask students to explain in writing what they think it means to say each of these expressions (then discuss):

couldn't care less
in less than no time
more or less

Suffix Practice,
Writing Sentences

Review *less* as a suffix. Have students add *less* to *help* (137), *name* (155), *home* (157), *end* (170), and *need* (221). Have students brainstorm for more words that can take the *less* suffix. Discuss the meanings of the words. Then have students write the words with the *less* suffix in sentences.

341 *wind*

Book Tie-In,
Writing Predictions

Use *The Sea-Breeze Hotel* (Marcia Vaughan, HarperCollins, 1992), a humorous story of a "boisterous, blustery breeze" that initially is perceived as a bad thing. Have students write predictions of the story solution before reading how the wind becomes a positive entity.

Synonyms

Have students write synonyms for *wind* and then sequence the synonyms by intensity.

Book Tie-In,
Writing a Summary

Use *What Makes the Wind?* (Laurence Santrey, Troll, 1982) as an introduction to the wind as a weather factor. Follow up by asking students to summarize in writing the answer to the question in the book's title.

Homograph Usage,
Writing Sentences

Review the homographs *use* (88), *does* (128), *read* (165), *live* (217), and *close* (328). Have students use *wind* in sentences to illustrate its two different meanings and pronunciations. Ask students to brainstorm for more homographs *(object, desert, present).*

Other Word Forms,
Writing Words

Have students brainstorm for common other word forms for the two homographs *wind: windy, windier, windiest, winds;* and *wind: winds, wound, winding.*

342 *behind*

Antonyms

Introduce antonyms of *behind,* the phrase *in front of,* or the word *ahead.*

Idiomatic Usage,
Writing Explanations

Ask students to explain in writing what they think it means to say each of these expressions (then discuss):

behind someone's back
behind the eight ball
behind the scenes
to get behind

Word Analysis,
Alphabetical Order

Have students brainstorm for *be _____* words *(because* [127], *between* [154], *below* [176], *began* [215], *before* [332], *became* [334], *become* [336], *beside, believe, belong).* Then have them write the words in alphabetical order.

343 *cannot*

Compound Words, Contractions

Have students write *cannot* and underline the two word parts of the compound. Then have them write the contraction *can't.* Review contractions by asking students to write contractions and the words that they comprise. Include *don't* (190), *didn't* (281), *I'm* (284), *I'll* (325).

Compound Words,
Writing Words

Have students brainstorm for compound words. Then play Spelling Baseball using the compounds (see *Spelling Sourcebook 1,* page 91).

344 *letter*

Book Tie-In, Writing a Letter
◆ Use *The Jolly Postman* (Janet and Allan Ahlberg, Little, 1986), a book of humorous postcards and letters sent to classic fairy tale characters. Ask students to add another letter to the collection.

Book Tie-Ins, Alliteration, Writing Sentences
◆ Use *Once Upon A to Z: An Alphabet Odyssey* (Jody Linscott, (Doubleday, 1991) and *The Horrendous Hullabaloo* (Margaret Mahy, Viking, 1992) to introduce alliteration to students. Follow up with students writing sentences made almost entirely of words beginning with the same letter.

Other Word Forms, Vocabulary Skills, Writing Sentences
◆ Have students brainstorm for common other word forms of *letter: letters, lettered, lettering*. Discuss unfamiliar words. Have students write the other word forms in sentences.

Multiple Meanings, Writing Sentences
◆ Brainstorm for meanings of *letter*. Then have students check a dictionary for verification. Ask students to write sentences to illustrate the different meanings. Review these words with multiple meanings: *side* (203), *kind* (214), *hand* (223), *light* (227), *country* (228), *second* (235), *paper* (241), *hard* (242), *room* (266), *top* (269), *point* (272), *play* (274), *turn* (289), *face* (291), *cut* (293), *short* (304), *run* (306), *order* (309), *ground* (311), *course* (317), *close* (328), *draw* (338). Have students write the words in sentences to illustrate their different meanings.

345 *among*

Usage, Writing Sentences
◆ Introduce appropriate usage of *among* and *between* (*among:* with 3 or more/*between:* with 2). Have students write the words in sentences.

Sorting Words
◆ Have students play Word Sorts (see **Spelling Sourcebook 1**, page 92) using these words: *among, long* (91), *about* (48), *around* (120), *thing* (258), *away* (140), *along* (171), *alone, belong*.

346 *able*

Other Word Forms, Vocabulary Skills, Writing Sentences
◆ Have students brainstorm for common other word forms for *able: abler, ablest, ably, ability*. Discuss unfamiliar words. Have students write the other word forms in sentences.

Prefix Practice
◆ Review the *un* prefix. Ask students to write *unable* and define it. Have students add the *un* prefix to *wind* (341), *open(ed)* (310), *true* (296), and *American* (319).

Suffix Practice, Spelling Rules, Writing Sentences
◆ Introduce *able* used as a suffix. Have students add *able* to *use* (88), *work* (124), *read* (165), *change* (264), *move* (290), and *live* (217). Review the spelling rule for adding suffixes to words that end in silent *e* (see **Spelling Sourcebook 1**, page 85). Then have students write the words with the *able* suffix in sentences.

347 *dog*

Book Tie-In, Writing Poetry
◆ Use *Dog Poems* (Myra Cohn Livingston, Holiday, 1990) as a catalyst for students' own canine poetry.

Book Tie-In, Writing Descriptions
◆ Use *Walt Disney's 101 Dalmatians: Illustrated Classic* (Ann Baybrooks, adapted from film, Disney, 1991), about Dalmatians and their human pets. Follow up by having students list breeds of dogs, beginning with Dalmatian, and tell one distinguishing feature of each.

Other Word Forms,
Writing Sentences

✦ Have students brainstorm for common other word forms for *dog: dogs, doggy.* Have students write the other word forms in sentences.

Idiomatic Usage,
Writing Explanations

✦ Ask students to explain in writing what they think it means to say each of these expressions (then discuss):

as sick as a dog
call the dogs off
to lead a dog's life
Let sleeping dogs lie.
to put on the dog
raining cats and dogs
You can't teach an old dog new tricks.
in the doghouse

348 *shown*

Other Word Forms, Vocabulary
Skills, Writing Sentences

✦ Have students brainstorm for common other word forms for *shown: show, shows, showed, showing, showy.* Discuss unfamiliar words. Have students write the other word forms in sentences.

Homophone Usage,
Writing Words

✦ Introduce the homophone of *shown,* the word *shone.* Have students write the homophones in sentences to differentiate them. Have students brainstorm for more homophone partners. Then play Connect the Dots using the homophones (see *Spelling Sourcebook 1*, page 87).

Sound-Symbol Awareness,
Writing Sentences

✦ Ask students to write *shown.* Then have them follow these directions to write new and review words:

Change *shown* to make *own* (163).
Change *shown* to make *grown.* (The tree has *grown* tall.)
Change *shown* to make *down* (84), *town, frown, clown.*
Change *shown* to make *show* (184).
Change *shown* to make *how* (49).
Change *shown* to make *shower.*

Have students write a sentence for each word they made.

349 *mean*

Multiple Meanings,
Writing Sentences

✦ Ask students to brainstorm for meanings of *mean.* Discuss meanings of *means.* Then have students check a dictionary for verification. Have students write the different meanings in sentences.

Book Tie-In, Choral Reading,
Synonyms

✦ Use *The Mean Old Mean Hyena* (Jack Prelutsky, Greenwillow, 1978), and have fun chorally reading this tongue-tangling rhyming tale. Ask students to think of synonyms for *mean* to describe the hyena.

Other Word Forms, Vocabulary
Skills, Writing Sentences

✦ Have students brainstorm for common other word forms of *mean: meaner, meanest, means, meant, meaning, meaningful, meanly, meanness.* Discuss unfamiliar words. Have students write the other word forms in sentences.

Sound-Symbol Awareness,
Sorting Words

✦ Have students write *mean,* say the word, and listen to the long *e* sound. Then have them collect more words with the long *e* sound to note the most frequent spellings for long *e* (most common: *ee [see], e [me], ea [eat], e-consonant-e [these]*). Create a list of long *e* words. Have students write the words in categories sorted by the spelling for the long *e.* Have one category for "other" to accommodate less common spellings.

350 *English*

Book Tie-In, Writing Reasons

Use *I Hate English* (Ellen Levine, Scholastic, 1989), a picture book about Chinese Mei Mei and her challenge to learn English as a second language. Ask students to give reasons why they think Mei Mei's dislike for English was justified or not justified.

Book Tie-In, Word Lore, Creating a Book

Use *Talk About English: How Words Travel and Change* (Janet Klausner, Crowell, 1990) as a catalyst to research word lore and create a class-made book of interesting word stories.

Capitalization

Ask students to write *English*. Then have them list other words that are always capitalized. Choices may include *American* (319), *United States* (305), *Canadian*, *Abe Lincoln*, *Cherry Lane*, *Monday*, *Maple School*, *Thanksgiving*, *Mrs.*, *I*, and *Lake Erie*.

Research and Writing, Public Speaking

Have students research one of the following topics, tell about their findings in writing, and then present the information orally to the class:

How the English language was formed
A comparison of spellings of some words in British
   and American English
Words in the English language that have been borrowed
   from other languages (*bouquet*, French; *pizza*, Italian)

351 *rest*

Multiple Meanings, Writing Sentences

Brainstorm for meanings of *rest*. Then have students check a dictionary for verification. Ask students to write sentences to illustrate the different meanings.

Other Word Forms, Vocabulary Skills, Writing Sentences

Have students brainstorm for common other word forms of *rest: rests, rested, resting, restless, restlessness, restful.* Discuss unfamiliar words. Have students write the other word forms in sentences.

Idiomatic Usage, Writing Explanations

Ask students to explain in writing what they think it means to say each of these expressions (then discuss):

to put something to rest
rest assured
to rest on your laurels

Other Word Forms, Writing Words

Have students play All in the Family using other word forms of *rest* and selected review words (see *Spelling Sourcebook 1*, page 86).

352 *perhaps*

Dictation and Writing

Dictate these partial sentences and have students complete them:

After school today, perhaps I will _____.
Perhaps the best book I ever read was _____.
Perhaps all Americans (Canadians) should _____.
If I had enough money, perhaps _____.

353 *certain*

Other Word Forms, Vocabulary Skills, Writing Sentences

Have students brainstorm for common other word forms of *certain: certainly, certainty.* Discuss unfamiliar words. Have students write the other word forms in sentences.

Multiple Meanings, Writing Sentences

Have students check the meanings of *certain* in a dictionary and then write sentences to illustrate the different meanings.

354 *six*

Book Tie-In,
Writing Predictions

◆ Use *Six Sleepy Sheep* (Jeffie Ross Gordon, Caroline, 1991), in which "Six sleepy sheep slumber on six soft pillows in one big bed . . . UNTIL one sheep snored." Then the scenario begins! Ask students to write predictions of what might follow. Then complete the reading.

Book Tie-In, Writing a Sequel

◆ *Six-Dinner Sid* (Inga Moore, Simon, 1991) reinforces the word *six* through Sid the Cat's six different owners who call him by six different names, provide him with six homes, six cat beds, six dinners, and six trips to the vet when he catches cold. Ask students to write sequels to the story creating new adventures for Sid and his six life styles.

Book Tie-In, Creating a Book

◆ *Six By Seuss* (Dr. Seuss, Random, 1991) features six of the doctor's most beloved books. Follow up with students compiling booklets of their six best writing pieces, assignments, and illustrations. Title the booklets *Six By* _____ (name of student).

Other Word Forms, Writing
Sentences, Spelling Rules,
Writing Plurals

◆ Have students brainstorm for common other word forms of *six: sixes, sixth, sixteen, sixty.* Have students write the other word forms in sentences. Introduce the spelling rule for plurals that applies to *six* (see **Spelling Sourcebook 1**, page 85). Have students find and write more singular and plural words that follow this spelling rule.

355 *feel*

Book Tie-In, Writing Poetry

◆ Use *The Way I Feel . . . Sometimes* (Beatrice De Regniers, Ticknor, 1988), poetry about feelings. Follow up with students writing a short poem about the way they feel . . . sometimes.

Other Word Forms, Vocabulary
Skills, Writing Sentences

◆ Have students brainstorm for common other word forms of *feel: feels, felt, feeling, feelings.* Discuss unfamiliar words and the two meanings of *felt.* Have students write the other word forms in sentences.

Idiomatic Usage,
Writing Explanations

◆ Ask students to explain in writing what they think it means to say each of these expressions (then discuss):

    to feel out of place
    to feel fit
    to feel put upon
    to get the feel of something
    to feel free to do something

Predicting Spellings, Homophone
Usage, Writing Sentences

◆ Have students write *feel.* Then have them predict the spellings of *steel, wheel, heel, feet* (201), *feed, flee, fee,* and *free.* Discuss unfamiliar words. Have students find and write the homophones among the words *(steel, heel, feet, flee)* and write their homophone partner words. Discuss meanings and have students write the homophones in sentences to differentiate them.

356 *fire*

Book Tie-In,
Creating a Guide Book

◆ Use *Summer of Fire: Yellowstone* 1988 (Patricia Lauber, Orchard, 1991), in which the massive fire is placed within the historical life cycle of forests. Ask students to create a fire safety guide for forest users (see page 138, Creating Classroom Books).

Book Tie-In, Career Awareness,
Writing a Summary

◆ Use *A Day in the Life of a Firefighter* (Betsy Smith, Troll, 1981), an introduction to the career of firefighting. Follow up with students interviewing a firefighter for more information about this job. Have students summarize the information in writing.

Book Tie-In,
Comparing and Contrasting

◆ Use *Matilda, Who Told Lies, and Was Burned to Death* (Hilaire Belloc, Knopf, 1992), an amusing poem that parallels "The Boy Who Cried Wolf." Ask students to research the original version. Then have them compare and contrast it to Belloc's version, which includes, "for every time she shouted 'Fire!'" / They only answered 'Little Liar!'"

Other Word Forms, Vocabulary
Skills, Writing Sentences

◆ Have students brainstorm for common other word forms of *fire: fires, fired, firing, fiery*. Discuss unfamiliar words. Have students write the other word forms in sentences.

Idiomatic Usage,
Writing Explanations

◆ Ask students to explain in writing what they think it means to say each of these expressions (then discuss):

to keep the home fires burning
to add fuel to the fire
to have too many irons in the fire
out of the fry pan and into the fire
under fire
Where there's smoke, there's fire.

Multiple Meanings,
Writing Sentences

◆ Brainstorm for meanings of *fire*. Then have students check a dictionary for verification. Ask students to write sentences to illustrate the different meanings.

357 *ready*

Other Word Forms, Vocabulary
Skills, Writing Sentences

◆ Have students brainstorm for common other word forms of *ready: readier, readiest, readies, readied, readying, readily, readiness*. Discuss unfamiliar words. Have students write the other word forms in sentences.

Analogies, Writing Sentences

◆ Review analogies (see 307, 319, 333) and the use of colons. Then have students write these analogies and complete them with the appropriate word:

sun : sunnier :: ready : _____ (readier)
three : four :: five : _____ (six [354])
relax : rest :: maybe : _____ (perhaps [352])
can : cannot :: more : _____ (less [340])
uncertain : certain :: unable : _____ (able [346])
city : country :: in front of : _____ (behind [342])
Have students write the answer words in sentences.

Sound-Symbol Awareness,
Writing Questions

◆ Ask students to write *ready*. Then have them follow these directions to write new and review words:

Change *ready* to make *read* (165).
Change *ready* to make *really* (313).
Change *ready* to make *steady*.
Have students write a question for each word they made.

358 *green*

Book Tie-In,
Writing Explanations

◆ Use *The Big Green Book* (Fred Pearce, Grosset & Dunlap, 1991), which tells how humans affect the earth. Have students write what they can do to make a difference in preserving the green freshness of our environment.

Other Word Forms, Vocabulary Skills, Writing Sentences

◆ Have students brainstorm for common other word forms of *green: greener, greenest, greens, greenery, greenish*. Discuss unfamiliar words. Have students write the other word forms in sentences.

Idiomatic Usage, Writing Explanations

◆ Ask students to explain in writing what they think it means to say each of these expressions (then discuss):

> green with envy
> The grass is always greener on the other side of the fence.
> to have a green thumb
> to get the green light

Remember . . .

Develop spelling accountability as students write—see *Spelling Sourcebook 1*, Article 8, page 33. Spelling mastery is achieved ONLY when students can spell and use words consistently correctly in writing.

359 *yes*

Antonyms, Writing Words

◆ Review the antonym of *yes*, the word *no* (71). Have students review antonyms by writing the antonym of each word you say.

Creating and Responding to a Questionnaire

◆ Have students create questionnaires that require a yes or no response, exchange questionnaires, and fill them out.

Synonyms

◆ Have students write synonyms of *yes* (all right, OK, certainly, sure, absolutely, of course).

360 *built*

Book Tie-In, Comparing and Contrasting

◆ Use *How They Built Long Ago* (Christopher Fagg and Adrian Sington, Warwick, 1981), which contrasts the ways modern and ancient structures were built. Have students compare and contrast in writing the skills and attributes of builders yesterday and today.

Choral Reading, Book Tie-In, Writing Explanations, Comparing and Contrasting

◆ Chorally read *The World That Jack Built* (Ruth Brown, Dutton, 1991). Then ask students to write in their own words the message the poem is sending. Compare and contrast the poem to the more familiar "The House That Jack Built." Use *The House That Jack Built* (Jenny Stow, Dial, 1992).

Other Word Forms, Vocabulary Skills, Writing Sentences

◆ Have students brainstorm for common other word forms of *built: build, builds, building, builder*. Discuss unfamiliar words. Have students write the other word forms in sentences.

Word Analysis, Writing Words

◆ Write *b _ _ lt* on the chalkboard. Ask students to fill in the vowels to make *built* and to then write the whole word. Extend the fill-in activity to include *ready* (357), *certain* (353), *though* (330), *brought* (327), *learned* (326), *early* (324), *course* (317), *ground* (311), *true* (296), *turn* (289), *money* (279), *usually* (278), *learn* (271), *against* (268), *several* (263), *heard* (262), *young* (256), *country* (228), earth (220), *enough* (209), *thought* (179), *people* (79), *through* (102), *around* (120), *because* (127), and *does* (128).

Then have students choose words to write without the vowels to continue the game with a partner.

361 *special*

Book Tie-Ins,
Creating a Family Calendar
✦ Use *Book of Holidays Around the World* (Alice van Straalen, Dutton, 1986) for a presentation of "special days." For craft ideas, recipes, puzzles, and jokes for these holidays, use *Amazing Days* (Randy Harelson, Workman, 1979). Then ask students to create a calendar of special days for their own family including birthdays of family members.

Other Word Forms, Vocabulary
Skills, Writing Sentences
✦ Have students brainstorm for common other word forms of *special: specialize, specialist, specialty, specially, especially.* Discuss unfamiliar words. Have students write the other word forms in sentences.

362 *ran*

Other Word Forms,
Alphabetical Order
✦ Review common other word forms of *ran: run* (306), *runs, running, runner.* Have students write the other word forms in alphabetical order.

Dictation and Writing
✦ Dictate these partial sentences and have students complete them:
> If I ran the world, I would _____.
> If we ran out of water, _____.
> When the animal ran toward me, _____.

Predicting Spellings,
Vocabulary Skills
✦ Have students write *ran* and then predict the spellings of *fan, pan, tan, rash, plan, van, bran, than* (73), *rat, rack,* and *rag.* Discuss unfamiliar words.

363 *full*

Other Word Forms,
Writing Sentences
✦ Have students brainstorm for common other word forms of *full: fuller, fullest, fully, fullness.* Note the double letter *l.* Have students write the other word forms in sentences.

Idiomatic Usage,
Writing Explanations
✦ Ask students to explain in writing what they think it means to say each of these expressions (then discuss):
> full of beans
> at full speed
> in full swing
> to have your hands full

Suffix Practice,
Visual Skill-Building
✦ Review the *ful* suffix, which may mean "full of." Have students brainstorm for words that use the *ful* suffix. Choices may include *rest* (351), *play* (274), *hand* (223), *thought* (179), *use* (88), *wonder, beauty, care.* Have students write the words with the *ful* suffix. Have students circle the single *l.*

364 *town*

Idiomatic Usage,
Writing Explanations
✦ Ask students to explain in writing what they think it means to say each of these expressions (then discuss):
> go to town
> out of town

Book Tie-In, Comparing and
Contrasting, Writing Stories
✦ Have students find different versions of "The Town (or City) Mouse and the Country Mouse." Then ask them to compare and contrast the versions. Next, have them write a version of their own.

Writing Words
✦ Have students play Password using *town* and selected review words (see ***Spelling Sourcebook 1***, page 89).

❖❖❖

Sound-Symbol Awareness, Writing Sentences ❖ Ask students to write *town*. Then have them follow these directions to write new and review words:

Change *town* to make *down* (84), *clown, gown, frown, brown*.
Change *town* to make *ton*.
Change *town* to make *tow*.
Change *town* to make *own* (163).
Change *town* to make *torn*.

Have students write a sentence for each word they made.

365 *complete*

Other Word Forms, Vocabulary Skills, Writing Sentences ❖ Have students brainstorm for common other word forms of *complete: completes, completed, completing, completion, completely, completeness*. Discuss unfamiliar words. Have students write the other word forms in sentences.

Suffix Practice, Writing Sentences ❖ Review the *ly* suffix. Have students add the *ly* suffix to *complete, special* (361), *certain* (353), *close* (328), *sad* (323), *order* (309), *short* (304), *true* (296), *sure* (251). Have students write the words with *ly* in sentences.

366 *oh*

Book Tie-In, Creating a Book, Reading, Public Speaking ❖ Use *Oh, Such Foolishness!* (William Cole, Harper, 1978), a book of humorous poems with illustrations to match! Following the sharing of selected poems, ask students to use this source or another to find one favorite humorous poem to include in a class collection. Have students read their choice to the class and tell why it was their favorite.

Book Tie-In, Creating a Book ❖ *Oh!* (Josse Goffin, Abrams, 1991) is a wordless lift-the-flap book that humorously juxtaposes two things when each flap is lifted. Using this book as a model, ask students to make their own *Oh!* books that reveal a surprise under the flaps.

Writing Exclamations ❖ Review exclamations (*my* [80], *man* [111]). Have students write exclamations using *oh* and other exclamatory words.

367 *person*

Writing Descriptions, Book Tie-In ❖ Ask students to write a description of the perfect person. Then use *Be a Perfect Person in Just Three Days* (Stephen Manes, Houghton, 1982), about a boy who decides to change his ways.

Other Word Forms, Vocabulary Skills, Writing Sentences ❖ Have students brainstorm for common other word forms of *person: persons, personal, personally, personality, personable*. Discuss unfamiliar words. Have students write the other word forms in sentences.

Writing Words ❖ Have students play the All-Play Spelling Bee (see **Spelling Sourcebook 1**, page 86) to reinforce other word forms of *person* and selected review words with their other word forms.

368 *hot*

Book Tie-In, Writing Explanations ❖ Use *The Queen's Holiday* (Margaret Wild, Watts, 1992), a humorous story describing the antics of the royal household cooling off at the seashore on a very hot day. When the day gets hotter and everyone gets silly, the Queen must take control. Before reading the Queen's solution to the disorder, have students write how they would regain the decorum of the group.

❖❖❖

Book Tie-In,
Writing a Summary

❖ Use *The Science Book of Hot and Cold* (Neil Ardley, Gulliver, 1992) for can-do experiments that explore hot and cold. While one student performs an experiment, others can write a summary of it.

Other Word Forms, Vocabulary
Skills, Writing Sentences

❖ Have students brainstorm for common other word forms of *hot: hotter, hottest, hotly.* Discuss unfamiliar words. Have students write the other word forms in sentences.

Idiomatic Usage,
Writing Explanations

❖ Ask students to explain in writing what they think it means to say each of these expressions (then discuss):

in the hot seat
full of hot air
hot under the collar
in hot water
Strike while the iron is hot.

Research and Writing,
Public Speaking

❖ Have students find the daily weather section in the newspaper and note over several days the cities that report the hottest temperatures. Then have them research the yearly climate of one of these cities and compare the climate with that of their own area. Have students report the information in writing and orally to the class.

369 *anything*

Sorting Words

❖ Have students play Word Sorts (see *Spelling Sourcebook 1*, page 92) using these words: *anything, anywhere, something* (178), *anyone, nothing* (329), *everything, someone.*

Compound Words,
Writing Words

❖ Have students play Bingo (see *Spelling Sourcebook 1*, page 87). Use the variation of the game, Compound Bingo, to reinforce *anything* and other compound words.

370 *hold*

Other Word Forms, Vocabulary
Skills, Writing Sentences

❖ Have students brainstorm for common other word forms of *hold: holds, held, holding, holder.* Discuss unfamiliar words. Have students write the other word forms in sentences.

Idiomatic Usage,
Writing Explanations

❖ Ask students to explain in writing what they think it means to say each of these expressions (then discuss):

Hold it!
Don't hold your breath.
Hold your horses.
hold up
Hold onto your hat.
Hold your tongue.
to hold a grudge
Hold the line.
to take hold
on hold

371 *state*

Book Tie-In,
Writing Descriptions
♦ Use *Anno's USA* (Anno Mitsumasa, Putnam, 1983), a wordless trek across the United States with imaginative drawings that could be used as models for students' drawings of a trek across their state. Ask students to include a written description of their trek.

Research and Writing, Creating a
Brochure, Writing to Persuade
♦ Have students research scenic and/or historical tourist attractions of their state. Then they write and illustrate a brochure to increase tourism to these sites.

Other Word Forms, Vocabulary
Skills, Writing Sentences
♦ Have students brainstorm for common other word forms of *state: states, stated, stating, stately, statement.* Discuss unfamiliar words. Have students write the other word forms in sentences.

Multiple Meanings,
Writing Sentences
♦ Brainstorm for meanings of *state.* Then have students check a dictionary for verification. Ask students to write sentences to illustrate the different meanings. Review these words with multiple meanings: *side* (203), *kind* (214), *hand* (223), *light* (227), *country* (228), *second* (235), *paper* (241), *hard* (242), *room* (266), *top* (269), *point* (272), *play* (274), *turn* (289), *face* (291), *cut* (293), *short* (304), *run* (306), *order* (309), *ground* (311), *course* (317), *close* (328), *draw* (338), *mean* (349), *rest* (351), and *fire* (356). Have students write the words in sentences to illustrate their different meanings.

Writing State Names,
Abbreviations
♦ Ask students to write the names of the states and the Post Office abbreviation for each.

Research and Writing,
Public Speaking
♦ Have students research one of the following topics, tell about their findings in writing, and then present the information orally to the class:

How a state got its name

Your state in comparison with another state or Canadian province

What you think causes people to move into or out of
your state

372 *list*

Other Word Forms, Vocabulary
Skills, Writing Sentences
♦ Have students brainstorm for common other word forms of *list: lists, listed, listing.* Discuss unfamiliar words. Have students write the other word forms in sentences.

Sound-Symbol Awareness,
Writing Sentences
♦ Ask students to write *list.* Then have them follow these directions to write new and review words:

Change *list* to make *last* (166).

Change *list* to make *fist, mist, wrist.*

Change *list* to make *lit.*

Change *list* to make *listen.*

Change *list* to make *lost.*

Have students write a sentence for each word they made.

Writing a List
♦ Have students create a list of words that they have trouble remembering how to spell. Then have them create and write a memory device for correctly spelling each word.

373 *stood*

Other Word Forms,
Writing Sentences
♦ Have students brainstorm for common other word forms of *stood: stand, stands, standing.* Have students write the other word forms in sentences.

Writing Questions and Answers ✦ Have students play Questions and Answers using *stood* and selected review words (see ***Spelling Sourcebook 1***, page 90).

Sound-Symbol Awareness ✦ Ask students to write *stood*. Then have them follow these directions to write new and review words:
> Change *stood* to make *stand*.
> Change *stood* to make *hood, good, wood* (fire wood)
> Change *stood* to make *food* (198), *stool*. (Note the different vowel sound.)
> Change *stood* to make *should* (156).

Alphabetical Order ✦ Have students list the words they made in alphabetical order.

374 *hundred*

Research, Writing Reasons ✦ Ask students to research whose pictures are on the one, five, ten, twenty, and one-hundred dollar bills (Washington, Lincoln, Hamilton, Jackson, and Franklin). Invent a new denomination and ask each student to choose a person to be featured on it. Have them write why that person is the best choice.

Other Word Forms,
Writing Number Words ✦ Have students brainstorm for common other word forms of *hundred: hundreds, hundredth*. Then ask them to write more number words.

375 *ten*

Other Word Forms, Vocabulary
Skills, Writing Sentences ✦ Have students brainstorm for common other word forms of *ten: tens, tenth, tenths*. Discuss unfamiliar words. Have students write the other word forms in sentences.

Analogies, Writing Sentences ✦ Review analogies (see 307, 319, 333, 357) and the use of colons. Then have students write these analogies and complete them with the appropriate word:
> hundred : hundredth :: ten : _____ (tenth)
> at : hat :: old : _____ (hold [370] or any word that rhymes
>   with *old*.)
> build : built :: stand : _____ (stood [373])
> green : color :: Texas : _____ (state [371])
> mean : meaner :: hot : _____ (hotter [hot 368])
> no thing : nothing :: any thing : _____ (anything [369])
> no : yes :: empty : _____ (full [363])
> clothes : close :: shone : _____ (shown [348])
> Have students write the answer words in sentences.

376 *fast*

Other Word Forms, Vocabulary
Skills, Writing Sentences ✦ Have students brainstorm for common other word forms of *fast: faster, fastest, fasts, fasted, fasting*. Discuss unfamiliar words. Have students write the other word forms in sentences.

Idiomatic Usage,
Writing Explanations ✦ Ask students to explain in writing what they think it means to say each of these expressions (then discuss):
> to get nowhere fast
> a hard-and-fast rule
> to make a fast buck
> to pull a fast one

Multiple Meanings,
Writing Sentences ✦ Brainstorm for meanings of *fast*. Then have students check a dictionary for verification. Ask students to write sentences to illustrate the different meanings.

Synonyms, Sequencing ◆ Have students write synonyms for *fast* and then sequence the words by relative speed.

Antonyms, Book Tie-In ◆ Introduce the antonym of *fast*, the word *slow*. Review antonyms with **Opposites** (Richard Wilbur, Harcourt, 1991), a book of rhymes and word games with opposites.

377 *felt*

Other Word Forms, Vocabulary Skills, Writing Sentences ◆ Have students brainstorm for common other word forms of *felt: feel, feels, feeling, feelings*. Discuss unfamiliar words. Have students write the other word forms in sentences.

Vocabulary Skills ◆ Discuss *felt* meaning "a kind of material." Have students brainstorm for items that are often made of felt.

Dictation, Proofreading ◆ Have students play Sentence Spelling to reinforce dictation and proofreading skills (see **Spelling Sourcebook 1**, page 91).

378 *kept*

Other Word Forms, Writing Sentences ◆ Have students brainstorm for common other word forms of *kept: keep, keeps, keeping, keeper*. Have students write the other word forms in sentences.

Writing Words ◆ Have students play Race Track Spelling using *kept* and selected review words (see **Spelling Sourcebook 1**, page 90).

379 *notice*

Other Word Forms, Vocabulary Skills, Writing Sentences, Suffix Practice ◆ Have students brainstorm for common other word forms of *notice: notices, noticed, noticing, noticeable, noticeably*. Discuss unfamiliar words. Have students write the other word forms in sentences. Point out that the silent *e* of *notice* is not dropped before the *able* suffix.

Vocabulary Skills, Writing a Notice ◆ Discuss *notice* meaning "bulletin," "warning," or "announcement." Have students write a notice about a real or make-believe school event.

Writing Words ◆ Have students play Spelling Baseball (see **Spelling Sourcebook 1**, page 91) using *notice* and selected review words.

380 *can't*

Idiomatic Usage, Writing Explanations ◆ Ask students to explain in writing what they think it means to say each of these expressions (then discuss):

> Beggars can't be choosers.
> can't carry a tune
> can't stand something
> You can't take it with you.
> You can't teach an old dog new tricks.

Writing Sentences ◆ Have students play Sentence Puzzles using *can't* and selected review words (see **Spelling Sourcebook 1**, page 91).

Writing a Definition ◆ Have students write a definition for *contraction*.

381 *strong*

Other Word Forms, Vocabulary Skills, Writing Sentences ◆ Have students brainstorm for common other word forms of *strong: stronger, strongest, strongly, strength, strengthen, strengthening*. Discuss unfamiliar words. Have students write the other word forms in sentences.

Sound-Symbol Awareness,
Writing Sentences

✦ Ask students to write *strong*. Then have them follow these directions to write new and review words:

Change *strong* to make *along* (171).
Change *strong* to make *among* (345).
Change *strong* to make *wrong, song, long* (91).
Change *strong* to make *string*.
Change *strong* to make *strange*.

Have students write a sentence for each word they made.

382 *voice*

Other Word Forms, Vocabulary
Skills, Writing Sentences

✦ Have students brainstorm for common other word forms of *voice: voices, voiced, voicing, voiceless, voicelessness*. Discuss unfamiliar words. Have students write the other word forms in sentences.

Writing Words

✦ Have students play Write and Fold Relay (see *Spelling Sourcebook 1*, page 93) using *voice* and selected review words.

Word Analysis,
Sound-Symbol Awareness

✦ Have students change *voice* to *choice* and then underline the parts of the words that are alike. Have students find and write other words that contain *oi* or end in *ce*.

383 *probably*

Using a Dictionary,
Pronunciation Key,
Writing Words

✦ Have students find *probably* in the dictionary and use the pronunciation key to check how the word should be said. Ask students to practice pronouncing each syllable to help them remember all the letters when spelling the word. Extend use of the dictionary pronunciation key for *February, often, library*, and other words that students often mispronounce. Have students both write and say the words.

Book Tie-In,
Writing a Definition

✦ Use *Do You Wanna Bet? Your Chance to Find Out About Probability* (Jean Cushman, Clarion, 1991), an entertaining introduction to probability. After the reading, have students define probability.

Other Word Forms, Vocabulary
Skills, Writing Sentences

✦ Have students brainstorm for common other word forms of *probably: probable, probability, improbable, improbability*. Discuss unfamiliar words. Have students write the other word forms in sentences.

Dictation and Writing

✦ Dictate these partial sentences and have students complete them:

Probably the most important thing to remember at school is _____.
Probably the best way to get plants to grow is _____.
It would probably make me sad if _____.
One change my mother would probably like to see is _____.

384 *area*

Writing Words

✦ Play 5-7-10 (see *Spelling Sourcebook 1*, page 93) using *area* and selected review words.

Syllables

✦ Ask students to note the number of syllables in *area* (3). Then have them find and write more words with three syllables.

385 *horse*

Book Tie-In, Hypothesizing,
Writing Speculations

✦ Use *Horse* (Juliet Clutton-Brock, Knopf, 1992) for facts and fine photographs of horses. Have students hypothesize in writing how life might have been different without the horse.

Homophone Usage,
Writing Sentences

◆ Introduce the homophone of *horse*, the word *hoarse*. Discuss the meaning of *hoarse*. Then have students write the homophones in sentences to differentiate them.

Book Tie-In, Writing Reasons

◆ Use *Herds of Thunder, Manes of Gold: A Collection of Horse Stories and Poems* (Bruce Coville, Doubleday, 1989), which includes excerpts from *Black Beauty* and *King of the Wind* that may entice students to read the longer versions. Have each student pick a favorite in the collection and write reasons why it is their choice.

Idiomatic Usage,
Writing Explanations

◆ Ask students to explain in writing what they think it means to say each of these expressions (then discuss):

> to change horses in midstream
> to eat like a horse
> Hold your horses!
> to work like a horse
> to get a Charley horse
> a horse of another color
> straight from the horse's mouth

Research and Writing,
Public Speaking

◆ Have students research one of the following topics, tell about their findings in writing, and then present the information orally to the class:

> miniature horses
> the career of a veterinarian
> the horseshoe as a good luck symbol

386 *matter*

Other Word Forms, Vocabulary
Skills, Writing Sentences

◆ Have students brainstorm for common other word forms of *matter: matters, mattered.* Discuss unfamiliar words. Have students write the other word forms in sentences.

Idiomatic Usage,
Writing Explanations

◆ Ask students to explain in writing what they think it means to say each of these expressions (then discuss):

> as a matter of fact
> to get to the heart of the matter
> no laughing matter
> no matter what

Word Analysis, Writing Words

◆ Have students write *matter* and underline the double letters. Then have students write more words that have double *t* (*letter* [344], *better* [245], *little* [92]). Expand the lesson to words that have double *o* (*stood* [373]), *l* (*full* [363]), *e* (*green* [358]), *n* (*cannot* [343]), *d* (*add* [335]), *s* (*across* [247]), and *f* (*different* [139]).

387 *stand*

Other Word Forms,
Writing Questions

◆ Review common other word forms of *stand: stood* (373), *stands, standing.* Have students write the other word forms in questions.

Idiomatic Usage,
Writing Explanations

◆ Ask students to explain in writing what they think it means to say each of these expressions (then discuss):

> to know where you stand
> to make someone's hair stand on end
> You don't stand a chance.
> Stand on your own two feet.
> to stand someone up

to take a stand
to take the stand
to stand by someone

388 *box*

Other Word Forms, Vocabulary Skills, Spelling Rules, Writing Sentences
♦ Have students brainstorm for common other word forms of *box: boxes, boxed, boxing, boxer, boxy*. Discuss unfamiliar words. Introduce the spelling rule for plurals of words that end in *x* (see **Spelling Sourcebook 1**, page 85). Have students write the other word forms in sentences.

Sound-Symbol Awareness, Word Analysis, Writing Words
♦ Write on the chalkboard *box, facts, rocks, marks*. Have students listen to the ending sounds of the words and note the letters spelling the sound. Then have students find and write more words that follow each of these spelling patterns.

389 *start*

Other Word Forms, Vocabulary Skills, Writing Sentences
♦ Have students brainstorm for common other word forms of *start: starts, started, starting, starter*. Discuss unfamiliar words. Have students write the other word forms in sentences.

Idiomatic Usage, Writing Explanations
♦ Ask students to explain in writing what they think it means to say each of these expressions (then discuss):
from start to finish
to get a head start
off to a running start
to start from scratch
to start with a clean slate
to get off to a bad start

Writing a Story Ending
♦ Have students play Finish the Story using *start* and selected review words (see **Spelling Sourcebook 1**, page 88).

390 *that's*

Sorting Words
♦ Have students play Word Sorts (see **Spelling Sourcebook 1**, page 92) using these words: *that's, they're, don't* (190), *it's* (253), *you're, didn't* (281), *we're, shouldn't, he's*.

Sound-Symbol Awareness, Writing Sentences
♦ Ask students to write *that's*. Then have them follow these directions to write new and review words:
Change *that's* to make *that is* (9, 7).
Change *that's* to make "more than one hat" (*hats*).
Change *that's* to make *than* (73).
Have students write a sentence for each word they made.

Contractions, Writing Words
♦ Have students play Bingo (see **Spelling Sourcebook 1**, page 87). Use the variation that reinforces contractions.

391 *class*

Other Word Forms, Spelling Rules, Vocabulary Skills, Writing Sentences
♦ Have students brainstorm for common other word forms of *class: classes, classy*. Introduce the spelling rule for adding plurals to words that end in *ss* (see **Spelling Sourcebook 1**, page 85). Discuss unfamiliar words. Have students write the other word forms in sentences.

Multiple Meanings, Writing Sentences
✦ Brainstorm for meanings of *class*. Then have students check a dictionary for verification. Ask students to write sentences to illustrate the different meanings.

Hypothesizing, Writing Predictions
✦ Ask students to hypothesize and write an answer to this question: What changes may need to be made if your class gets ten new students tomorrow?

Book Tie-In, Hypothesizing, Writing Speculations
✦ Use *Miss Nelson Is Missing* (Harry Allard, Houghton, 1977) to introduce the character Miss Viola Swamp. Tell students Miss Swamp be their substitute teacher tomorrow. Have them hypothesize what Miss Swamp will say and do in class tomorrow. Then have them write about one incident.

392 *piece*

Homophone Usage, Writing Sentences
✦ Introduce the homophone of *piece*, the word *peace*. Discuss both meanings. Then have students use the homophones in written sentences to differentiate them. Have students brainstorm for more homophone partners and then play Connect the Dots using the homophones (see **Spelling Sourcebook 1**, page 87).

Other Word Forms, Vocabulary Skills, Writing Sentences
✦ Have students brainstorm for common other word forms of *piece: pieces, pieces, piecing*. Discuss unfamiliar words. Have students write the other word forms in sentences.

Idiomatic Usage, Writing Explanations
✦ Ask students to explain in writing what they think it means to say each of these expressions (then discuss):
    to go to pieces
    a piece of cake
    to speak one's piece
    thrilled to pieces
    to give someone a piece of your mind

393 *surface*

Other Word Forms, Vocabulary Skills, Writing Sentences
✦ Have students brainstorm for common other word forms of *surface: surfaces, surfaced, surfacing*. Discuss unfamiliar words. Have students write the other word forms in sentences.

Other Word Forms, Writing Words
✦ Have students play All in the Family using other word forms of *surface* and selected review words (see **Spelling Sourcebook 1**, page 86).

Prefix Practice, Answering Questions
✦ Review the *re* prefix. Then have students answer these questions:
    Why might a street be resurfaced?
    Why might someone ask you to restate your name when you're introduced? (*state* [371])
    Why might a building be rebuilt? (*built* [360])
    If you are told to remove your coat, what do you do? (*move* [290])
    If you are told to return to your seat, what do you do? (*turn* [289])
    Why might you need to be retold to do something? (*told* [255])
    If your bedroom is being repapered, what is happening? (*paper* [241])
    How do you restudy your spelling words? (*study* [234])
    What experience would you most like to relive? (*live* [217])
    What story would you like reread to you? (*read* [165])
    Why might a light bulb need to be replaced? (*place* [131])
    If you cannot recall the spelling of a word, what might you do? (*called* [96])

394 *river*

Book Tie-In,
Writing Explanations

✦ Use *A River Ran Wild* (Lynne Cherry, Harcourt, 1992), an environmental history of the pollution of the Nashua River and the solution. The true account inspires youngsters to try to make a difference in the world. Ask students what they have done or hope to do to make a difference.

Vocabulary Skills,
Writing Words

✦ Have students write words that name waterways or bodies of water (*river, creak, stream, lake, pond, pool, puddle, sea, ocean, slough, inlet, bay*).

Hypothesizing,
Writing Predictions

✦ Have students hypothesize and write an answer to this question: How might life change if one of North America's major rivers (Mississippi, Columbia, Saskatchewan) suddenly went dry?

395 *common*

Other Word Forms, Vocabulary
Skills, Writing Sentences

✦ Have students brainstorm for common other word forms of *common: commoner, commonest, commonly, commons*. Discuss unfamiliar words. Have students write the other word forms in sentences.

Writing Words,
Other Word Forms

✦ Have students play the All-Play Spelling Bee (see ***Spelling Sourcebook 1***, page 86) to reinforce other word forms of *common* and selected review words with their other word forms.

Prefix Practice, Answering
Questions, Vocabulary Skills,
Writing Sentences

✦ Review the *un* prefix. Discuss the meaning of *uncommon*. Ask students to answer these questions:

From what you know about pets, what pet do you think might be considered an uncommon one?

What would the advantages and disadvantages be of having an unlisted phone number? (*list* [372])

Then have students write these words in sentences: *unkept* (*kept* [378]), *unnoticed* (*notice* [379]), *uncertain* (*certain* [353]), *unbecoming* (*become* [336]), *unusually* (*usually* [278]).

396 *stop*

Other Word Forms,
Writing Sentences

✦ Have students brainstorm for common other word forms of *stop: stops, stopped, stopper, stopping*. Have students write the other word forms in sentences.

Spelling Rules, Suffix Practice,
Writing Reasons

✦ Review the spelling rule for doubling the final consonant before adding a suffix (see ***Spelling Sourcebook 1***, page 85.) Have students determine which of these words would double the consonant before *ing, en, er,* or *ed: list* (372), *sad* (323), *open* (310), *run* (306), *turn* (289), *point* (272), *hard* (242), *let* (230), *keep* (199), *end* (170), *put* (138). Have students write the words with the appropriate suffixes and tell why or why not the consonant doubles with its addition.

Sound-Symbol Awareness,
Writing Sentences

✦ Ask students to write *stop*. Then have them follow these directions to write new and review words:

Change *stop* to make *top* (269).

Change *stop* to make *step*.

Change *stop* to make *stoop*.

Change *stop* to make *shop*.

Change *stop* to make *strap*.

Change *stop* to make *stock*.

Have students write a sentence for each word they made.

**Antonyms,
Creating a Word Puzzle**

◆ Introduce the antonym of *stop*, the word *go*. Then brainstorm for other antonym pairs. Have students create a crossword puzzle with the antonym pairs using one partner in the puzzle and the other as the word clue (use the grid paper on page 108 of *Spelling Sourcebook 1*).

Research and Writing

◆ Have students research traffic signs and write the words they find *(stop, yield, slow, merge left/right, keep left/right, reduce speed ahead, do not pass)*.

397 *am*

**Sound-Symbol Awareness,
Alphabetical Order**

◆ Ask students to write *am*. Then have them follow these directions to write new and review words:

Change *am* to make *I'm* (284).
Add letters to *am* to make *dam, ham, jam, ram, yam*.
Add letters to *am* to make *same* (115), *came* (122), *name* (155), *became* (334).
Add letters to *am* to make *American* (319).
Add letters to *am* to make *among* (345).

Have students write the words they made in alphabetical order.

398 *talk*

**Book Tie-In,
Research and Writing**

◆ Use *Ahyoka and the Talking Leaves* (Peter and Connie Roop, Lothrop, 1992), a brief, easy-to-understand, fictionalized account of Sequoyah's work to develop a written language for the Cherokee. Follow up with students researching and writing about an aspect of the Cherokee that was introduced in the book.

Writing Comics

◆ Cut out comic strips from the newspaper. Use white correction fluid to cover the conversation in the talk balloons. Then enlarge and copy the strips. Ask students to write talk inside the balloons using the pictures as a clue.

**Book Tie-In,
Writing a Summary**

◆ Use *Bees Dance and Whales Sing: The Mysteries of Animal Communication* (Margery Facklam, Sierra, 1992) to introduce fascinating scientific information about how animals "talk." Have students summarize in writing key ideas in the book.

**Other Word Forms, Vocabulary
Skills, Writing Sentences**

◆ Have students brainstorm for common other word forms of *talk: talks, talked, talking, talker, talkative*. Discuss unfamiliar words. Have students write the other word forms in sentences.

**Research and Writing,
Public Speaking**

◆ Have students research one of the following topics, tell about their findings in writing, and then present the information orally to the class:

talk shows on television and radio
tips on giving a talk in public
how to help babies learn to talk

399 *whether*

**Homophone Usage,
Writing Words**

◆ Introduce the sound-alike word for *whether*, the word *weather*. Have students brainstorm for more sound-alike words, including homophones. Then play Mystery Word using these tricky words (see *Spelling Sourcebook 1*, page 89.)

Dictation, Proofreading

◆ Have students play Sentence Spelling to reinforce dictation and proofreading skills (see *Spelling Sourcebook 1*, page 91). Focus the activity on sound-alike words, homophones, and other tricky spellings.

400 *fine*

Other Word Forms, Vocabulary Skills, Writing Sentences

◆ Have students brainstorm for common other word forms of *fine: finer, finest, fines, fined, fining, finely, finery.* Discuss unfamiliar words. Have students write the other word forms in sentences.

Sound-Symbol Awareness, Sorting Words

◆ Have students write *fine.* Ask students to listen to the long *i* sound in the word. Then have them collect more words with the long *i* sound and sort them to note the most frequent spellings for long *i* (most common: *igh [might], y [my], i [mind], i-*consonant-*e [smile]*). Have one category for "other" to accommodate less common spellings.

Multiple Meanings, Writing Sentences

◆ Brainstorm for meanings of *fine.* Then have students check a dictionary for verification. Ask students to write sentences to illustrate the different meanings. Then have students find and write words with multiple meanings. Have students write the words in sentences to illustrate their different meanings.

A Reading and Writing Partnership

Spelling Sourcebook 2 contains many suggestions for class-made and student-made books. The catalysts for the book-making projects are often books themselves—literature references are abundant in these activities. By reading, thinking, writing, creating their own books and reading them too, students are experiencing the full circle of language. And within that circle are varied language-building opportunities, including spelling and proofreading.

In a class-made book, each student participates in writing the book. Perhaps each student writes one page in the book. Perhaps students work in small groups to produce the book. Or a third strategy for making a class book is to have the class as a whole develop the story together, as an experience chart might be made in the primary grades. The final product in a class-made book is the result of input from the whole class. However, a student-made book is an individual's original book. A single student is the author. It is likely to be shorter than a class-made book.

When writing pieces are "published," such as in the production of class-made and student-made books, a writing-as-a-process approach is often used. This kind of writing, as opposed to everyday writing, strives for error-free final copies. There are various writing process models. Each model progresses through several stages of refinement to the published, perfectly proofread piece.

The class-made and student-made published books should resemble "actual" library books as closely as possible. They might include a section "about the author(s) or illustrator(s)," illustrations, a table of contents, page numbers, chapter titles, an index, a library card, and a cover.

The books can be assembled by the students, a teacher, or volunteer helpers. A school or classroom publishing house may be an efficient way to do this. With all the materials at hand, the books can be bound with ease.

Convenient bindings include construction paper and staples, report folders, file folders, poster board (railroad board) and tape, wallpaper and staples or tape, fabric and heavy thread or yarn. The paper books last longer if they are laminated or covered with clear, adhesive shelf-lining paper.

Novelty-style books include "accordion" books, "canned" books, and "shape" books. An accordion book is easy to make by taping pages accordion-pleated-fashion and attaching cover paper to the two end pages. Canned books are written on narrow paper, such as cash register tape, wound, and fitted inside a clean soup can that announces its title on a decorated paper label. Shape books have covers and pages cut into a shape appropriate for the book's content. For example, a book explaining the history and myth of Halloween might be shaped like a jack o' lantern.

The books produced at school can be cataloged in a classroom or school library, each with a library card for check-out. Some of the books could have an accompanying audio tape of the story text for check-out. Students can make these audio tapes. In fact, trying to record well-read stories on tape sharpens students' oral reading skills. But people other than students can read the stories on tape. For example, the school principal or office secretary can become the occasional audio tape story reader. Students enjoy having different familiar voices on the tapes.

The value of read-aloud time in the classroom is undisputed. Students of all ages who are afforded read-aloud time show growth in reading skills, writing development, and related language learning that can be attributed to the oral reading. The literature suggestions in *Spelling Sourcebook 2* can be shared orally, or parts of them can be. But the students' class-made and student-made books should also be chosen for read-alouds.

Story readers can be students, school personnel, or community visitors invited to the classroom to be readers. The community readers might be "special" personalities, such as the local newscaster, a firefighter, or the mayor. These special read-alouds might be video-taped for replay. Students can invite the readers through written invitations . . . and thank them for being a guest through written thank-you letters— authentic examples of writing with built-in reasons to spell and proofread with accuracy.

Book-making activities provide one of many possibilities for reading and writing partnerships in the classroom. The marriage of reading and writing in the instructional program affords gains in student skill development, as well as increased student interest in both reading and writing. Combine the two through an ongoing production of class-made and student-made books in your classroom!

page	word	page	word	page	word	page	word
7	a	115	before	41	day	70	food
119	able	76	began	31	did	10	for
20	about	118	behind	97	didn't	69	form
75	above	83	being	49	different	53	found
87	across	62	below	19	do	74	four
116	add	87	best	46	does	13	from
35	after	86	better	119	dog	110	front
50	again	54	between	67	don't	125	full
93	against	56	big	101	done	107	gave
112	ago	104	black	100	door	37	get
57	air	98	body	31	down	56	give
16	all	106	book	117	draw	38	go
76	almost	64	both	87	during	68	going
60	along	133	box	20	each	36	good
43	also	72	boy	112	early	77	got
64	always	113	brought	77	earth	51	great
136	am	124	built	104	eat	123	green
111	American	15	but	60	end	108	ground
119	among	14	by	121	English	101	group
18	an	35	called	73	enough	116	grow
7	and	44	came	46	even	15	had
73	animal	17	can	85	ever	102	half
44	another	118	cannot	53	every	78	hand
92	answer	130	can't	91	example	85	hard
41	any	97	car	100	face	24	has
127	anything	121	certain	99	family	13	have
11	are	91	change	78	far	9	he
131	area	70	children	129	fast	74	head
43	around	95	city	81	father	90	hear
11	as	133	class	122	feel	91	heard
66	asked	114	close	71	feet	49	help
12	at	108	cold	130	felt	25	her
50	away	44	come	64	few	48	here
38	back	135	common	32	find	79	high
12	be	126	complete	137	fine	26	him
115	became	27	could	122	fire	96	himself
46	because	81	country	28	first	11	his
116	become	110	course	102	fish	127	hold
28	been	101	cut	96	five	55	home

page	word	page	word	page	word
130	strong	101	true	23	would
83	study	89	try	39	write
47	such	99	turn	79	year
89	sun	94	turned	124	yes
88	sure	25	two	117	yet
134	surface	58	under	8	you
109	table	105	United States	89	young
48	take	69	until	18	your
136	talk	21	up		
52	tell	98	upon		
129	ten	59	us		
28	than	33	use		
9	that	96	usually		
133	that's	34	very		
7	the	131	voice		
18	their	68	want		
21	them	10	was		
22	then	33	water		
17	there	32	way		
23	these	17	we		
12	they	47	well		
90	thing	51	went		
43	think	16	were		
12	this	15	what		
64	those	16	when		
114	though	35	where		
63	thought	136	whether		
45	three	18	which		
37	through	61	while		
26	time	84	white		
7	to	29	who		
87	today	90	whole		
66	together	48	why		
89	told	20	will		
41	too	118	wind		
74	took	11	with		
93	top	72	without		
96	toward	35	words		
125	town	44	work		
110	tree	67	world		

Increasing Student Spelling Achievement..

in everyday writing across the curriculum

Rebecca Sitton's Spelling Seminar Handbook

for follow-along use during the seminar and for follow-up use after the seminar with over 100 pages of teacher-reference information and teaching aids

Rebecca Sitton's
Spelling Sourcebook Series

The SPELLING SOURCEBOOK provides an alternative to traditional workbook spelling. It is your source for teacher-customized spelling instruction designed to complement the writing-rich classroom. Develop your own research-based, spelling-for-writing program using the SPELLING SOURCEBOOK options and resources.

SPELLING SOURCEBOOK 1   Provides the "how-to" and "why" for developing and implementing your own spelling program. It contains extensive reference material, including the list of 1200 high-frequency writing words, and all the blackline masters that will make your new program easy to use.

SPELLING SOURCEBOOKS 2, 3, &4   are the activity books. They provide abundant suggestions for teaching and extending every high-use word 1-1200 within a literature-based, language-centered classroom.

SPELLING SOURCEBOOK 2   Provides exciting activity ideas for teaching the words within frequencies 1-400

SPELLING SOURCEBOOK 3   Provides exciting activity ideas for teaching the words within frequencies 401-800

SPELLING SOURCEBOOK 4   Provides exciting activity ideas for teaching the words within frequencies 801-1200

Rebecca Sitton's Spelling Sourcebook

VIDEO SERIES

In these three NEW video tape programs, Rebecca reinforces and extends the how-tos and whys of the Spelling Sourcebook methodology. Teachers new to the process, as well as experienced users will benefit from the insights Rebecca shares…and, you asked for it, a video for parents!

TAPE I   Introduction to Teachers (70 minutes)

Rebecca introduces educators to the commonsense methodology and research-based strategies outlined in the SOURCEBOOKS for developing, implementing, and authentically assessing a language-centered spelling curriculum. This tape is a "must" for educators who are considering developing their own spelling program (one without student books!), for beginning users of the methodology, or for experienced users who need a fast-paced refresher.

TAPE II   Introduction to Parents (40 minutes)

In this video, Rebecca visits with parents about the challenge of teaching students to spell and proofread in their writing every day, *not* just on Friday Spelling Tests! She assures parents that the focus of the SOURCEBOOK approach to spelling growth parallels real-world use of spelling…spelling well in daily writing…and outlines the steps for achieving it.

TAPE III   Management & Record Keeping Options (70 minutes)

Rebecca offers multiple how-to suggestions for organizing the daily use of the SOURCEBOOK methodology. This video includes a comparison of Core Words and Priority Words, considerations for identifying Priority Words, selecting and marking everyday writing papers for spelling performance feedback, grading, time-effective record keeping, and managing the Individualized List to complement learning.

For an **ON-LOAN** video preview of the *Spelling Sourcebook Series*, contact Egger Publishing, Inc.

**Questions?
Contact:**

Egger Publishing, Inc.
P.O. Box 4466, Spokane, WA 99202
(509) 534-1000 • fax: (509) 534-6971

OR

Rebecca Sitton
2336 South Pittsburg, Spokane, WA 99203
(509) 535-5500

Here's how to order:

Spelling Seminar Handbooks

Increasing Student Spelling Achievement   **1-49 books $15 each   •   50 or more books $9 each**

Number of books _____   Price per copy $_____   Handbook Net $ _____

Spelling Sourcebooks

Spelling Sourcebook 1 Guidelines for Developing and Implementing Your Own Language-Integrated Spelling Program

1-49 copies $26.50 each .... number of copies _____ Total $ _____

50 or more* $21.50 each .... number of copies _____ Total $ _____

Spelling Sourcebook 2 Activity Ideas for Words with Frequencies 1-400

1-49 copies $26.50 each .... number of copies _____ Total $ _____

50 or more* $21.50 each .... number of copies _____ Total $ _____

Spelling Sourcebook 3 Activity Ideas for Words with Frequencies 401-800

1-49 copies $26.50 each .... number of copies _____ Total $ _____

50 or more* $21.50 each .... number of copies _____ Total $ _____

Spelling Sourcebook 4 Activity Ideas for Words with Frequencies 801-1200

1-49 copies $26.50 each .... number of copies _____ Total $ _____

50 or more* $21.50 each .... number of copies _____ Total $ _____

* Any combination of Sourcebooks
1, 2, 3 and 4 totaling 50 copies or more   **Sourcebook Net $ _____**

Spelling Sourcebook VIDEOS

Tape I Introduction to Teachers
$150 each tape .... Number of tapes_____ Total $ _____

Tape II Introduction to Parents
$100 each tape .... Number of tapes_____ Total $ _____

Tape III Management and Record Keeping Options
$150 each tape .... Number of tapes _____ Total $ _____

Tape Set (one of each tape)
$350 each set .... Number of sets _____ Total $ _____

Multiple Tape Sets (10 or more sets)
$300 each set .... Number of sets _____ Total $ _____

Contract for special broadcast and duplication rights, contact Egger Publishing, Inc.

Video Net $ _____

Seminar Handbook Net $ _____

Spelling Sourcebook Net $ _____

Video Net $ _____

TOTAL NET $ _____

Add tax: 8.25% in CA; 8.1% in WA $ _____

Add postage & handling:

	U.S. ($4.00 Min.)	CANADA ($8.00 Min.)	$ _____
$0-500:	8%	14%	
$500-1,000:	$40.00	$70.00	
$1,000 & up:	4%	7%	

TOTAL ORDER $ _____

Canadian orders must be in U.S. funds

** Prices subject to change
without notice

CHOOSE YOUR PAYMENT METHOD:

☐ Bill school / district:
Purchase order no. _____

☐ Check enclosed (prepay personal orders)

☐ VISA or ☐ MasterCard Expir. date ☐☐ - ☐☐
Card
Acct. No. ☐☐☐☐☐☐☐☐☐☐☐☐☐☐☐☐

Authorized Signature _____

Does this confirm an order already submitted by phone or fax? _____

BILL TO:

District _____
Address _____
City _____ State _____ Zip _____
Phone _____ Fax _____

SHIP TO (if different):

Name _____
Address _____
City _____ State _____ Zip _____
Phone _____ Fax _____

Here's where to send your order:

Northwest Textbook
17970 SW McEwan Rd.
Portland, OR 97224
(503) 639-3193
fax: (503) 639-2559

Questions? Contact:

Egger Publishing, Inc.
P.O. Box 4466
Spokane, WA 99202
(509) 534-1000
fax: (509) 534-6971